D1562519

THE FATHERS
OF THE CHURCH

MEDIAEVAL CONTINUATION

VOLUME 16

THE FATHERS
OF THE CHURCH

MEDIAEVAL CONTINUATION

PETER THE VENERABLE

WRITINGS AGAINST THE SARACENS

Translated by

IRVEN M. RESNICK

THE CATHOLIC UNIVERSITY OF AMERICA PRESS
Washington, D.C.

Library of Congress Cataloging-in-Publication Data
Names: Peter, the Venerable, approximately 1092–1156, author.
Title: Writings against the Saracens / Peter the Venerable ;
translated by Irven M. Resnick.
Description: Washington, D.C. : Catholic University of America Press, 2016. |
Series: The fathers of the church, medieval continuation ; VOLUME 16 |
Includes bibliographical references and index.
Identifiers: LCCN 2015035573 | ISBN 9780813228594 (cloth : alk. paper)
Subjects: LCSH: Christianity and other religions–Islam–Early works to 1800. |
Islam–Relations–Christianity–Early works to 1800. |
Islam–Controversial literature–Early works to 1800.
Classification: LCC BP172 .P45413 2016 | DDC 239—dc23
LC record available at http://lccn.loc.gov/2015035573

CONTENTS

ABBREVIATIONS
AND SIGLA

Abbreviations

CC CM	*Corpus Christianorum Continuatio Mediaevalis*
CC SL	*Corpus Christianorum Series Latina*
CSEL	*Corpus Scriptorum Ecclesiasticorum Latinorum*
The Pseudo-Historical Image of the Prophet Mohammad	Michelina Di Cesare. *The Pseudo-Historical Image of the Prophet Mohammad in Medieval Latin Literature: A Repertory.* Studien zur Geschichte und Kultur des islamischen Orientis 26. Berlin and Boston: De Gruyter, 2011.
Encyclopedia of Islam	*Encyclopedia of Islam.* Second edition. Edited by P. Bearman, Th. Blanquis, C. E. Bosworth, E. van Donzel, W. P. Heinrichs. Brill Online, 2015. Accessed at the University of Tennessee at Chattanooga.
Eusebius, *Hist. eccles.*	*Historia ecclesiastica.* Turnhout: Brepols, 2012; CD ROM.
FOTC	Fathers of the Church
FOTC, MC	Fathers of the Church, Mediaeval Continuation
Glei	*Petrus Venerabilis Schriften zum Islam.* Corpus Islamo-Christiana, Series Latina 1. Ed. Reinhold Glei. Altenberge: CIS-Verlag, 1985.
Jerome, *De viris ill.*	*De viris illustribus* (PL 23: 602–726)
MGH	*Monumenta Germaniae Historica*
SS	*Scriptores*
SS rer. Germ.	*Scriptores rerum Germanicarum in usum scholarum*

Petrus Alfonsi, *Dialogue*	Petrus Alfonsi. *Dialogue Against the Jews.* Trans. Irven M. Resnick. Fathers of the Church, Mediaeval Continuation 8. Washington, DC: The Catholic University of America Press, 2006.
PG	*Patrologiae Cursus Completus, Series Graeca*
PL	*Patrologiae Cursus Completus, Series Latina*
Rescriptum Christiani	Fernando González Muñoz. *Exposición y refutación del Islam. La version Latina de las epistolas de al-Hāšimī y al-Kindī.* A Coruña: Universidade da Coruña, 2005.
Vulg.	Vulgate

Sigla

< >	Brackets enclosing words inserted by editor of Latin edition
[ ]	Brackets enclosing words inserted by translator

SELECT BIBLIOGRAPHY

Primary Sources

Alberic of Trois-Fontaines. *Chronicon*. Edited by Paul Scheffer-Boichorst. MGH, SS 23. Hanover: 1874.

Albert the Great. *Albert the Great's Questions Concerning Aristotle's* On Animals. Translated by Irven M. Resnick and Kenneth F. Kitchell, Jr. FOTC, MC 9. Washington DC: The Catholic University of America Press, 2008.

———. *Quaestiones super de animalibus*. In *Opera omnia Alberti Magni* 12. Edited by E. Filthaut. Monasterii Westf.: Aschendorff, 1955.

Alonso de Cartagena. *Defensorium unitatis Christianae (Tratado en favor de los judíos conversos)*. Edited by Manuel Alonso. Madrid: Consejo Superior de Investigaciones Científicas, 1943.

Amboise, F. *Apologetica praefatio pro Petro Abaelardo*. PL 178: 71–104.

Anastasius Bibliothecarius [the Librarian]. *Chronographia et Anastasii Bibliothecarii Historia Ecclesiastica sive Chronographia tripartita*. Edited by Carl de Boor. Leipzig: G. Teubner, 1883–85. Reprint, Hildesheim: G. Olms, 1980.

———. *Historia ecclesiastica sive Chronographia tripertita*. Paris: e typographia regia, 1649.

Anon. *In Evangelia excerpta*. In *Scriptores Hiberniae Minores*. CC SL 108B.1. Turnhout: Brepols, 1973.

Anselm of Canterbury. *Cur Deus Homo*. In *S. Anselmi Cantuariensis Archiepiscopi opera omnia*. Edited by F. S. Schmitt, 2. 6 vols. Rome and Edinburgh: Thomas Nelson and Sons, 1938–61. Pp. 37–133.

Arnold of Lübeck. *Chronica Slavorum*. Edited by J. M. Lappenberg. MGH, SS rer. Germ. 14. Hannover: Hahn, 1868.

Augustine. *Against Julian*. Translated by Matthew A. Schumacher. FOTC 35. Washington, DC: The Catholic University of America Press, 1957.

———. *Confessiones*. Edited by Luc Verheijen. CC SL 27. Turnhout: Brepols, 1981.

———. *Contra Donatistas*. Edited by Michael Petschenig. CSEL 53. Vienna: F. Tempsky, 1910.

———. *Contra Faustum*. Edited by Joseph Zycha. CSEL 25.1 Vienna: F. Tempsky, 1891.

———. *Contra Fortunatum*. Edited by Joseph Zycha. CSEL 25.1. Vienna: F. Tempsky, 1891.

————. *De civitate dei*. Edited by Bernhard Dombart and Alfons Kalb. CC SL 47–48. Turnhout: Brepols, 1955.

————. *De consensu evangelistarum*. Edited by Franz Weihrich. CSEL 43. Vienna: F. Tempsky, 1904.

————. *De haeresibus*. Edited by R. Vander Plaetse and C. Beukers. CC SL 46. Turnhout: Brepols, 1969. CD ROM.

————. *Four Anti-Pelagian Writings*. Translated by John A. Mourant and William J. Collinge. FOTC 86. Washington, DC: The Catholic University of America Press, 1992.

————. *Sermo 241: De resurrectione corporum, contra Gentiles*. PL 38: 1134–38.

Bartholomew of Lucca. *Continuatio Thomae de Aquino: De regimine principum*. In *Opuscula philosophica Thomae Aquinatis*. Edited by Raymund M. Spiazzi. Turin: Marietti, 1954; Turnhout: Brepols, 2013. CD ROM.

Basil of Caesarea. *Against Eunomius*. Translated by Mark DelCogliano and Andrew Radde-Gallwitz. FOTC 122. Washington, DC: The Catholic University of America Press, 2011.

————. *Contra Sabellianos et Arium et Anomoeos*. PG 31: 600–617.

Bede, the Venerable. *Histoire ecclésiastique du peuple anglais*. Edited by André Crépin, Michel Lapidge, Pierre Monat, and Phillipe Robin. Sources chrétiennes 489–91. Paris: Éditions du Cerf, 2005.

Bernard of Clairvaux. *Epistola 363*. In *Sancti Bernardi opera genuina*. Edited by the Monks of St. Benedict. 8 vols. Lyons and Paris: Perisse Frères, 1854. 8:316.

————. *The Letters of St. Bernard of Clairvaux*. Translated by Bruno Scott James. Chicago: Henry Regnery Company, 1953.

Bullarum sacri ordinis Cluniacensis. Edited by P. Symon. Lyons: Antonius Jullieron, 1680.

Chronica Adefonsi Imperatoris. Edited by Emma Falque, Juan Gil, Antonio Maya. CC CM 71. Turnhout: Brepols, 1990. CD ROM.

Chronicles of the Reigns of Stephen, Henry II, and Richard I, vol. 4: *The Chronicle of Robert of Torigni* [*Chronica Roberti*]. London: Public Record Office, 1889.

Concilia oecumenica et generalia Ecclesiae catholicae—Concilium Nicaenum I a. 325 (transl. latina). Turnhout: Brepols, 2013. CD ROM.

Ekkehardus Uraugiensis. *Chronicon universale*. Edited by G. Waitz. MGH, SS 6. Turnhout: Brepols Publishers, 2013. CD ROM.

Ephrem the Syrian. *Hymns on Faith*. Translated by Jeffrey Wickes. FOTC 130. Washington, DC: The Catholic University of America Press, 2015.

Freculphus of Lisieux. *Historiarum libri XII*. Edited by Michael I. Allen. CC CM 169A. Turnhout: Brepols, 2002. CD ROM.

Fredegar the Scholastic. *Chronicum*. PL 71: 605–64.

Gregory the Great. *Homiliae in Hiezechihelem prophetam*. Edited by Marcus Adriaen. CC SL 142. Turnhout: Brepols, 1971. CD ROM.

Hilary of Poitiers. *De trinitate*. Edited by P. Smulders. CC SL 62. Turnhout: Brepols, 1979.

Horace. *Ars poetica*. Translated by H. R. Fairclough. Loeb Classical Library 194. Cambridge, MA: Harvard University Press, 1929.

Hugh of Flavigny. *Chronicon.* PL 154: 9–403.

Irenaeus. *Adversus haereses (Against Heresies).* Edited by A. Rousseau and Louis Doutreleau. Sources chrétiennes 264. Paris: Éditions du Cerf, 1979; Turnhout: Brepols, 2010. CD ROM.

Jacques de Vitry. *Libri dvo, quorum prior Orientalis, siue hierosolymitanæ: Alter, Occidentalis Historiae nomine inscribitur.* Edited by F. Moschus. Douai: B. Belleri, 1597.

Jerome. *Commentarii in Ezechielem.* Edited by F. Glorie. CC SL 75. Turnhout: Brepols, 1964.

———. *De viris illustribus.* PL 23: 602–726.

———. *Epistulae.* Edited by Isidore Hilberg. CSEL 54. Vienna: F. Tempsky, 1910. CD ROM.

Justinian, Emperor. *The Institutes of Justinian.* Translated by Thomas Collett Sandars. 1st American edition. Chicago: Callaghan & Company, 1876.

Muhammad ibn Jarir al-Tabari. *The History of al-Tabari.* Translated by W. Montgomery Watt and M. V. McDonald. Volume 6. Albany: SUNY Press, 1987.

Optatus of Mileve. *Optatus: Against the Donatists.* Translated by Mark Edwards. Liverpool: Liverpool University Press, 1997.

Paulinus of Aquileia. *Libellus sacrosyllabus contra Elipandum.* PL 99: 151–66.

Peter Abelard. *Collationes.* Edited and translated by John Marenbon and Giovanni Orlandi. Oxford: Clarendon Press, 2001.

———. *Dialogus inter Philosophum, Iudaeum, et Christianum.* Edited by Rudolf Thomas. Stuttgart-Bad Cannstatt: Friedrich Frommann Verlag, 1970.

Peter of Poitiers. *Capitula Petri Pictaviensis ad domnum Petrum abbatem.* PL 189: 661A–662A.

Peter the Venerable. *Adversus Iudeorum inveteratam duritiem.* Edited by Yvonne Friedman. CC CM 58. Turnhout: Brepols, 1985.

———. *Against the Inveterate Obduracy of the Jews.* Translated by Irven M. Resnick. FOTC, MC 14. Washington, DC: The Catholic University of America Press, 2013.

———. *Carmina cum Petri Pictaviensis Panegyrico/ Pierre le Vénérable: Poèmes avec le panegyrique de Pierre de Poitiers.* Edited by Franz Dolveck. Auteurs latins du Moyen Âge 27. Paris: Les belles lettres, 2014.

———. *Contra Petrobrusianos hereticos.* Edited by James Fearns. CC CM 10. Turnhout: Brepols, 1968.

———. *De miraculis.* Edited by D. Bouthillier. CC CM 83. Turnhout: Brepols, 1988.

———. *The Letters of Peter the Venerable.* Edited by Giles Constable. 2 vols. Cambridge, MA: Harvard University Press, 1967.

———. *Peter the Venerable: Selected Letters.* Edited by Janet Martin with Giles Constable. Toronto: Pontifical Institute of Mediaeval Studies, 1974.

———. *Schriften zum Islam.* Edited and translated [into German] by Reinhold Glei. Corpus Islamo-Christianum, Series Latina, 1. Altenberge: CIS-Verlag, 1985.

Petrus Alfonsi. *Dialogue Against the Jews.* Translated by Irven M. Resnick. FOTC,

MC 8. Washington, DC: The Catholic University of America Press, 2006.

Petrus Damiani. *Die Briefe des Petrus Damiani*. Edited by Kurt Reindel. MGH, Epp. Kaiserzeit 3. Munich: MGH, 1983–93.

Physiologus Latinus (recension B). Edited by F. J. Carmody. Paris: Librairie E. Droz, 1939.

Pseudo Al-Kindi. "Al-Kindi, Apologia del Cristianismo." Edited by José Muñoz Sendino. In *Miscellanea Comillas* 11–12 (1949): 337–460.

———. *Exposición y refutación del islam: La versión latina de las epístolas de al-Hasimi y al-Kindi*. Edited by Fernando González Muñoz. A Coruña, Spain: Universidade da Coruña, 2005.

Pseudo Athanasius. *Contra Sabellianos*. PG 28: 96–121.

Ralph of Caen. *Gesta Tancredi*. In *Recueil des historiens des croisades. Historiens Occidentaux*. 5 vols. Paris: Academie des Inscriptions et Belles-Lettres, 1844–95.

Robert of Ketton. *Roberti Retenensis praefatio in libro legis saracenorum, quam alcoran vocant, a se translato. Ad domnum petrum abbatem cluniacensem*. PL 189: 657–60.

Robert the Monk. *Historia Iherosolomitana*. In *Recueil des historiens des croisades. Historiens occidentaux*. 5 vols. Paris: Academie des Inscriptions et Belles-Lettres, 1844–95.

Sigebert of Gembloux. *Chronographia*. Edited by L. Bethmann. MGH, SS 6. Turnhout: Brepols, 2013.

Tertullian. *Adversus Hermogenem*. Edited by E. Kroymann. CC SL 1. Turnhout: Brepols, 1954. CD ROM.

———. *Adversus Iudaeos*. Edited by E. Kroymann. CC SL 2. Turnhout: Brepols, 1954. CD ROM.

———. *De carne Christi*. Edited by E. Kroymann. CC SL 2. Turnhout: Brepols, 1954. CD ROM.

———. *De ieiunio aduersus psychicos*. Edited by A. Reifferscheid and G. Wissowa. CC SL 2. Turnhout: Brepols, 1954. CD ROM.

Vincent of Beauvais. *Speculum quadruplex, sive, Speculum maius: naturale, doctrinale, morale, historiale*. Duaci, 1624. Reprint, Graz, Austria: Akademische Druck- u. Verlagsanstalt; ex officina typographica Baltazaris Belleri, 1964–1965.

Vincent of Lérins. *Tractatus Peregrini pro Catholicae fidei antiquitate et universitate adversus prophanas omnium haereticorum novitates*. PL 50: 637–77.

William of St. Thierry. *Meditationes deuotissimae (Meditatiuae orationes)*. Edited by P. Verdeyen. CC CM 89. Turnhout: Brepols, 2005. CD ROM.

Secondary Sources

Akbari, Suzanne Conklin. *Idols in the East: European Representations of Islam and the Orient, 1100–1450*. Ithaca and London: Cornell University Press, 2009.

Beckingham, Charles F., and Bernard Hamilton, eds. *Prester John, the Mongols and the Ten Lost Tribes*. London: Variorum, 1996.

Berry, Virginia. "Peter the Venerable and the Crusades." In *Petrus Venerabilis 1156–1956: Studies and Texts Commemorating the Eighth Centenary of His Death.* Edited by Giles Constable and James Kritzeck. Studia Anselmiana 40. Rome: Herder, 1956. Pp. 140–62.

Billet, Bernard. "Notes de mariologie. La dévotion mariale de Pierre le Vénérable (1092–1156)." *Esprit et vie* 87.37 (1977): 465–72.

Bishko, Charles Julian. "Liturgical Intercession at Cluny For the King-Emperors of Leon." *Studia Monastica* 7 (1961): 53–76.

————. "Peter the Venerable's Journey to Spain." In *Petrus Venerabilis 1156–1956: Studies and Texts Commemorating the Eighth Centenary of His Death.* Edited by Giles Constable and James Kritzeck. Studia Anselmiana 40. Rome: Herder, 1956. Pp. 163–75.

Blum, Christopher Olaf. "Vézelay: The Mountain of the Lord." *Logos: A Journal of Catholic Thought and Culture* 8.3 (2005): 141–64.

Blumenthal, Uta-Renate. "Pope Gregory VII and the Prohibition of Nicolaitism." In *Medieval Purity and Piety: Essays on Medieval Clerical Celibacy and Religious Reform.* Edited by Michael Frassetto. New York: Garland Publishing, Inc., 1998. Pp. 239–67.

Bobzin, Harmut. "Latin Translations of the Koran, a Short Overview." *Der Islam* 70 (1993): 193–206.

Bohn, Henry G. *A Polyglot of Foreign Proverbs.* London: H. G. Bohn, 1857.

Bredero, Adriaan H. "Saint Bernard in His Relations with Peter the Venerable." In *Bernardus Magister,* Cistercian Studies Series 135. Edited by John R. Sommerfeldt. Western Michigan University: Cistercian Publications, Inc., 1992. Pp. 315–48.

————. *Cluny et Cîteaux au douzième siècle: L'histoire d'une controverse monastique.* Amsterdam: Holland University Press, 1988.

————. "Pierre le Vénérable: Les commencements de son abbatiat à Cluny (1122–1132)." In *Pierre Abélard—Pierre le Vénérable: Les courants philosophiques, littéraires et artistiques en Occident au milieu du XIIe siècle; [actes et mémoires du colloque international],* Abbaye de Cluny, 2 au 9 juillet 1972, Colloques internationaux du Centre National de la Recherche Scientifique, no. 546. Paris: Éditions du Centre National de la Recherche Scientifique, 1975. Pp. 98–116.

————. "The Controversy Between Peter the Venerable and Saint Bernard of Clairvaux." In *Petrus Venerabilis 1156–1956: Studies and Texts Commemorating the Eighth Centenary of His Death.* Edited by Giles Constable and James Kritzeck. Studia Anselmiana 40. Rome: Herder, 1956. Pp. 53–71.

Bruce, Scott G. *Cluny and the Muslims of La Garde-Freinet. Hagiography and the Problem of Islam in Medieval Europe.* Ithaca and London: Cornell University Press, 2015.

————. "An Abbot between Two Cultures: Maiolus of Cluny Considers the Muslims of La Garde-Freinet." *Early Medieval Europe* 15.4 (2007): 426–40.

Burman, Thomas E. "Nicholas of Cusa and Peter the Venerable's Request." In *Nicholas of Cusa and Islam. Polemic and Dialogue in the Late Middle Ages.* Edited by Ian Christopher Levy, Rita George-Tvrtković, and Donald F. Duclow. Leiden: Brill, 2014. Pp. xiii–xx.

———. *Reading the Qur'ān in Latin Christendom, 1140–1560*. Philadelphia: University of Pennsylvania Press, 2007.

———. "'Tathlîth al-wahdânîyah' and the Twelfth-Century Andalusian-Christian Approach to Islam." In *Medieval Christian Perceptions of Islam*. Edited by John Victor Tolan. New York and London: Routledge, 1996. Pp. 109–28.

———. *Religious Polemic and the Intellectual History of the Mozarabs, ca. 1050–1200*. Leiden: E. J. Brill, 1994.

Burnett, Charles. "The Works of Petrus Alfonsi: Questions of Authenticity." *Medium Aevum* 66.1 (1997): 42–79.

———. *The Introduction of Arabic Learning into England*. The Panizzi Lectures, 1996. London: The British Library, 1997.

———. "Hermann of Carinthia." In *A History of Twelfth-Century Western Philosophy*. Edited by P. Dronke. Cambridge: Cambridge University Press, 1988. Pp. 386–404.

———. "Some Comments on the Translating of Works from Arabic into Latin in the Mid-Twelfth Century." In *Orientalische Kultur und europäisches Mittelalter*. Edited by Albert Zimmermann, Ingrid Craemer-Ruegenberg, and Gudrun Vuillemin-Diem. Miscellanea Mediaevalia 17. Berlin and New York: Walter de Gruyter, 1985. Pp. 161–70.

———. "Arabic into Latin in Twelfth-Century Spain: The Works of Hermann of Carinthia." *Mittellateinisches Jahrbuch* 13 (1978): 100–134.

Cahn, Walter B. "The 'Portrait' of Muhammad in the Toledan Collection." In *Reading Medieval Images. The Art Historian and the Object*. Edited by Elizabeth Sears and Thelma K. Thomas. Ann Arbor: University of Michigan Press, 2002. Pp. 51–60.

Cecini, Ulisse. *Alcoranus latinus. Eine sprachliche und kulturwissenschaftliche Analyse der Koranübersetzungen von Robert von Ketton und Marcus von Toledo*. Berlin: Lit Verlag, 2012.

Châtillon, Jean. "Pierre le Vénérable et les Pétrobrusiens." In *Pierre Abélard—Pierre le Vénérable: Les courants philosophiques, littéraires et artistiques en Occident au milieu du XIIe siècle; [actes et mémoires du colloque international]*, Abbaye de Cluny, 2 au 9 juillet 1972, Colloques internationaux du Centre National de la Recherche Scientifique, no. 546. Paris: Éditions du Centre National de la Recherche Scientifique, 1975. Pp. 165–76.

Chazan, Robert. *European Jewry and the First Crusade*. Berkeley: University of California Press, 1996.

Cohen, Jeremy. *Living Letters of the Law: Ideas of the Jew in Medieval Christianity*. Berkeley: University of California Press, 1999.

Conant, Kenneth John. "Cluny Studies, 1968–1975." *Speculum* 50.3 (1975): 383–90.

———. "Édifices marquants dans l'ambiance de Pierre le Vénérable et Pierre Abélard." In *Pierre Abélard—Pierre le Vénérable: Les courants philosophiques, littéraires et artistiques en Occident au milieu du XIIe siècle; [actes et mémoires du colloque international]*, Abbaye de Cluny, 2 au 9 juillet 1972, Colloques internationaux du Centre National de la Recherche Scientifique, no. 546. Paris: Éditions du Centre National de la Recherche Scientifique, 1975. Pp. 727–29.

———. "Medieval Academy Excavations at Cluny, X." *Speculum* 45.1 (1970): 1–35.

———. "Cluniac Building during the Abbacy of Peter the Venerable." In *Petrus Venerabilis 1156–1956: Studies and Texts Commemorating the Eighth Centenary of His Death*. Edited by Giles Constable and James Kritzeck. Studia Anselmiana 40. Rome: Herder, 1956. Pp. 121–27.

Constable, Giles. "Cluny in the Twelfth Century: From Hugh I to Hugh V." In *The Abbey of Cluny: A Collection of Essays to Mark the Eleven-Hundredth Anniversary of its Foundation*. Berlin: Lit Verlag, 2010. Pp. 265–80.

———. "The Reception-Privilege of Cluny." In *Le gouvernement d'Hugues de Semur à Cluny*, Actes du colloque scientifique international, Cluny, September 1988. Cluny: Musée Ochier, 1990. Pp. 59–74. Reprinted in *The Abbey of Cluny: A Collection of Essays to Mark the Eleven-Hundredth Anniversary of its Foundation*. Berlin: Lit Verlag, 2010. Pp. 163–78.

———. "The Monastic Policy of Peter the Venerable." In *Cluniac Studies*. London: Variorum Reprints, 1980. Pp. 119–38.

———. "The Second Crusade as Seen by Contemporaries." *Traditio* 9 (1953): 213–79.

Cutler, Allan. "Peter the Venerable and Islam." *Journal of the American Oriental Society* 86 (1966): 184–98.

Cutler, Allan H., and Helen E. Cutler. *The Jew as Ally of the Muslim: Medieval Roots of Anti-Semitism*. Notre Dame, IN: University of Notre Dame Press, 1986.

d'Alverny, M. T. "Alain de Lille et l'Islam. Le 'Contra paganos.'" *Cahiers de Fanjeaux* 18 (1983): 301–50.

———. "Quelques manuscrits de la 'collectio Toletana.'" In *Petrus Venerabilis 1156–1956: Studies and Texts Commemorating the Eighth Centenary of His Death*. Edited by Giles Constable and James Kritzeck. Studia Anselmiana 40. Rome: Herder, 1956. Pp. 202–18.

———. "Pierre le Vénérable et la légende de Mahomet." In *A Cluny Congrès Scientifique Fêtes et cérémonies liturgiques en l'honneur des saints Abbés Odon et Odilo, 9–11 juillet 1949*. Dijon: Société des Amis de Cluny, 1950. Pp. 161–70.

Di Cesare, Michelina. "Petrus Alfonsi and Islamic Culture: Literary and Lexical Strategies." In *Petrus Alfonsi and his Dialogus. Background, Context, Reception*. Edited by Carmen Cardelle de Hartmann and Philipp Roelli. Micrologus Library 66. Florence: SISMEL-Edizioni del Galluzzo, 2014. Pp. 203–25.

———. *The Pseudo-Historical Image of the Prophet Mohammad in Medieval Latin Literature: A Repertory*. Studien zur Geschichte und Kultur des islamischen Orientis 26. Berlin and Boston: De Gruyter, 2011.

Duby, Georges. "Un inventaire des profits de la seigneurie Clunisienne à la mort de Pierre le Vénérable." In *Petrus Venerabilis 1156–1956: Studies and Texts Commemorating the Eighth Centenary of His Death*. Edited by Giles Constable and James Kritzeck. Studia Anselmiana 40. Rome: Herder, 1956. Pp. 128–40.

El-Cheikh, Nadia Maria. "Muhammad and Heraclius: A Study in Legitimacy." *Studia Islamica* 89 (1999): 5–21.

Encyclopedia of Islam. Second edition. Edited by P. Bearman, Th. Blanquis, C. E. Bosworth, E. van Donzel, and W. P. Heinrichs. Brill Online, 2015.

Ferrari, Angel. "El cluniacense Pedro de Poitiers y la 'Chronica Adefonsi Imperatoris' y Poema de Almeria." *Boletin de la Real Academia de la Historia* 158 (1963): 153–204.

Ferreiro, Alberto. *Simon Magus in Patristic, Medieval and Early Modern Traditions.* Leiden: Brill, 2005.

———. "Simon Magus, Nicolas of Antioch, and Muhammad." *Church History* 72.1 (2003): 53–70.

———. "Priscillian and Nicolaitism." *Vigiliae Christianae* 52.4 (1998): 382–92.

Fichtenau, Heinrich. *Heretics and Scholars in the High Middle Ages 1000–1200.* Translated by Denise A. Kaiser. University Park, PA: Pennsylvania State University Press, 1998.

Forey, Alan. "The Siege of Lisbon and the Second Crusade." *Portuguese Studies* 20 (2004): 1–13.

Forster, Regula. "Der abwesende Dritte. Die Darstellung des Islam im *titulus V* des *Dialogus* des Petrus Alfonsi." In *Petrus Alfonsi and his Dialogus. Background, Context, Reception.* Edited by Carmen Cardelle de Hartmann and Philipp Roelli. Micrologus Library 66. Florence: SISMEL-Edizioni del Galluzzo, 2014. Pp. 159–82.

Friedman, John Block. *The Monstrous Races in Medieval Art and Thought.* Syracuse, NY: Syracuse University Press, 2000.

Gandeul, Jean-Marie, and Robert Caspar. "Textes de la tradition musulmane concernant le tahrîf des écritures." *Islamochristiana* 6 (1980): 61–104.

Glassé, Cyril. *The Concise Encyclopedia of Islam.* New York: Harper Collins, 1991.

Gow, Andrew Colin. *The Red Jews: Antisemitism in an Apocalyptic Age 1200–1600.* Leiden: E. J. Brill, 1995.

Graf, David F., and M. O'Connor. "The Origin of the Term Saracen and the Rawwāfā Inscriptions." *Byzantine Studies* 4.1 (1977): 52–66.

Griffith, Sidney H. "Arguing from Scripture: The Bible in the Christian/Muslim Encounter in the Middle Ages." In *Scripture and Pluralism: Reading the Bible in the Religiously Plural Worlds of the Middle Ages and Renaissance.* Edited by Thomas Heffernan and Thomas Burman. Leiden: Brill, 2005. Pp. 29–58.

Guiley, Rosemary Ellen. *The Encyclopedia of Angels.* Second edition. New York: Facts on File/Checkmark Books, 2004.

Hagemann, Ludwig B. "Die erste lateinische Koranübersetzung-Mittel zur Verständigung zwischen Christen und Muslimen im Mittelalter?" In *Orientalische Kultur und europäisches Mittelalter.* Edited by Albert Zimmermann, Ingrid Craemer-Ruegenberg, and Gudrun Vuillemin-Diem. Miscellanea Mediaevalia 17. Berlin and New York: Walter de Gruyter, 1985. Pp. 45–58.

Halevi, Leor. "*Lex Mahomethi:* Carnal and Spiritual Representations of Islamic Law and Ritual in a Twelfth-Century Dialogue by a Jewish Convert to Christianity." In *The Islamic Scholarly Tradition. Studies in History, Law, and Thought in Honor of Professor Michael Allen Cook.* Edited by Asad Q. Ahmed, Behnam Sadeghi, and Michael Bonner. Leiden and Boston: Brill, 2011. Pp. 315–42.

Harris, Jennifer A. "Building Heaven on Earth: Cluny as *Locus Sanctissimus* in the Eleventh Century." In *From Dead of Night to End of Day: The Medieval Customs of Cluny/Du coeur de la nuit à la fin du jour: Les coutumes Clunisiennes au moyen âge.* Edited by Susan Boynton and Isabelle Cochelin. Disciplina Monastica 3. Turnhout: Brepols, 2005. Pp. 131–52.

Haseldine, Julian. "Friendship, Intimacy and Corporate Networking in the Twelfth Century: The Politics of Friendship in the Letters of Peter the Venerable." *English Historical Review* 126.519 (2011): 251–80.

Hunt, Noreen. *Cluny under St. Hugh 1049–1109.* Notre Dame, IN: University of Notre Dame Press, 1967.

Iogna-Prat, Dominique. "The Creation of a Christian Armory Against Islam." In *Medieval Religion: New Approaches.* Edited by Constance Hoffman Berman. New York and London: Routledge, 2005. Pp. 325–46.

———. *Order and Exclusion: Cluny and Christendom Face Heresy, Judaism, and Islam (1000–1150).* Translated by Graham Robert Edwards. Ithaca, NY: Cornell University Press, 2002.

Jansen, Katherine Ludwig. "Mary Magdalen and the Contemplative Life." In *Medieval Religion: New Approaches.* Edited by Constance Hoffman Berman. New York and London: Routledge, 2005. Pp. 249–71.

Jeauneau, Édouard. "La bibliothèque de Cluny et les oeuvres de L'Érigene." In *Pierre Abélard—Pierre le Vénérable: Les courants philosophiques, littéraires et artistiques en Occident au milieu du XIIe siècle;* [*actes et mémoires du colloque international*], *Abbaye de Cluny, 2 au 9 juillet 1972, Colloques internationaux du Centre National de la Recherche Scientifique,* no. 546. Paris: Éditions du Centre National de la Recherche Scientifique, 1975. Pp. 703–25.

Jolivet, Jean. "Abélard et le philosophe (occident et Islam aux XIIe siècle)." *Revue de l'histoire des religions* 164 (1963): 181–89.

Kardong, Terrence G. "Saint Benedict and the Twelfth-Century Reformation." *Cistercian Studies Quarterly* 36.3 (2001): 279–309.

Keating, Sandra Toenies. "Revisiting the Charge of Taḥrīf: The Question of Supersessionism in Early Islam and the Qur'an." In *Nicholas of Cusa and Islam. Polemics and Dialogue in the Late Middle Ages.* Edited by Ian Christopher Levy, Rita George-Tvrtković, and Donald F. Duclow. Leiden: Brill, 2014. Pp. 202–17.

Knight, Gillian. "Politics and Pastoral Care: Papal Schism in Some Letters of Peter the Venerable." *Revue Bénédictine* 109, no. 3–4 (1999): 359–90.

Knowles, David. "The Reforming Decrees of Peter the Venerable." In *Petrus Venerabilis 1156–1956: Studies and Texts Commemorating the Eighth Centenary of His Death.* Edited by Giles Constable and James Kritzeck. Studia Anselmiana 40. Rome: Herder, 1956. Pp. 1–20.

Koningsveld, P. Sj. Van. "La apologia de Al-Kindi en la España del siglo XII. Huellas toledanos de un 'Animal disputax.'" In *Estudios sobre Alfonso VI y la Reconquista de Toledo. Actes del II Congreso Internacional de Estudios Mozárabes (Toledo, 20–26 Mayo 1985).* Series historica 5. Toledo: Instituto de Estudios Visigótico-Mozárabes, 1989. Pp. 107–29.

Kritzeck, James. "De l'influence de Pierre Abélard sur Pierre le Vénérable dans ses oeuvres sur l'Islam." In *Pierre Abélard—Pierre le Vénérable: Les courants philosophiques, littéraires et artistiques en Occident au milieu du XIIe siècle; [actes et mémoires du colloque international]*, Abbaye de Cluny, 2 au 9 juillet 1972, *Colloques internationaux du Centre National de la Recherche Scientifique*, no. 546. Paris: Éditions du Centre National de la Recherche Scientifique, 1975. Pp. 205–12.

———. *Peter the Venerable and Islam*. Princeton, NJ: Princeton University Press, 1964.

———. "Peter the Venerable and the Toledan Collection." In *Petrus Venerabilis 1156–1956: Studies and Texts Commemorating the Eighth Centenary of His Death*. Edited by Giles Constable and James Kritzeck. Studia Anselmiana 40. Rome: Herder, 1956. Pp. 176–201.

Lawrence, Bruce. *The Qur'an: Books that Changed the World*. London: Atlantic Books, 2007.

Leclerq, Jean. "Pierre le Vénérable et l'invitation au salut." *Bulletin des Missions* 20 (1946): 145–56.

Lejbowicz, Max. "Développement autochtone assumé et acculturation dissimulée." In *Les relations culturelles entre chrétiens et musulmans au moyen âge: Quelles leçons en tirer de nos jours? Colloque organisé à la Fondation Singer-Polignac le mercredi 20 octobre 2004 par Rencontres médiévales européennes*. Edited by Max Lejbowicz. Turnhout: Brepols, 2005: 57–81.

Lemay, Richard. "Apologetics and (bad) Latin." *Middle East Forum* 49 (1965): 41–44.

Lohrmann, Dietrich. "Pierre le Vénérable et Henri Ier, Roi d'Angleterre." In *Pierre Abélard—Pierre le Vénérable: Les courants philosophiques, littéraires et artistiques en Occident au milieu du XIIe siècle; [actes et mémoires du colloque international]*, Abbaye de Cluny, 2 au 9 juillet 1972, *Colloques internationaux du Centre National de la Recherche Scientifique*, no. 546. Paris: Éditions du Centre National de la Recherche Scientifique, 1975. Pp. 191–203.

Luchitskaja, Svetlana. "The Image of Muhammad in Latin Chronography of the Twelfth and Thirteenth Centuries." *Journal of Medieval History* 26.2 (2000): 115–26.

Mandonnet, P. F. "Pierre le Vénérable et son activité littéraire contre l'Islam." *Revue Thomiste* 1 (1893): 328–42.

Martínez Gázquez, José. "Trois traductions médiévales latines du Coran: Pierre le Vénérable-Robert de Ketton, Marc de Tolède et Jean de Segobia." *Revue des études latines* 80 (2003): 223–36.

Metlitzki, Dorothee. *The Matter of Araby in Medieval England*. New Haven: Yale University Press, 2005.

Meyvaert, Paul. "Bede and the Church Paintings at Wearmouth-Jarrow." *Anglo-Saxon England* 8 (1979): 63–77.

Monnot, Guy. "Les citations coraniques dans le 'Dialogus' de Pierre Alphonse." *Cahiers de Fanjeaux, Collection d'Histoire religieuse du Languedoc au XIIIe et au début du XIVe siècle: Islam et chrétiens du Midi (XIIe-XIVe S.)* 18. Edited by Edouard Privat. Fanjeaux: Centre d'études historiques de Fanjeaux, 1983. Pp. 261–77.

Morawski, Joseph, ed. *Proverbes français anterieurs au XVe siècle*. Paris: Librairie Ancienne Edouard Champion, 1925.

Morris, Colin. *The Papal Monarchy: The Western Church from 1050 to 1250*. Oxford: Oxford University Press, 1989. Reprint, 2001.

Obeidat, Marwan M., and Ibrahim Mumayiz. "Anglo-American Literary Sources on the Muslim Orient: The Roots and the Reiterations." *Journal of American Studies of Turkey* 13 (2001): 47–72.

Phillips, Jonathan. *The Second Crusade: Extending the Frontiers of Christendom*. New Haven: Yale University Press, 2007.

———. "St. Bernard of Clairvaux, the Low Countries and the Lisbon Letter of the Second Crusade." *Journal of Ecclesiastical History* 48.3 (1997): 485–97.

Poole, Kevin R. "Beatus of Liébana: Medieval Spain and the Othering of Islam." In *End of Days: Essays on the Apocalypse from Antiquity to Modernity*. Edited by Karolyn Kinane and Michael A. Ryan. Jefferson, NC: McFarland & Co., Publishers, 2009. Pp. 47–66.

Puig, Josef. "The Polemic Against Islam in Medieval Catalan Culture." In *Wissen über Grenzen. Arabisches Wissen und lateinisches Mittelalter*. Edited by Andreas Speer and Lydia Wegener. Miscellanea Mediaevalia 33. Berlin: Walter de Gruyter, 2006. Pp. 238–58.

Reichert, Michelle. "Hermann of Dalmatia and Robert of Ketton: Two Twelfth-Century Translators in the Ebro Valley." In *Science Translated. Latin and Vernacular Translations of Scientific Treatises in Medieval Europe*. Leuven: Leuven University Press, 2008. Pp. 47–58.

Resnick, Irven M. "Falsification of Scripture and Medieval Christian-Jewish Polemics." *Medieval Encounters* 2.3 (1996): 345–80.

———. "Peter Damian on Cluny, Liturgy, and Penance." *Journal of Religious History* 15.1 (1988): 61–75. Reprinted in *Studia Liturgica* 18.2 (1988): 170–87.

Roggema, Barbara. *The Legend of Sergius Baḥīrā. Eastern Christian Apologetics and Apocalyptic in Response to Islam*. Leiden: E. J. Brill, 2009.

Rosenwein, Barbara H., ed. *Reading the Middle Ages. Sources from Europe, Byzantium, and the Islamic World*. Second edition. Toronto: University of Toronto Press, 2014.

Saurette, Marc. "Thoughts on Friendship in the Letters of Peter the Venerable." *Revue Bénédictine* 120.2 (2010): 321–46.

———. "Tracing the Twelfth-Century *Chronica* of Richard of Poitiers, Monk of Cluny." *Memini. Travaux et documents* 8 (2005/06): 303–50.

Strickland, Debra Higgs. *Saracens, Demons, and Jews: Making Monsters in Medieval Art*. Princeton, NJ: Princeton University Press, 2003.

Stroll, Mary. *The Jewish Pope: Ideology and Politics in the Papal Schism of 1130*. Leiden: E. J. Brill, 1987.

Tabbernee, William. *Fake Prophecy and Polluted Sacraments. Ecclesiastical and Imperial Reactions to Montanism*. Leiden: Brill, 2007.

Thérel, Marie-Louise. "Pierre le Vénérable et la creation iconographique au XIIe siècle." In *Pierre Abélard—Pierre le Vénérable: Les courants philosophiques, littéraires et artistiques en Occident au milieu du XIIe siècle; [actes et mémoires du colloque international*], *Abbaye de Cluny, 2 au 9 juillet 1972, Colloques internationaux du Centre National de la Recherche Scientifique*, no. 546. Paris: Éditions du Centre National de la Recherche Scientifique, 1975. Pp. 733–43.

Thomas, David, and Alex Mallett, eds. *Christian-Muslim Relations. A Bibliographical History; Vol. 3 (1050–1200)*. Leiden: Brill, 2011.

Tischler, Matthias M. "*Lex Mahometi*. Die Erfolgsgeschichte eines vergleichenden Konzepts der christlichen Religionspolemik." In *Das Gesetz—The Law—La Loi*. Edited by Andreas Speer and Guy Guldentops. Berlin: Walter de Gruyter, 2014. Pp. 527–73.

———. "Modes of Literary Behaviours in Christian-Islamic Encounters in the Iberian Peninsula: *Pseudo-Turpin* versus Peter the Venerable." In *Languages of Love and Hate: Conflict, Communication, and Identity in the Medieval Mediterranean*. Edited by Sarah Lambert and Helen Nicholson. Turnhout: Brepols, 2012. Pp. 201–22.

Tolan, John. "European Accounts of Mohammad's Life." In *Cambridge Companion to Muhammad*. Edited by Jonathan Brockopp. Cambridge: Cambridge University Press, 2009. Pp. 226–50.

———. *Saracens: Islam in the Medieval European Imagination*. New York: Columbia University Press, 2002.

———. "Peter the Venerable on the 'Diabolical Heresy of the Saracens.'" In *The Devil, Heresy and Witchcraft in the Middle Ages: Essays in Honor of Jeffrey B. Russell*. Edited by Alberto Ferreiro. Leiden: Brill, 1998. Pp. 345–67.

———. *Petrus Alfonsi and his Medieval Readers*. Gainesville, FL: University Press of Florida, 1993.

Torrell, Jean-Pierre. "La notion de prophétie et la méthode apologétique dans la *Contra Saracenos* de Pierre le Vénérable." *Studia monastica* 17 (1975): 257–82.

Torrell, Jean-Pierre, and Denis Bouthillier. *Pierre le Vénérable et sa vision du monde*. Leuven: Spicilegium Sacrum Lovaniense, 1986.

Van den Eynde, D. "Les principaux voyages de Pierre le Vénérable." *Benedictina* 15 (1968): 58–110.

Vones, Ludwig. "Zwischen Kulturaustausch und religioser Polemik. Von den Möglichkeiten und Grenzen christlich-muslimischer Verständigung zur Zeit des Petrus Venerabilis." In *Wissen über Grenzen. Arabisches Wissen und lateinisches Mittelalter*. Edited by Andreas Speer and Lydia Wegener. Miscellanea Mediaevalia 33. Berlin: Walter de Gruyter, 2006. Pp. 217–37.

Wallis, Faith, ed. *Medieval Medicine: A Reader*. Toronto: University of Toronto Press, 2010.

Watt, W. M. *Muslim-Christian Encounters: Perceptions and Misperceptions*. London: Routledge, 1991.

Werckmeister, O. K. "Cluny III and the Pilgrimage to Santiago of Compostela." *Gesta* 27.1–2 (1988): 103–12.

White, Hayden. "Pontius of Cluny, the *Curia Romana* and the End of Gregorianism in Rome." *Church History* 27.3 (1958): 195–219.

Williams, Daniel H. "The Anti-Arian Campaigns of Hilary of Poitiers and the 'Liber contra Auxentium.'" *Church History* 61.1 (1992): 7–22.

INTRODUCTION

INTRODUCTION

The Benedictine monastery at Cluny, founded in 909 CE, enjoyed a remarkable nine-hundred-year history in France. When in February 1790 the National Constituent Assembly determined that it would no longer recognize monastic vows and ordered the suppression of religious orders and congregations, it brought an abrupt end to Cluny's renowned history.

After the suppression of the order, what remained of its extensive monastic library was dispersed.[1] And yet even before 1790, Cluny had ceased to be a powerful monastic institution, and its abbots were no longer the great feudal lords they once had been. On 21 April 1798, the great abbey church was sold at auction, and over the next twenty-six years (1798–1824) Cluny was dismantled piece by piece. The Mayor of Cluny properly chastised government officials who, he insisted, would be remembered as "a disgrace to all humanity" for the demolition of the monastic buildings.[2] Today, only one arm of one transept of the abbey church remains as a pale reminder of what had once stood at the center of an international monastic community.

Before their demolition, Cluny's immense structures were visible symbols of the glory and success of medieval Benedictinism. When its rebuilt abbey church, Cluny III, was completed

1. In fact, much of the library had been destroyed as early as the sixteenth century. For some discussion of its fate in the early modern era, see Édouard Jeauneau, "La bibliothèque de Cluny et les oeuvres de L'Érigene," in *Pierre Abélard—Pierre le Vénérable. Les courants philosophiques, littéraires et artistiques en Occident au milieu du XIIe siècle, Abbaye de Cluny 2 au 9 juillet 1972, Colloques internationaux du Centre National de la Recherche Scientifique*, no. 546 (Paris: Éditions du Centre National de la Recherche Scientifique, 1975): 703–25, but especially 711–14.

2. "Vous serez la honte de l'humanité," quoted by Kenneth John Conant, "Cluny Studies, 1968–1975," *Speculum* 50.3 (1975), 386.

during the first half of the twelfth century and consecrated by Pope Innocent II in 1130 during the reign of the Cluniac abbot Peter the Venerable, the length of Cluny III surpassed even the Gothic cathedral at Rheims, the royal coronation church of France. It accommodated more than twelve hundred people and was the largest church in the world until the construction of St. Peter's in Rome.[3] The design of Cluny III may have been intended to establish Cluny itself as a pilgrimage destination, in order to expand the monastery's revenues,[4] although, if this was Abbot Hugh's intention, it remained unrealized. Nonetheless, Cluny III endured as "a capital church for a monastic empire."[5]

Peter the Venerable (d. 1156), Ninth Abbot of Cluny

Peter of Montboissier (b. 1092) was elected ninth abbot of Cluny in 1122 when the Benedictine abbey was at the height of its reputation. For more than one hundred years it had developed, embellished, and expanded the monastic liturgy on an unprecedented scale, although not without eliciting criticism from other orders.[6] When Peter's great-uncle, Abbot Hugh I, died in 1109, Cluny had perhaps three hundred monks. Since their liturgical performances were understood to benefit not only the monks themselves but all of Christendom, in the years before Hugh's death additional donations and new members had been drawn to the abbey,[7] justifying perhaps

3. See Kenneth John Conant, "Medieval Academy Excavations at Cluny, X," *Speculum* 45.1 (1970), 3.

4. See O. K. Werckmeister, "Cluny III and the Pilgrimage to Santiago of Compostela," *Gesta* 27, 1.2 (1988): 103–12.

5. Kenneth John Conant, "Cluny Studies, 1968–1975," 384.

6. See, for example, my "Peter Damian on Cluny, Liturgy, and Penance," *Journal of Religious History* 15.1 (1988): 61–75; reprinted in *Studia Liturgica* 18.2 (1988): 170–87.

7. As Giles Constable has pointed out, many of these had come from other religious houses, often without the permission of their superiors, under a controversial papal privilege granted to Cluny under Abbot Hugh I. See Constable, "The Reception-Privilege of Cluny," originally published in *Le gouvernement d'Hughes de Semur à Cluny*, Actes du colloque scientifique international, Cluny, September 1988 (Cluny: Musée Ochier, 1990), 59–74; reprinted in *The Abbey of Cluny: A Collection of Essays to Mark the Eleven-Hundredth Anniversary of its*

Hugh's dramatic building program. Many other monasteries adopted the Cluniac custom and accepted its sovereignty to share in its privileges and prestige. In 1064 St. Peter Damian, a sometime critic of Cluny's liturgical excesses, wrote to Abbot Hugh I and praised Cluny, nonetheless, as a spiritual arena where heaven and earth meet.[8] Before his death in 1117 the eremitic advocate and reformer Robert of Arbrissel, the founder of Fontevrault, ranked Cluny among the chief holy places of Christendom just after Bethlehem, Jerusalem, and Rome.[9] At the election of Peter of Montboissier—remembered as Peter the Venerable—Cluny had grown to become a large family that comprised some ten thousand monks found in the mother abbey and daughter cells, along with hundreds of affiliated houses and their dependencies, spread throughout England, Germany, Spain, Italy, and even the Holy Land. Before Peter's death, the mother house of Cluny, having completed its ambitious project of building and renovation, reached its peak population of 460 monks.[10]

Peter's family, although from the second rank of the nobility, enjoyed much prestige in central Auvergne.[11] At age sixteen

---

Foundation (Berlin: Lit Verlag, 2010), 163–78. For life at Cluny under Hugh I, see Noreen Hunt, *Cluny under St. Hugh 1049–1109* (Notre Dame, IN: University of Notre Dame Press, 1967).

8. "Cluniacus praeterea spiritalis quidam campus est, ubi caelum et terra congreditur ..." See *Epist.* 113, in Petrus Damiani, *Die Briefe des Petrus Damiani,* ed. Kurt Reindel, Epp. Kaiserzeit (Munich: MGH, 1983–93), 3: 292, ln. 1.

9. Cited by Giles Constable, "The Monastic Policy of Peter the Venerable," in *Cluniac Studies* (London: Variorum Reprints, 1980), 136. For further discussion of Cluny as an especially holy place, see Jennifer A. Harris, "Building Heaven on Earth: Cluny as *Locus Sanctissimus* in the Eleventh Century," in *From Dead of Night to End of Day: The Medieval Customs of Cluny/Du coeur de la nuit à la fin du jour: Les coutumes Clunisiennes au moyen âge,* ed. Susan Boynton and Isabelle Cochelin, Disciplina Monastica 3 (Turnhout: Brepols, 2005), 131–52.

10. See Kenneth J. Conant, "Cluniac Building during the Abbacy of Peter the Venerable," in *Petrus Venerabilis 1156–1956: Studies and Texts Commemorating the Eighth Centenary of His Death,* ed. Giles Constable and James Kritzeck, Studia Anselmiana 40 (Rome: Herder, 1956): 121–27; and Conant, "Édifices marquants dans l'ambiance de Pierre le Vénérable et Pierre Abélard," in *Pierre Abélard—Pierre le Vénérable,* 727–29.

11. For Peter's family and genealogy, see especially *The Letters of Peter the Venerable,* ed. Giles Constable, 2 vols. (Cambridge, MA: Harvard University

Peter was offered to the Benedictine Order at Sauxillanges in Auvergne, a neighboring Cluniac priory patronized by the family Montboissier. Indeed, Peter's father, Maurice, took the monastic habit at Sauxillanges before his death and conferred an estate upon the priory.[12] Peter was educated there, and made his own monastic profession at Cluny shortly before the death of Abbot Hugh I. He quickly advanced to important priorates at Vézelay and at Domène, near Grenoble, where he came to admire the contemplative life at La Grande Chartreuse, the mother-house of the Carthusian Order.[13]

Although Peter had left Vézelay by 1120, his elder brother Pontius[14] became abbot of Vézelay from 1138 to 1161 and continued its ties to Cluny, although almost immediately after his death Pope Alexander III declared Vézelay's autonomy; thereafter it became the special property of the papacy.[15] Vézelay was an important site on the pilgrimage route to Compostela, and since the eleventh century the abbey had received papal approval for its claim that it possessed the relics of Mary Magdalene, for whom Peter himself composed a hymn.[16] The popularity of her cult brought great wealth to the monastery and led to the construction of the abbey church, Sainte-Marie-Madeleine, which was begun before 1100. It was certainly during the ab-

---

Press, 1967), 2: 233–46; and see Jean-Pierre Torrell and Denis Bouthillier, *Pierre le Vénérable et sa vision du monde* (Leuven: Spicilegium Sacrum Lovaniense, 1986), 3–19.

12. See Peter's *Letter* 53, "Item ad germanos suos eiusdem matris <sue> epitaphium," in *Peter the Venerable: Selected Letters,* ed. Janet Martin with Giles Constable (Toronto: Pontifical Institute of Mediaeval Studies, 1974), p. 32 and n. 98.

13. See, for example, Peter's *Letter* 24, "Ad Cartusienses," in *Peter the Venerable: Selected Letters,* 19–24.

14. Pontius was evidently quite unlike his brother Peter in temperament and piety, and the two had a turbulent relationship. See Jean-Pierre Torrell and Denis Bouthillier, *Pierre le Vénérable et sa vision du monde,* 12–13.

15. For an account, see Giles Constable, "Cluny in the Twelfth Century: From Hugh I to Hugh V," in *The Abbey of Cluny: A Collection of Essays to Mark the Eleven-Hundredth Anniversary of its Foundation,* 265–80, esp. 278.

16. For a useful discussion of medieval religious perceptions of Mary Magdalene, see Katherine Ludwig Jansen, "Mary Magdalen and the Contemplative Life," in *Medieval Religion: New Approaches,* ed. Constance Hoffman Berman (New York and London: Routledge, 2005): 249–71.

batial office of Peter's brother that the decoration of the abbey church—its sculpted capitals and tympanum—was completed.[17] Peter the Venerable may have contributed something to the imagery on the tympanum, on which was depicted the mission of the apostles surrounded by scenes that depicted the monstrous races, including the dog-headed creatures (*Cynocephali*) that Strickland has suggested may have symbolized both Jews and Muslims.[18] It was also at Vézelay that St. Bernard of Clairvaux called for a Second Crusade just after Easter 1146, placing this French monastic community very near the center of political and religious life.[19]

Other family members also were important figures in France. Peter's brothers Jordanus (d. 1157–1158) and Armannus[20] became abbots of La-Chaise-Dieu (*Casa Dei*) and Manglieu respectively. La-Chaise-Dieu, founded in the eleventh century by Robert of Brioude, would become one of the most prosperous Benedictine foundations in Auvergne. Like Vézelay, La-Chaise-Dieu was on a pilgrimage route. Another brother, Heraclius, a secular cleric, was provost of the chapter of Saint-Julian at Brioude and then later archbishop of Lyon (1153–d. 1163). Of three other brothers, one died as a youth; a second brother,

17. For a discussion of the decoration, see Christopher Olaf Blum, "Vézelay: The Mountain of the Lord," *Logos: A Journal of Catholic Thought and Culture* 8.3 (2005): 141–64 (especially 152–64). For a brief discussion of the decoration in relation to Peter the Venerable, see also Dominique Iogna-Prat, *Order and Exclusion: Cluny and Christendom Face Heresy, Judaism, and Islam (1000–1500)*, trans. Graham Robert Edwards (Ithaca and London: Cornell University Press, 2002), 268–69.

18. See Debra Hicks Strickland, *Saracens, Demons, and Jews: Making Monsters in Medieval Art* (Princeton: Princeton University Press, 2003), 160. Cf. Christopher Olaf Blum, "Vézelay: The Mountain of the Lord," 158; John Block Friedman, *The Monstrous Races in Medieval Art and Thought* (Syracuse, NY: Syracuse University Press, 2000), 77–79. For Peter's influence on Christian iconography in the sculpted tympanums at La Charité-sur-Loire, see Marie-Louise Thérel, "Pierre le Vénérable et la creation iconographique au XIIe siècle," in *Pierre Abélard—Pierre le Vénérable*, 733–43. The author attributes to Peter's influence the depiction there of the Transfiguration of Christ as well as Mary's bodily assumption.

19. Robert Chazan, *European Jewry and the First Crusade* (Berkeley: University of California Press, 1987), 174.

20. Armannus had been prior at Cluny until 1149.

Dissutus, a knight, married and had two daughters who became nuns at Marcigny,[21] as did Peter's mother, Raingard (d. 1135); the third and youngest brother, Eustace, remained a layman and a knight.

Following the death of Abbot Hugh I, his successor, Pontius of Melgueil (r. 1109–1122), resigned his office after a troubled reign and departed on a pilgrimage to the Holy Land. His successor, Hugh II of Marcigny, died in 1122 after only a few months in office. Peter traveled then to Cluny to elect a new abbot, and he was himself raised up to the abbatial throne. But his abbacy was soon beset by challenges to his rule. Although Pontius of Melgueil had remained in the East for a year, he returned to Italy in 1124 to settle in a little monastery he built in Treviso. There he stayed until spring 1125, at which time he crossed the Alps, and, aided by some of Cluny's monks and by local supporters, he seized Cluny again by force of arms while Peter was absent, visiting Cluniac houses in Aquitaine. In spring 1126 Pontius was summoned by Pope Honorius II to Rome to stand trial. Because Pontius refused to appear before Honorius II, he was arrested, convicted without hearing, and imprisoned in Rome, where he languished until his death in December 1126. Later his body was collected by Peter the Venerable and returned to Cluny.[22]

21. Marcigny-les-Nonnains, a double monastery under the jurisdiction of Cluny, founded in 1055 by Geoffrey II de Semur-en-Brionnais and his brother, Abbot Hugh I of Cluny.

22. Historians have largely disagreed on the causes of Pontius's "fall." Some have argued that Pontius represented an older, decadent Gregorian spirit in the Church that was now challenged by a new guard in the papal curia, influenced by a new spirituality emphasized by the Cistercians. For one such account, see Hayden White, "Pontius of Cluny, the *Curia Romana* and the End of Gregorianism in Rome," *Church History* 27.3 (1958): 195–219. Others have seen the conflict as rooted instead in currents of change internal to Cluny and, in particular, have seen Pontius as an ardent reformer of Cluniac life who was unable to overcome opposition from monastic traditionalists, including Peter the Venerable (his later efforts at reform in Cluny notwithstanding). For this explanation, see Adriaan H. Bredero, *Cluny et Cîteaux au douzième siècle: L'histoire d'une controverse monastique* (Amsterdam: Holland University Press, 1988); cf. Adriaan Bredero, "Pierre le Vénérable: Les commencements de son abbatiat à Cluny (1122–1132)," in *Pierre Abélard—Pierre le Vénérable*, 98–116. Perhaps the most helpful summary of the issues of historical interpretation can

Dissension within Cluny itself was not Peter's only challenge, however. The Cluniac discipline was coming under growing criticism from advocates for change to the religious life. Principal among these was the Cistercian Bernard of Clairvaux; Peter and Bernard emerged as the chief spokesmen for two diverging paths of Benedictine monasticism.[23] The Cistercian yearning for monastic simplicity and austerity influenced Peter as well, who would attempt to reform Cluniac life and to adapt its customs to a new spirituality arising during the twelfth-century renaissance.[24] His success is marked by continued growth and expansion in the Cluniac family, despite the challenges of innovative religious alternatives that included a new emphasis on eremitic experiments and vigorous efforts to conform to the ideals of the apostolic life.[25] Growth at Cluny appeared despite severe pressures on the monastery's finances that stemmed both from debts that Peter inherited and from costs associated with its expansion and growth.[26] Peter himself was greatly admired outside the monastic world: it was not a Cluniac monk but Frederick Barbarossa, who reigned as emperor of the Holy Roman Empire from 1155, who conferred upon him the title

be found in Mary Stroll, *The Jewish Pope: Ideology and Politics in the Papal Schism of 1130* (Leiden: E. J. Brill, 1987), chaps. 3–4. Stroll suggests that a strong case can be made that the underlying cause behind the fall of Abbot Pontius was papal and episcopal efforts to expand control over Cluny and its resources.

23. For their relationship, see especially Adriaan H. Bredero, "Saint Bernard in His Relations with Peter the Venerable," in *Bernardus Magister,* Cistercian Studies Series 135, ed. John R. Sommerfeldt (Western Michigan University: Cistercian Publications, Inc., 1992): 315–48. Here the author seems to modify some of the conclusions of his earlier "The Controversy Between Peter the Venerable and Saint Bernard of Clairvaux," in *Petrus Venerabilis 1156–1956,* 53–71.

24. See David Knowles, "The Reforming Decrees of Peter the Venerable," in *Petrus Venerabilis 1156–1956,* 1–20.

25. For a snapshot of reform currents, see Lester K. Little, "Intellectual Training and Attitudes toward Reform, 1075–1150," in *Pierre Abélard—Pierre le Vénérable,* 235–54; for a summary of the differing emphases of Cluniac and Cistercian reform efforts, see Terrence G. Kardong, "Saint Benedict and the Twelfth-Century Reformation," *Cistercian Studies Quarterly* 36.3 (2001): 279–309.

26. For the financial conditions at Cluny during Peter's abbacy, see especially Georges Duby, "Un inventaire des profits de la seigneurie Clunisienne à la mort de Pierre le Vénérable," in *Petrus Venerabilis 1156–1956,* 128–40.

"the Venerable."[27] Following his death on 25 December 1156, Peter was buried in the abbey church at Cluny.[28]

Peter's Literary Work

Peter the Venerable produced an extensive literary legacy that includes poems,[29] a large letter collection, and polemical treatises. His letters appear in two collections. The first collection was likely assembled before 1142 by Peter and his *notarius* or secretary, Peter of Poitiers,[30] and includes his polemical attack on the Petrobrusians (*Tractatus contra Petrobrusianos haereticos*).[31] A second and larger letter collection, compiled perhaps just before or after Peter's death in 1156, was divided into six books and contained 196 letters and several treatises. Between the two collections there are some differences in content as well as stylistic variations, suggesting that revisions were made, probably by Peter himself. The first printed edition of the letters, published in 1522 and edited by the Cluniac monk

27. Reinhold Glei, *Petrus Venerabilis Schriften zum Islam*, Corpus Islamo-Christianum, Series Latina 1 (Altenberge: CIS-Verlag, 1985), xiv.

28. See Conant, "Medieval Academy Excavations at Cluny, X," 9, for a diagram showing the location of the abbots' tombs.

29. Peter's poetic compositions have appeared in a Latin-French critical edition, *Petrus Venerabilis. Carmina cum Petri Pictaviensis Panegyrico/Pierre le Vénérable: Poèmes avec le Panegyrique de Pierre de Poitiers*, ed. Franz Dolveck, Auteurs latins du Moyen Âge 27 (Paris: Les belles lettres, 2014). I have not been able to consult this work yet.

30. Peter of Poitiers was the secretary or *notarius* to Peter the Venerable and assisted Peter of Toledo to produce his Latin translations. He is identified as a *notarius* already in 1136/37, in Peter the Venerable's *Letter* 24 to Guigo du Châtel, prior of the Carthusians. See *Peter the Venerable: Selected Letters*, 24, lns. 125–26. For a discussion of his life, see *The Letters of Peter the Venerable*, ed. Giles Constable, 2: 331–43.

31. For the critical edition, see *Contra Petrobrusianos hereticos*, ed. James Fearns, CC CM 10 (Turnhout: Brepols, 1968). For discussion of the heresy, see Jean Châtillon, "Pierre le Vénérable et les Pétrobrusiens," in *Pierre Abélard—Pierre le Vénérable*, 165–76; Heinrich Fichtenau, *Heretics and Scholars in the High Middle Ages 1000–1200*, trans. Denise A. Kaiser (University Park, PA: Pennsylvania State University Press, 1998), 57–63. For more detailed discussion of the *Tractatus contra Petrobrusianos haereticos*, see especially Dominique Iogna-Prat, *Order and Exclusion*, part II, chap. 3; and Torrell and Bouthillier, *Pierre le Vénérable et sa vision du monde*, 162–71. This work was first composed ca. 1138.

Pierre de Montmartre, is based on a no longer extant manuscript probably from Cluny itself. It contains not only more letters than any other collection, but also the rare polemic *Against
the Sect of the Saracens* (*Contra sectam sive haeresim Saracenorum*),
written late in Peter's life. Peter's longest polemical treatise was
directed against a third enemy, namely, the Jews. Peter's *Against
the Inveterate Obduracy of the Jews* (*Adversus Iudeorum inveteratam
duritiem*),[32] in five chapters, was written in the years between
Against the Petrobrusians and *Against the Saracens.* These polemical treatises were not incidental to Peter's concern, despite the
many challenges he faced within his own monastery and in the
Church at large. Indeed, Peter of Poitiers, in a letter translated
below,[33] recalls his abbot's polemical campaign and encourages
Peter the Venerable to prevail equally over the Muslims:

I want you to confound them, then, just as you have confounded the
Jews and the heretics from our region.[34] Indeed, in our time you are
the only one who has cut down with the sword of the divine word[35]
the three greatest enemies of holy Christianity—I mean the Jews, the
heretics, and the Saracens—and you have shown that Mother Church
is not so deprived or despoiled of good sons but that she has still, by
a gracious Christ, such ones as can supply "to each one demanding
it a reason for the hope" and faith "that are in us,"[36] and can humble
all the devil's arrogance and pride "that raises itself up against the
height of God."[37]

Peter the Venerable's polemics seem to constitute a unified program, then, intended to defeat the most significant contemporary challenges to Christian faith and power.

The Translations

The Catholic University of America Press published my English translation of Peter the Venerable's *Against the Inveterate
Obduracy of the Jews* in 2013.[38] The present volume will make

32. Peter the Venerable, *Adversus Iudeorum inveteratam duritiem,* ed. Yvonne
Friedman, CC CM 58 (Turnhout: Brepols, 1985).
33. *Epistola Petri Pictaviensis 3,* found in the Appendix, *infra,* pp. 163–66.
34. A reference, in all likelihood, to Peter's polemic *Against the Petrobrusians.*
35. Cf. Eph 6.17.   36. 1 Pt 3.15.
37. Cf. 2 Cor 10.5.
38. Peter the Venerable, *Against the Inveterate Obduracy of the Jews,* trans.

available Peter the Venerable's twin polemics against Islam: *A Summary of the Entire Heresy of the Saracens (Summa totius haeresis Saracenorum)* and *Against the Sect of the Saracens (Contra sectam Saracenorum)*. Together, these two texts represent the whole of Peter the Venerable's systematic attack upon the teachings of Islam. They should not be divorced, however, from Peter's political theology. For example, Peter wrote a long letter to King Louis VII (r. 1137–1180) in support of the Second Crusade (1146–49 CE), in which Peter praised the king for his plan to march to the East, "armed with the cross of Christ" in order to attack "the wicked Arab or Persian people." Louis VII, Peter incorrectly predicted, "will destroy the Saracens, enemies of the true faith, and will toil to conquer their lands for God." Moreover, Peter saw a link between the armed Crusade against the Saracens, and the treatment of Jews within Christian Europe: "as the Christian army which sets out against the Saracens does not spare its own lands and money out of its love for Christ, let it not spare the treasures of the Jews amassed through vile means. Let their lives be spared but their money taken away, so that through the power of the Christians, fortified by the wealth of the blasphemous Jews, the audacity of the Saracen infidels may be overcome."[39]

As the abbot of perhaps the greatest monastery in Europe, Peter was not destined to take up military arms against the Saracens. Although he discouraged monks from taking up the crusader's cross, he certainly encouraged the military ranks, the warriors or *bellatores,* to assume this task.[40] In his own way,

---

Irven M. Resnick, FOTC, MC 14 (Washington, DC: The Catholic University of America Press, 2013).

39. *Letter* 130. For the Latin text, see *The Letters of Peter the Venerable,* 1: 327–30. I have relied here on Jeremy Cohen's translation, which will appear in the forthcoming *Twelfth-Century Renaissance: A Reader,* ed. Alex Novikoff (Toronto: University of Toronto Press).

40. For contemporary views and source materials on the Second Crusade, see especially Giles Constable, "The Second Crusade as Seen by Contemporaries," *Traditio* 9 (1953): 213–79. For Peter's own relationship to the Second Crusade, see Virginia Berry, "Peter the Venerable and the Crusades," in *Petrus Venerabilis 1156–1956,* 140–62. The aims of the Crusade in the East were not realized, but in the West the Crusaders did capture the city of Lisbon—one of their few achievements. See Jonathan Phillips, "St. Bernard of Clairvaux, the

however, Peter made a real contribution by creating a literary arsenal with which to defeat the enemies of the Christian faith. Peter developed "a verbal martial art with precise rules of engagement,"[41] and, as such, his polemics served as a literary parallel to the military effort of the crusaders.[42] Again, Peter of Poitiers would later exhort his abbot to complete his polemical campaign armed "with the sword of the divine word." As the Crusades were intended to restore a divinely ordained order to the world, so Peter's polemics were meant to defend the spiritual order of Christendom against contemporary challengers. These challengers—Petrobrusians, Jews, and Muslims—all seemed to Peter more inclined toward this world than the next and challenged, as a result, the power that Christianity (and monasticism in particular) claimed for itself to open for its adherents the gates to heaven.

Peter's polemics against Islam, then, are not unrelated to the crusading ideology of the mid-twelfth century.[43] The first text, the *Summary of the Entire Heresy of the Saracens,* was likely completed soon after Peter returned to Cluny from Spain in early summer, 1143. The second and much longer text, *Against the Sect of the Saracens,* was likely completed not long before Peter's death in 1156, and may have been composed, in part, during

---

Low Countries and the Lisbon Letter of the Second Crusade," *Journal of Ecclesiastical History* 48.3 (1997): 485–97. But cf. Alan Forey, "The Siege of Lisbon and the Second Crusade," *Portuguese Studies* 20 (2004): 1–13.

41. Dominique Iogna-Prat, *Order and Exclusion,* 122.

42. Torrell and Bouthillier remark quite properly that for Peter "le dialogue est en réalité un autre forme de combat, la manière propre de se battre de ceux qui, comme lui, ne peuvent pas porter les armes." *Pierre le Vénérable et sa vision du monde,* 180.

43. Moreover, Peter would surely have been aware that one of Cluny's early abbots, Maiolus of Cluny (d. 994), and his entourage had been kidnaped in 972 and held for ransom by Muslim brigands from La Garde-Freinet, in southeastern France. As Scott G. Bruce has noted, the story had been retold as late as the first quarter of the twelfth century by the Cluniac monk Nalgod in his *Vita sancti Maioli.* See Scott G. Bruce, "An Abbot between Two Cultures: Maiolus of Cluny Considers the Muslims of La Garde-Freinet," *Early Medieval Europe* 15.4 (2007): 426–40; idem, *Cluny and the Muslims of La Garde-Freinet. Hagiography and the Problem of Islam in Medieval Europe* (Ithaca and London: Cornell University Press, 2015).

his second visit to England. The date for this visit has been a subject of controversy.

It is certain that Peter made his first journey to England in 1130. Cluny enjoyed the patronage of many members of the nobility in England, moreover, and the special patronage of King Henry I (d. 1135), whose gifts to the abbey, according to abbatial documents, surpassed those of other monarchs, including Alfonso VI in Spain.[44] Most scholars date Peter's second visit to England to 1155–1156, based in part on a letter from Peter of Poitiers,[45] which Constable dated to the end of 1155.[46] In addition, we have the witness of Robert de Torigny, who asserts that in 1155 Bishop Henry of Winchester (Henry of Blois) had secretly sent his wealth from England to Cluny with its abbot, Peter the Venerable.[47] Van den Eynde, however, argued for an earlier date for this second journey to England—namely, 1148/49;[48] Yvonne Friedman was inclined to support Van den Eynde's conclusion, and has suggested 1149 as a *terminus ante quem* for the letter from Peter of Poitiers.[49] Subsequently, however, Torrell and Bouthillier argued persuasively that Peter's second visit to England must have occurred in late 1155 or early 1156. Their conclusion is based especially on a text in his *De miraculis* in which Peter the Venerable describes a certain miracle that he attributes to St. Maiolus, who, he notes, had died 162 years earlier.[50] Since

---

44. See Dietrich Lohrmann, "Pierre le Vénérable et Henri Ier, Roi d'Angleterre," *Pierre Abélard—Pierre le Vénérable*, 191–203, citing 191–92.

45. *Infra*, pp. 163–66.

46. *The Letters of Peter the Venerable*, ed. Giles Constable, 2 vols. (Cambridge, MA: Harvard University Press, 1967), 2: 268.

47. See *Chronicles of the Reigns of Stephen, Henry II, and Richard I*, vol. 4: *The Chronicle of Robert of Torigni* [*Chronica Roberti*] (London: Public Record Office, 1889), p.186. Henry of Winchester was brother to King Stephen (of Blois). After Henry II came to the throne in 1154, Henry of Winchester evidently feared that the new king would seize his wealth.

48. See D. Van den Eynde, "Les principaux voyages de Pierre le Vénérable," *Benedictina* 15 (1968): 58–110, esp. 89–94.

49. See *Adversus Iudeorum inueteratam duritiem*, lxiii. Her conclusion is based on the identification of Godfrey/Godefridus as constable in Peter of Poitiers' *Letter*. Since Godfrey held this position only until 1146–1147, and had been replaced by Leontfridus in 1149, she infers that the letter (and the visit to England) must have been completed before then.

50. *De miraculis* 2, cap. 32 (31).

St. Maiolus died in 994, this chapter can be dated precisely to 1156. Moreover, the chapter immediately precedes another in which Peter mentions having returned from his second visit to England,[51] providing strong evidence that this second visit to England had occurred in 1155 or 1156.[52]

To these two texts—*Summary of the Entire Heresy of the Saracens* and *Against the Sect of the Saracens*—I have joined a translation of three related documents. The first is Peter the Venerable's *Letter [to Bernard of Clairvaux] on His Translation (Epistola de translatione sua)*, which Peter wrote in 1144 to Bernard, the Cistercian abbot of Clairvaux, in an effort to recruit the latter to his project, namely, a refutation of the errors of Islam. The second is the *Letter of Peter of Poitiers (Epistola Petri Pictaviensis)*, in which Peter of Poitiers, the secretary or *notarius* to Abbot Peter the Venerable, replies to the Cluniac abbot and promises to reconstruct the lost chapter headings for *Against the Sect of the Saracens*. According to this letter, the chapter headings had been lost by the monk John, a member of Peter the Venerable's entourage, during the course of the abbot's travel to England. The third document contains Peter of Poitiers' *capitula,* or chapter headings themselves, reconstructed to satisfy his promise to his abbot.

These documents help to establish the historical background to Peter the Venerable's project. The letter to St. Bernard reveals the importance that Peter attached to his polemical campaign against Islam, insofar as he sought—albeit unsuccessfully—to persuade Bernard, whose reputation was solidly established in Christendom, to compose a comprehensive refutation of Islam, soon after Peter wrote his own brief *Summary of the Entire Heresy of the Saracens.* Not only was Bernard a well-known literary figure and preacher, but only two years after Peter composed his letter to Bernard, the latter went to Vézelay (just after Easter 1146), accompanied by King Louis VII, and called for a Second Crusade.[53] Although Bernard never replied directly to Peter's

---

51. *De miraculis* 2, cap. 33 (32).

52. See Jean-Pierre Torrell and Denis Bouthillier, *Pierre le Vénérable et sa vision du monde*, pp. 57–59, 133 n. 85, and 172.

53. For Bernard's preaching of the Crusade, see, for example, *Epist.* 363.6 in *Sancti Bernardi Opera genuina*, ed. Monks of St. Benedict, 8 vols. (Lyons and Paris: Perisse Frères, 1854), 8: 316. This letter is addressed to the English peo-

appeal, his later support for the Second Crusade provides some reason to believe that Bernard would not be unsympathetic to Peter's goal.

The letter written by Peter the Venerable's *notarius,* Peter of Poitiers, is significant for other reasons. Not only does this letter help us to assign a date to *Against the Sect of the Saracens,* which Peter the Venerable likely completed not long before his death in 1156, but the letter also creates something of a conundrum for the historian, not least because Peter of Poitiers' summary of the chapter headings and outline of chapter contents in Peter the Venerable's *Against the Sect of the Saracens* suggest a much longer treatise in four books, whereas the one that has been preserved for us contains only two books. To make matters somewhat worse, the *Chronicon Cluniacense* indicates that there were five books.[54] Kritzeck argued that Peter did not follow the chapter divisions suggested by Peter of Poitiers, and that "what remains to us is the entirety of the work completed by Peter."[55] It remains possible, nonetheless, that Peter had *planned* but failed to produce a work longer and more complete than what we have in *Against the Sect of the Saracens.*[56]

The complete text of *Against the Sect of the Saracens* is found in a single twelfth-century manuscript, MS 381 of the Bibliothèque municipale de Douai, which also contains most of Peter the Venerable's correspondence and his *Against the Inveterate Obduracy of the Jews,* as well as Peter of Poitiers's *capitula,* mentioned above. This unique manuscript was the basis for the subsequent edition in Migne's *Patrologia,*[57] although several contemporary scholars have suggested significant corrections to the readings

---

ple and exhorts them to participate in the Second Crusade. It can be found in translation (as *Letter* 391) in *The Letters of St. Bernard of Clairvaux,* trans. Bruno Scott James (Chicago: Henry Regnery Company, 1953), 460–63. For a broad discussion of Bernard and Cistercian crusading ideology, see Jonathan Phillips, *The Second Crusade: Extending the Frontiers of Christendom* (New Haven: Yale University Press, 2007), chap. 4.

54. PL 189: 30C.

55. James Kritzeck, *Peter the Venerable and Islam* (Princeton: Princeton University Press, 1964), 156.

56. For discussion, see Glei, xxi–xxviii.

57. PL 189: 663–720.

found there.[58] The *Summary of the Entire Heresy of the Saracens* is found in MS 1162 of the Bibliothèque de l'Arsenal; in addition, brief selections from the *Summary of the Entire Heresy of the Saracens* are found in two later medieval MSS.[59] The manuscript tradition and the relationship between these texts have been treated admirably by James Kritzeck[60] and M. T. d'Alverny.[61] In addition, Kritzeck published a historical investigation followed by a helpful, although sometimes flawed, English paraphrase of the *Summary of the Entire Heresy of the Saracens* and *Against the Sect of the Saracens*.[62]

Peter the Venerable's two texts were not the first to convey to a Latin audience Islam's fundamental theological claims. Indeed, the fifth titulus of Petrus Alfonsi's *Dialogue Against the Jews*,[63] which appeared almost forty years before the *Summary of the Entire Heresy of the Saracens* and which reflected the author's familiarity with the Arabic sources for Islam, was in many ways a better informed discussion of contemporary Islamic ritual and practice.[64] It also was an important source for Peter the

58. For a summary of necessary corrections, see Jean-Pierre Torrell, "La notion de prophétie et la méthode apologétique dans le *Contra Saracenos* de Pierre le Vénérable," *Studia Monastica* 17 (1975): 281–82; Glei, xxx–xxxi.

59. See Kritzeck, "Peter the Venerable and the Toledan Collection," in *Petrus Venerabilis 1156–1956: Studies and Texts Commemorating the Eighth Centenary of His Death*, ed. Giles Constable and James Kritzeck, Studia Anselmiana 40 (Rome: Herder, 1956), 184 n. 33; and idem, *Peter the Venerable and Islam*, 28. These are identified as a late (unnumbered) MS belonging to the Chapter of Le Puy, fol. 55v, and MS 2261 of the Bibliothèque municipale de Troyes, fols. 27v–28r.

60. James Kritzeck, "Peter the Venerable and the Toledan Collection," 176–201.

61. M. T. d'Alverny, "Quelques manuscrits de la 'collectio Toletana,'" in *Petrus Venerabilis 1156–1956*, 202–18.

62. James Kritzeck, *Peter the Venerable and Islam*. For perhaps the harshest review of Kritzeck's volume, see Richard Lemay, "Apologetics and (bad) Latin," *Middle East Forum* 49 (1965): 41–44. Lemay concludes, on pp. 43–44, both that "Kritzeck's mastery of the Latin language is at best very shaky" and that "the introductory material is surely of scant interest."

63. See *Petrus Alfonsi, Dialogue Against the Jews*, trans. Irven M. Resnick, FOTC, MC 8 (Washington, DC: The Catholic University of America Press, 2006).

64. For this conclusion, see also John V. Tolan, *Saracens: Islam in the Medieval*

Venerable's biography of Mohammad in the latter's *Summary of the Entire Heresy of the Saracens*. Nonetheless, Peter's twin compositions reflect an engagement with Islam's texts in Latin translation that had not been possible for earlier polemicists. This engagement was made possible when, during his journey to Spain in 1142–43, Peter the Venerable commissioned, at significant expense, the translation of a body of texts: the so-called Toledan Collection.[65] For this reason, Glei's assessment that Peter the Venerable was the initiator of Islamic studies in the West, and Tischler's claim that the Toledan Collection Peter commissioned led to substantial growth in the knowledge of Islam and to a "revolutionary shift" in efforts to refute it, are not exaggerations.[66]

European Imagination (New York: Columbia University Press, 2002), 163–64; Michelina di Cesare, "Petrus Alfonsi and Islamic Culture: Literary and Lexical Strategies," in *Petrus Alfonsi and his* Dialogus. *Background, Context, Reception,* ed. Carmen Cardelle de Hartmann and Philipp Roelli, Micrologus Library 66 (Florence: SISMEL-Edizioni del Galluzzo, 2014), 203–25; and Regula Forster, "Der abwesende Dritte. Die Darstellung des Islam im *titulus V* des *Dialogus* des Petrus Alfonsi," *op. cit.*, 159–82. For the dialogic tension in Alfonsi's account between a "Jewish" or carnal account of Islam and its origins, and a Christian, revisionist interpretation, see esp. Leor Halevi, "*Lex Mahomethi:* Carnal and Spiritual Representations of Islamic Law and Ritual in a Twelfth-Century Dialogue by a Jewish Convert to Christianity," in *The Islamic Scholarly Tradition. Studies in History, Law, and Thought in Honor of Professor Michael Allen Cook,* ed. Asad Q. Ahmed, Behnam Sadeghi, and Michael Bonner (Leiden and Boston: Brill, 2011), 315–42.

65. *Collectio Toledana,* also known as the *Corpus Cluniacense.* Already at the end of the 19th century Mandonnet drew attention to the scope and importance of the collection as a vehicle for transmitting to Latin Europe knowledge of Islam as a *religious* and not merely scientific culture. See P. F. Mandonnet, "Pierre le Vénérable et son activité littéraire contre l'Islam," *Revue Thomiste* 1 (1893): 328–42. Peter does not tell us how much he invested in this project, and, as Charles Burnett points out, this is the only instance of which he is aware in which payment was made for translation. See Charles S. F. Burnett, "Some Comments on the Translating of Works from Arabic into Latin in the Mid-Twelfth Century," in *Orientalische Kultur und europäisches Mittelalter,* ed. Albert Zimmermann, Ingrid Craemer-Ruegenberg, and Gudrun Vuillemin-Diem, Miscellanea Mediaevalia 17 (Berlin and New York: Walter de Gruyter, 1985), 161–70, citing 164.

66. Glei, ix; Matthias M. Tischler, "Modes of Literary Behaviours in Christian-Islamic Encounters in the Iberian Peninsula: *Pseudo-Turpin* versus Peter the Venerable," in *Languages of Love and Hate: Conflict, Communication, and Identity in*

The Toledan Collection resulted from Peter the Venerable's growing awareness of the religious threat that Islam represented to Christendom; Peter was also very aware that few European Christians outside Spain had the linguistic skills to study Islam's source materials. In Spain, however, there were numerous translators working to make Arabic texts available to a Latin audience. Peter became acquainted with several during his first visit there in 1142.

Peter had departed Cluny in 1142 with a large entourage to visit Cluniac monasteries in Spain, but also perhaps to go on pilgrimage to the shrine of Santiago de Compostela, leaving the care of all Cluniac monasteries during his absence to Archbishop Geoffrey of Bordeaux. In addition, he seems to have been invited to a meeting by Emperor Alfonso VII (d. 1157).[67] The emperor's father, Alfonso VI, had doubled his father Ferdinand's gift to Cluny and pledged an annual census donation of two thousand gold *metcales* or dinars.[68] Given Cluny's financial burdens and the fact that the donation was in arrears, Peter evidently hoped that the meeting would lead to an advantageous financial settlement. Although in a diploma of July 29, 1142, Alfonso VII ceded to Cluny the Castilian abbey of San Pedro de Cardeña, as well as certain minor properties near Burgos, Peter received only a small percentage of the funds owed the monastery and obtained only a pledge for a sharply reduced annual stipend from royal revenues. After he received reports that conditions at Cluny urgently required his presence, Peter began his return journey and arrived back at Cluny by summer 1143.

As Charles Burnett noted, between 1116 and 1187, at least 116 works were translated from Arabic to Latin in Spain by

---

the Medieval Mediterranean, ed. Sarah Lambert and Helen Nicholson (Turnhout: Brepols, 2012), 201–22, citing 211.

67. Bishko regards this as the most compelling factor to account for Peter's journey to Spain, which had been visited on two previous occasions by the Cluniac abbots Hugh I and Pontius. See Charles Julian Bishko, "Peter the Venerable's Journey to Spain," in *Petrus Venerabilis 1156–1956,* 163–75.

68. For Cluny's relationship to Alfonso VI (d. 1109) and his father, Ferdinand I (d. 1065), see especially Charles Julian Bishko, "Liturgical Intercession at Cluny for the King-Emperors of Leon," *Studia Monastica* 7 (1961): 53–76.

known authors.[69] In Spain, where Christians had long engaged in anti-Muslim polemic,[70] Peter had learned of a Christian book written in Arabic—the *Apology of [Ps.] Al-Kindi*[71]—that challenged or refuted Islamic doctrines, and he turned to Peter of Toledo to translate it. Puig may exaggerate slightly when he describes the Latin translation of this work as "the most influential source of anti-Muslim polemic ... in Medieval Europe."[72] Peter the Venerable recognized its utility, however. Because Peter of Toledo did not know Latin as well as he knew Arabic, Peter also assigned his own *notarius* Peter of Poitiers as an assistant to the translator to polish the Latin translation.[73] To-

69. Charles S. F. Burnett, "Some Comments on the Translating of Works from Arabic into Latin in the Mid-Twelfth Century," 161.

70. For Mozarabic polemic and intellectual currents before Peter's journey to Spain, see Ludwig Vones, "Zwischen Kulturaustausch und religioser Polemik. Von den Möglichkeiten und Grenzen christlich-muslimischer Verständigung zur Zeit des Petrus Venerabilis," in *Wissen über Grenzen. Arabisches Wissen und lateinisches Mittelalter*, ed. Andreas Speer and Lydia Wegener, Miscellanea Mediaevalia 33 (Berlin: Walter de Gruyter, 2006), 217–37.

71. The anti-Muslim polemic of pseudo-al-Kindi, the *Risālah (Apology)*, consists of two letters. The first purports to have been written to a Christian by a Muslim closely related to the caliph Al-Ma'mūn (r. 813–33), to encourage him to convert to the faith of Islam. The second is a much longer reply to the first, and was allegedly written by a Christian in the caliph's service. This text was available in medieval Spain only in Arabic, until it was translated into Latin in 1142 by Peter of Toledo. For the Latin translation, see José Muñoz Sendino, "Al-Kindi, Apologia del Cristianismo," in *Miscellanea Comillas* 11–12 (1949): 337–460. The Latin text itself appears on pp. 377–460. This edition is based on only two manuscripts, however: Oxford MS 184, Corpus Christi College, fols. 272–353; and Paris, MS Lat. 6064, Bibl. Nat., fols. 83–105; and it failed to take into account variant readings in MS 1162 of the Bibliothèque de l'Arsenal. For a newer edition, see Fernando González Muñoz, *Exposición y refutación del islam: La versión latina de las epístolas de al-Hasimi y al-Kindi* (A Coruña, Spain: Universidade da Coruña, 2005).

72. Josef Puig, "The Polemic Against Islam in Medieval Catalan Culture," in *Wissen über Grenzen*, 238–58, citing 241.

73. The identity of Peter of Toledo, evidently a convert to Christianity, remains controversial and much discussed. Glei (p. xviii) remarks, "Über die Person des Petrus von Toledo wissen wir so gut wie nichts." Most recently, it has been argued again that Peter of Toledo and Petrus Alfonsi, a Jewish convert to Christianity in Spain in 1106 and the author of the polemical *Dialogue Against the Jews*, may have been one and the same. See especially P. Sj. van Koningsveld, "La apologia de Al-Kindi en la España del siglo XII. Huellas toledanos de un

gether, from the Arabic text of the *Apology of [Ps.] Al-Kindi* they produced the *Letter of a Saracen with a Christian Response (Epistola Saraceni cum Rescripto Christiani)*. In addition, Peter also commissioned in Spain the Englishman Robert of Ketton, Herman of Dalmatia (or Carinthia), and a Muslim named Mohammad to translate other Arabic texts found in the Toledan Collection. This collection included the following: the *Fables of the Saracens (Fabulae Saracenorum)*, translated by Robert of Ketton and containing a potpourri of Islamic *hadith* traditions; the *Teaching of Mohammad (Doctrina Mahumet)*[74] and a "life" of the prophet Mohammad (*Liber generationis Mahumet*), both translated by Herman of Dalmatia;[75] and the first Latin translation of the whole of the Qur'an (*Lex Mahumet* or *Lex Sarracenorum*),[76] translated by Robert of Ketton, in which he not only expanded the number of surahs from 114 to 123, but to which he also introduced marginal notations for Latin readers to draw their attention to its "diabolical" claims.[77] Although Gospel texts had been avail-

---

'Animal disputax,'" in *Estudios sobre Alfonso VI y la Reconquista de Toledo. Actes del II Congreso Internacional de Estudios Mozárabes (Toledo, 20–26 Mayo 1985)*, Series Historica 5 (Toledo: Instituto de Estudios Visigótico-Mozárabes, 1989): 107–29; Allan H. Cutler and Helen E. Cutler, *The Jew as Ally of the Muslim: Medieval Roots of Anti-Semitism* (Notre Dame, IN: University of Notre Dame Press, 1986), 52–80; cf. Charles Burnett, "The Works of Petrus Alfonsi: Questions of Authenticity," *Medium Aevum* 66.1 (1997), 49–50; John Tolan, *Petrus Alfonsi and his Medieval Readers* (Gainesville: University Press of Florida, 1993), 210–11; and, for a summary of this controversy, see also Petrus Alfonsi, *Dialogue Against the Jews*, 22–24.

74. Based on the *Masā'il 'Absillāh ibn-Salām*, i.e., the "questions" of 'Abdallāh ibn-Salām. For further description, see James Kritzeck, *Peter the Venerable and Islam*, 89–96.

75. Herman based his translation upon the *Kitāb Nasāb Rasūl Allāh* by Sa'īd ibn-'Umar. See James Kritzeck, *Peter the Venerable and Islam*, 84–88.

76. As Matthias M. Tischler points out, identifying the Qur'an as a *Lex Mahumet/Mahometi* is intended to characterize the Qur'an as the product of Mohammad himself, a pseudo-prophet, rather than a work of divine inspiration, in contrast to the scriptures of Judaism and Christianity. See "*Lex Mahometi*. Die Erfolgsgeschichte eines vergleichenden Konzepts der christlichen Religionspolemik," in *Das Gesetz—The Law—La Loi*, ed. Andreas Speer and Guy Guldentops (Berlin: Walter de Gruyter, 2014), 527–73.

77. For discussion of Robert of Ketton's Latin translation of the Qur'an, completed in June or July 1143, see José Martínez Gázquez, "Trois traductions médiévales latines du Coran: Pierre le Vénérable-Robert de Ketton, Marc de

able in Arabic already since the ninth century, the absence of a
Latin translation of the Qur'an resulted in an asymmetry that
Peter the Venerable sought to remedy. Ultimately the translations that formed the Toledan Collection were collected into
a single volume,[78] perhaps with Peter of Poitiers as editor. The
Toledan Collection, preserved in the twelfth-century MS 1162
of the Bibliothèque de l'Arsenal (which also contains the earliest medieval illumination to depict the prophet Mohammad),[79]

Tolède et Jean de Segobia," *Revue des études latines* 80 (2003): 223–36. Very
helpful to understanding Robert's work is also Thomas E. Burman, *Reading
the Qur'an in Latin Christendom, 1140–1560* (Philadelphia: University of Pennsylvania Press, 2007), chaps. 3–4, pp. 60–123. Of special note is Burman's remark that, on the one hand, when compared to Later Latin translations of the
Qur'an, none is "so relentlessly hostile to Islam" while, "On the other hand,
very few other sources demonstrate such detailed familiarity with Islam and
Qur'ān exegesis ..."; *Reading the Qur'ān in Latin Christendom,* 74. The identity
of the author of the annotations to the translation has been debated, with Peter of Poitiers and Peter of Toledo the most likely candidates. For discussion,
see Thomas E. Burman in his *Religious Polemic and the Intellectual History of the
Mozarabs, ca. 1050–1200* (Leiden: E. J. Brill, 1994), 84–88. For some of the prob-
lems stemming from Robert of Ketton's translation, see also Ludwig B. Hagemann, "Die erste lateinische Koranübersetzung—Mittel zur Verständigung
zwischen Christen und Muslimen im Mittelalter?" in *Orientalische Kultur und
europäisches Mittelalter,* ed. Albert Zimmermann, Ingrid Craemer-Ruegenberg,
and Gudrun Vuillemin-Diem, Miscellanea Mediaevalia 17 (Berlin and New
York: Walter de Gruyter, 1985), 45–58, esp. 47ff. The conclusion of Obeidat
and Mumayiz is far too polemical: "The translation [of the Qur'an], by three
[*sic*] Christian scholars and an Arab was inaccurate, shallow, and full of errors." See Marwan M. Obeidat and Ibrahim Mumayiz, "Anglo-American Literary Sources on the Muslim Orient: The Roots and the Reiterations," *Journal of
American Studies of Turkey* 13 (2001): 47–72, citing 49.

78. Max Lejbowicz remarks that the collection would perhaps better be
known as the Cluniac Collection, since it had little significance in Spain. See
Max Lejbowicz, "Développement autochtone assumé et acculturation dissimulée," in *Les relations culturelles entre chrétiens et musulmans au moyen âge: Quelles
leçons en tirer de nos jours?* Colloque organisé à la Fondation Singer-Polignac le
mercredi 20 octobre 2004 par Rencontres médiévales européennes, ed. Max
Lejbowicz (Turnhout: Brepols, 2005): 57–81; it has been reprinted in English
translation as "Between Autochthonous Tradition and Concealed Acculturation," in *Wissen über Grenzen,* 32–46.

79. See Walter B. Cahn, "The 'Portrait' of Mohammad in the Toledan Collection," in *Reading Medieval Images. The Art Historian and the Object,* ed. Elizabeth Sears and Thelma K. Thomas (Ann Arbor: University of Michigan Press,

was widely read by late medieval Christian polemicists. Subsequently it was published by Thomas Bibliander in Basel in 1543;[80] Bibliander's print edition—which has its own fascinating history—led to even wider diffusion, and also became the basis for a number of vernacular translations of the Qur'an in the late sixteenth and seventeenth centuries.[81]

Not only did the Toledan Collection assemble essential elements in Latin translation for a study of Islam, but some of its texts, such as the *Letter of a Saracen with a Christian Response,* also provided Peter the Venerable with a literary armory necessary to construct his own polemics against Islam. By virtue of his access to sources in Latin translation, then, Peter the Venerable was able to produce an attack upon Islam based on textual sources, and one that would have some significant influence upon later medieval Christian images of Islam. Thanks in part to Peter's efforts, Christian clerics from the second half of the twelfth century could acquire a far superior historical knowledge of the prophet Mohammad,[82] of the teachings of Islam, and of its perceived threat to Christianity.[83] One of these may

---

2002), 51–60. The "portrait" of Mohammad appears in Bibliothèque de l'Arsenal, MS 1162, fol. 11r.

80. A digital edition is available at http://www.wdl.org/en/item/9922/view/1/5/.

81. For a brief survey of its history, see Harmut Bobzin, "Latin Translations of the Koran, a Short Overview," *Der Islam* 70 (1993): 193–206, esp. 193–98.

82. See M.-Th. D'Alverny, "Pierre le Vénérable et la Légende de Mahomet," in *A Cluny Congrès Scientifique Fêtes et cérémonies liturgiques en l'honneur des saints Abbés Odon et Odilo, 9–11 juillet 1949* (Dijon: Société des Amis de Cluny, 1950), 161–70. Access to superior historical sources did not eliminate the polemical treatment Mohammad received in Latin Christendom, but it did help to correct some of the more egregious errors that had circulated. For an overview of the evolution of Mohammad's biography in the West, see John Tolan, "European Accounts of Mohammad's Life," in *Cambridge Companion to Muhammad,* ed. Jonathan Brockopp (Cambridge: Cambridge University Press, 2009): 226–50.

83. D'Alverny remarks, "En ce qui concerne l'Islam, l'effort de Pierre le Vénérable n'avait pas été vain, car les notions des clercs de la fin du XIIe siècle sont moins élémentaires que celles de leurs prédécesseurs." Marie-Thérèse d'Alverny, "Alain de Lille et l'Islam. Le 'Contra paganos,'" *Cahiers de Fanjeaux* 18 (1983): 301–50, citing 305. This judgment is confirmed by the Cistercian chronicler Alberic of Trois-Fontaines (d. after 1252), who credits Peter with

have been Peter's own Cluniac confrère, Richard of Cluny (d. 1174), who dedicated to his mentor, Peter the Venerable, his mid-twelfth-century *Chronicon*, which included some discussion of the prophet Mohammad and the origins of Islam.[84] William of Tyre (d. 1183) presents another witness: his very popular *History of the Deeds done Beyond the Sea* seems to quote certain passages from Peter the Venerable's *Summary of the Entire Heresy of the Saracens*.[85]

Only one of the texts included in the Toledan Collection has received a critical edition: the *Apology of [Ps.] Al-Kindi*. Numerous contemporary scholars are working to produce critical editions of its remaining component elements, under the direction of Professor José Martínez Gázquez in Barcelona.[86] Selections from many of these Latin texts of the Toledan Collection, as well as from later medieval Latin treatments of Mohammad and Islam, can be found in *The Pseudo-Historical Image of the Prophet Mohammad*. This volume includes Latin selections from both Peter the Venerable's *Summary of the Entire Heresy of the Saracens* and *Against the Sect of the Saracens,* based on the Latin text prepared by Reinhold Glei.[87] Glei corrected certain errors of transcription found in Kritzeck's Latin texts. For this reason, Glei's Latin-German edition provides the basis for our English translation of Peter the Venerable's texts on the Saracens and Islam.

---

having the Qur'an translated in 1143 in order to reveal to the Church its foolish content: "Quo anno per industriam abbatis Petri Cluniacensis, liber qui dicitur Alcoranus cum tota secta impii et pseudopropheta Mahumet de Arabico in Latinum translatus est, hac ratione ut sciat catholica ecclesia, quam vilis et quam frivola et quam apertis mendaciis plena sit ista seductoris illius doctrina." *Chronicon*, ed. Paul Scheffer-Boichorst, MGH, SS 23 (Hanover: 1874), 837.

84. For Richard and his text, see Marc Saurette, "Tracing the Twelfth-Century *Chronica* of Richard of Poitiers, Monk of Cluny," *Memini: Travaux et documents* 8 (2005/06): 303–50. Richard's *Chronica* was edited by Georg Waitz in MGH, SS 26 (Hanover: 1882). For the brief section treating Mohammad and Islam, see *The Pseudo-Historical Image of the Prophet Mohammad*, 165–67 (full reference in the list of abbreviations in the front matter of the present volume).

85. See *The Pseudo-Historical Image of the Prophet Mohammad*, 171.

86. See http://grupsderecerca.uab.cat/islamolatina/content/proyectos.

87. *Petrus Venerabilis Schriften zum Islam*, Corpus Islamo-Christianum, Series Latina 1 (Altenberge: CIS-Verlag, 1985).

WRITINGS AGAINST
THE SARACENS

LETTER
[TO BERNARD OF CLAIRVAUX]
ON HIS TRANSLATION

(*Epistola de translatione sua*)[1]

<Inscription: "*The Letter of the Lord Abbot Peter to the Lord Abbot Bernard of Clairvaux concerning his translation, by which he caused the teaching,[2] that is, the heresy, of the Saracens to be translated from Arabic into Latin.*">

ROTHER PETER, humble abbot of Cluny, revering the lord abbot Bernard of Clairvaux with a singular veneration and embracing the inseparable friend of my heart with the arms of all [my] love, [prays for] the eternal salvation, for which he yearns.

1. In 1144, after having returned from Spain in 1143, where Peter the Venerable had commissioned a translation into Latin of the texts that formed the Toledan collection, Peter sent this letter to Bernard of Clairvaux (d. 1153), urging the latter to compose a refutation of those Islamic doctrines that impugned or introduced error to Christian teachings. For the relationship between this letter and the longer *Letter* 111, which resembles it, in Peter the Venerable's corpus, see esp. *The Letters of Peter the Venerable,* 2: 275–90. It is not likely that Bernard ever replied to his request directly, and his silence may be construed, then, as a refusal. As Kritzeck points out (*Peter the Venerable and Islam,* p. 45, n. 152), Bernard and Peter seem to have been increasingly estranged about this time, "because of the rivalry between their orders, disputed elections, and the controversy over tithes." Indeed, the competition between the Cluniac and Cistercian orders was intensifying, and sometimes resulted in monks shifting from one order to the other. A good example is Idung of Prüfening, a Cluniac who became a Cistercian toward the middle of the twelfth century and was a vocal critic of Cluniac monastic organization and customs. See Colin Morris, *The Papal Monarchy: The Western Church from 1050 to 1250* (Oxford: Oxford University Press, 1989; repr., 2001),

2. I am sending to you, my dearest,[3] our new translation that engages in debate with the very bad, wicked heresy of Mohammad,[4] which, when not long ago I was tarrying in Spain, was turned from Arabic to Latin by my effort. I had it translated, moreover, by a man skilled in both languages: master Peter of Toledo.[5] But because the Latin language was not as familiar or

---

252–53. Since Bernard failed to take up the challenge, Peter the Venerable felt compelled to undertake this task himself: having already composed the *Summary of the Entire Heresy of the Saracens,* Peter later produced his *Against the Sect of the Saracens.* Bernard's interest lay elsewhere, and by 1146 he had been commissioned by his former disciple, Pope Eugene III (r. 1145–1153), to preach the second Crusade. Still, as Tom Burman has recently remarked, it is strange that Peter appealed to Bernard to take up this task, since Bernard knew little of Islam and since Peter was acquainted already with figures in Spain (e.g., Robert of Ketton and Herman of Dalmatia) who might have produced just such a refutation. Burman suggests further that although Bernard failed to accept the challenge, several centuries later Nicholas of Cusa would do so with the composition of his *Cribatio Alkorani (Sifting of the Qur'an),* completed in 1460–1462. See Thomas E. Burman, "Nicholas of Cusa and Peter the Venerable's Request," in *Nicholas of Cusa and Islam. Polemic and Dialogue in the Late Middle Ages,* ed. Ian Christopher Levy, Rita George-Tvrtković, and Donald F. Duclow (Leiden: Brill, 2014), xiii–xx, esp. xiii–xv.

2. "Teaching": Lat., *secta,* which can be understood to mean "teaching" or "sect." Indeed, I have elected to translate the title of Peter's *Contra sectam Saracenorum* as *Against the Sect of the Saracens.*

3. "Dearest": *carissime.* For consideration of this form of epistolary address and others (for example, the reference to Peter of Poitiers as his "beloved friend" just below), see Julian Haseldine, "Friendship, Intimacy and Corporate Networking in the Twelfth Century: The Politics of Friendship in the Letters of Peter the Venerable," *English Historical Review* 126.519 (2011): 251–80. Cf. also Marc Saurette, "Thoughts on Friendship in the Letters of Peter the Venerable," *Revue Bénédictine* 120.2 (2010): 321–46.

4. The reference here, as Kritzeck argued (see "Peter the Venerable and the Toledan Collection," 179), is to the *Epistola Saraceni et Rescriptum Christiani,* Peter of Toledo's Latin translation of the *Risālat al-Kindī.* This text was a well-known Christian apology, originally in Arabic, and contains two "letters"—one allegedly written by a Muslim, Al-Hashimi, during the reign of the Caliph Al-Ma'mun (813–33), while the second represents a reply written by a Christian, Al-Kindi. According to Charles Burnett, errors in proper names in the text show that Peter of Toledo was reading it in a manuscript in Hebrew letters, leading some scholars to the assumption that he was a converted Jew. See Charles Burnett, "The Works of Petrus Alfonsi: Questions of Authenticity," *Medium Aevum* 66/1 (1997): 42–79, citing 49.

5. For brief discussion of Peter of Toledo and contemporary scholarship

known to him as Arabic, I provided to him a learned man as a coworker, our notary and beloved son and brother, Peter,[6] well known, it seems to me, to your reverence. He perfected [the translation], polishing the Latin words that had been produced by him that were very often awkward or confused, and ordering the letter, or rather the little treatise, so that, as I believe, it would become useful to many people by bringing to light things that were unknown. But also I contracted to bring out the entire impious teaching and life of that wicked man,[7] and the law, which he called the Qur'an[8] (that is, the collection of precepts

---

concerning his identity, see the Introduction, p. 20, and also *Christian-Muslim Relations. A Bibliographical History; Vol. 3 (1050–1200),* ed. David Thomas and Alex Mallett (Leiden: Brill, 2011), 478–79.

6. Peter of Poitiers, a monk at Cluny, and Peter the Venerable had a long-standing and close relationship. The former is identified as the abbot's *notarius* already in 1136/37, in Peter the Venerable's *Letter* 24 to Guigo du Châtel, prior of the Carthusians. See *Peter the Venerable: Selected Letters,* 24, lns. 125–26.

7. This seems to be a reference to several texts in the Toledan Collection: the *Liber generationis Mahumeth* and *Doctrina Mahumet,* which were translated by Herman of Dalmatia, and the *Fabulae Sarracenorum,* translated by Robert of Ketton.

8. For a brief but useful discussion of Robert of Ketton's translation of the Qur'an, and the linguistic and interpretative challenges he faced, one may consult Bruce Lawrence, *The Qur'an: Books that Changed the World* (London: Atlantic Books, 2007), 99–107. A more detailed account may be found in Thomas E. Burman, *Reading the Qur'ān in Latin Christendom, 1140–1560* (Philadelphia: University of Pennsylvania Press, 2007), esp. 60–103. Robert of Ketton's Latin translation was not the only source for contemporary knowledge of the Qur'an: Petrus Alfonsi included numerous passages from the Qur'an in Latin translation in his popular *Dialogue Against the Jews,* written about 1109. Alfonsi's translation of select passages has been described as simpler and less "florid" than Robert of Ketton's translation, which introduced the whole of the Qur'an. See Guy Monnot, "Les citations coraniques dans le 'Dialogus' de Pierre Alphonse," *Cahiers de Fanjeaux, Collection d'Histoire religieuse du Languedoc au XIIIe et au début du XIVe siècle: Islam et chrétiens du Midi (XIIe–XIVe S.)* 18, ed. Edouard Privat (Fanjeaux: Centre d'études historiques de Fanjeaux, 1983): 261–77, esp. 272. According to José Martínez Gázquez, Peter the Venerable was inspired to commission the translation of the Qur'an during his visit in 1142 to Spain, where he saw Cluniac monks living in close proximity to Muslims; he may have come to believe that they needed better tools with which to defend their beliefs. See José Martínez Gázquez, "Trois traductions médiévales latines du Coran: Pierre le Vénérable, Robert de Ketton, Marc de Tolède et

which he persuaded utterly wretched men had been borne to
him from heaven by the angel Gabriel), translated from Arabic
to Latin through men skilled in each language, namely Robert
of Ketton[9] of England, who is now an archdeacon of the church
of Pamplona, and also Herman of Dalmatia,[10] a scholar having
the sharpest and most learned ability, both of whom I found in
Spain near the Ebro,[11] studying the astrological art,[12] and I employed them at great expense.[13]

Jean de Segobia," *Revue des études latines* 80 (2003): 223–36. Robert of Ketton's
translation was probably completed during summer 1143.

9. Robert of Ketton was an Englishman who had settled by 1136 in Barcelona to study with Plato of Tivoli and who became active in the work of
translating scientific materials from Arabic to Latin. For a useful biograph-
ical overview, see Dorothee Metlitzki, *The Matter of Araby in Medieval England*
(New Haven: Yale University Press, 2005), 30–35. Robert of Ketton did become archdeacon of Pamplona and, later, canon of Tudela; he also served in
some capacity the king of Navarre, Garcia Ramirez. See Michelle Reichert,
"Hermann of Dalmatia and Robert of Ketton: Two Twelfth-Century Translators in the Ebro Valley," in *Science Translated. Latin and Vernacular Translations
of Scientific Treatises in Medieval Europe* (Leuven: Leuven University Press, 2008),
47–58.

10. On Herman of Dalmatia (also known as Herman of Carinthia), see especially Charles Burnett, "Hermann of Carinthia," in *A History of Twelfth-Century Western Philosophy*, ed. P. Dronke (Cambridge: Cambridge University Press,
1988), 386–404. Herman was formerly a pupil of Thierry of Chartres and
possibly a priest. His literary work includes *De generatione Mahumet, Doctrina
Mahumet,* his own original composition *De essentiis,* and about a dozen translations from Arabic, including treatises from the Jewish scholar Sahl ibn Bisch'r
(Zael), and Abū Ma'shar (Albumasar). With Robert of Ketton, he also translated the "Astronomical Tables" of Al-Khwarizmi. For his work as translator, see
Charles Burnett, "Arabic into Latin in Twelfth-Century Spain: The Works of
Hermann of Carinthia," *Mittellateinisches Jahrbuch* 13 (1978): 100–134.

11. I.e, the Ebro River, the longest river in Spain.

12. Indeed, in his preface to his translation of the Qur'an, Robert of Ketton
remarks that once he had accepted Peter the Venerable's commission, he was
compelled "to pass beyond my principal study of astronomy and geometry"
("astronomiae geometriaeque studium meum principale praetermittere").
See *Roberti Retenensis praefatio in libro legis saracenorum, quam alcoran vocant, a se
translato. Ad domnum petrum abbatem cluniacensem* (PL 189: 659A).

13. We do not know how much Peter the Venerable spent on this project,
but he mentions on other occasions the great effort and expense involved. In
the last paragraph of his *Summary of the Entire Heresy of the Saracens,* he notes
that the project succeeded only with *magno studio et impensis.* Similarly, in his

3. It was my intention in this effort, moreover, to follow the practice of the Fathers, in which they never passed over in silence even the most trivial heresy, so to speak, of their times, but rather they would withstand it with all of the powers of the faith and they would demonstrate both in written texts and in debates that it should be detested and is deserving of condemnation. I have chosen to do so for this the chief error of errors, for this the dregs of all heresies, into which have flowed the remnants of all the diabolical sects that have arisen since the very advent of the Savior, so that just as it is recognized that nearly half of the world is infected by its lethal plague, so too, once its foolishness and turpitude have been revealed, it will be acknowledged by those unfamiliar with it that it must be condemned and trod into the dust. By reading it you will acknowledge and, I think, rightly you will weep that such a large part of the human race has been deceived by such wicked and abject filth, and has so easily been turned away from their Creator by the wicked teaching (*secta*) of the foulest man, even after the grace of the Redeemer.

4. I have brought this to your attention especially, moreover, in order to inform so great a friend of our efforts and to arouse your splendor of religious teaching, which God has conferred upon you in a singular manner in our days, to write against so pernicious an error. For even though it cannot profit those who are lost, in my opinion, nonetheless just as it is fitting to have an appropriate response to other heresies, so too it is fitting to have a Christian arsenal against this plague as well.[14] If anyone shall allege that this is unnecessary, since they are not

---

Against the Sect of the Saracens 17, he remarks that he persuaded Christian scholars (Herman of Dalmatia and Robert of Ketton) "both by entreaty and with money, to translate from the Arabic language into Latin" texts treating Mohammad and his teachings and, finally, the Qur'an itself (Glei, 54, lns. 14–16). Whatever the cost, it came at a time when Cluny was itself suffering financial difficulty, providing additional evidence of the importance Peter attached to the project.

14. For the importance of developing a forensic "arsenal" with which to defend Christian teachings, see Dominique Iogna-Prat, "The Creation of a Christian Armory Against Islam," in *Medieval Religion: New Approaches,* ed. Constance Hoffman Berman (New York and London: Routledge, 2005): 325–46.

in the presence of those they ought to oppose when supported by such arms, he should know that some things are done in the realm of a great king for protection, and some things are done for honor, and some are done for both reasons. Now, the peace-loving Solomon made arms for safety,[15] even though they were less necessary in his day. The expenses, the provisions, and accoutrements designated for the beautification and construction of the divine Temple were prepared by David.[16] They did not serve any purpose in his day,[17] but rather they passed to divine uses after his days. And so for some time they remained unused, but when the need arose, those that had lain idle for a long time appeared fruitful. Nor, in my view, should I call this effort idle even at this time, since, according to the Apostle, it is incumbent upon you and upon all learned men to attack, to destroy, and to tread into the dust "every knowledge that exalts itself against the height of God,"[18] with every undertaking in word and text.[19]

5. If those who err cannot be converted by this, the learned man or teacher, if he possesses a zeal for justice, should not fail to provide for and to offer counsel to those that are weak in the Church, who are wont to be scandalized or to be secretly disturbed even by trivial affairs. I propose to you, then, that all the Fathers, and especially Father Augustine, who, even though he was unable to convert the Pelagian Julian[20] or the Manichean Faustus[21] to the correct faith with words and with his effort, nonetheless did not fail to compose volumes against them con-

15. See 2 Chr 9.15.

16. See 1 Chr 22.1–6, 14–16.

17. Because it was not David but rather his son Solomon who constructed the Temple. See 2 Chr 3.1–8.1 and 1 Kgs 6.1.

18. Cf. 2 Cor 10.5.

19. "word and text": *verbo et scripto.* Cf. 1 Tm 5.17, which praises priests who "labor in word and doctrine" ("qui laborant in verbo et doctrina").

20. Julian of Eclanum (d. 454), the semi-Pelagian Bishop of Eclanum in southern Italy. See Augustine's *Against Julian,* trans. Matthew A. Schumacher, FOTC 35 (Washington, DC: The Catholic University of America Press, 1957).

21. Augustine composed an extensive work against Faustus the Manichean's treatise entitled *The [thirty-three] Chapters;* Augustine's response, written in 397–398 in thirty-three books, is found in his *Against Faustus (Contra Faustum),* ed. Joseph Zycha, CSEL 25.1 (Vienna: Tempsky, 1891).

cerning their great error. Acting thus toward the remaining, contemporary heretics (and toward those who were not contemporaries), acting thus toward Jews, acting thus toward pagans, he not only armed men against those of his own time, but also transmitted to us and to all our posterity a divine gift of the greatest edification and instruction.

6. If, therefore, it shall be the will of your reverence to toil against them with God inspiring you (for through his grace the skill cannot be lacking), write us back, and we will send a book which we have not yet sent to you,[22] so that from your mouth a "benevolent Spirit"[23] may respond, filled with its praise, to the spirit of wickedness, and may provide treasures to its Church from the wealth of your wisdom.

---

22. There is much disagreement over what this book may have been: perhaps he refers to the remaining texts that comprised the Toledan Collection, including the Latin translation of the Qur'an. But cf. Yvonne Friedman, *Adversus Iudeorum inveteratam duritiem,* lxii–lxiii, who infers that Peter may refer here to the yet unwritten *Contra sectam Saracenorum,* for which he and Peter of Poitiers had only produced an outline.

23. Wis 1.6.

A SUMMARY OF
THE ENTIRE HERESY OF
THE SARACENS

(Summa totius haeresis Saracenorum)

HIS IS A SUMMARY of the entire heresy and of the diabolical teaching of the Saracens, that is, the Ishmaelites.[24]

First and foremost, their first and greatest error that ought to be cursed is that they deny the Trinity in the unity of the

24. The term *Saracen* was used in Roman antiquity especially to identify speakers of Arabic. See, for example, David F. Graf and M. O'Connor, "The Origin of the Term Saracen and the Rawwāfā Inscriptions," *Byzantine Studies* 4.1 (1977): 52–66. As such, it did not originally imply religious difference. For medieval Europe, *Saracen* was never a term applied to Christian speakers of Arabic. First it identified pagans in general, and only later did it distinguish a racial, ethnic, and religious group. See Suzanne Conklin Akbari, *Idols in the East: European Representations of Islam and the Orient, 1100–1450* (Ithaca and London: Cornell University Press, 2009), chap. 4. Later medieval Christian thinkers often struggled to explain the source of the term. In the thirteenth century, both Jacques de Vitry and the Dominican Vincent of Beauvais remark that Saracens should properly be called *Hagarenes,* that is, those descended from Abraham's maidservant Hagar through her son Ishmael, but that they prefer the term *Saracen,* which derives from Sarah, Abraham's free-born wife (cf. Gal 4.22–26). See Jacques de Vitry, *Historia Orientalis* 1.5, ed. F. Moschus (Douai: Belleri, 1597); and Vincent of Beauvais, *Speculum maius,* vol. 2: *Speculum doctrinale* 9.39 (Graz: Akademische Druck-u. Verlagsanstalt, 1965). Both "Saracen" and "Hagarene," then, came to refer to Muslims as a religious and ethnic group. On the Iberian peninsula, the term "Moor" also became common. According to Alonso de Cartagena (d. 1456), "Mohammedans" are called Moors, in the vulgar tongue, because in the past Mohammad's "error" quickly spread throughout Mauritania. Even contemporary European Christians, he added, if they apostatize and become Muslims, are called Moors. See his *Defensorium unitatis Christianae (Tratado en favor de los judíos conversos),* 2.4.27, ed. Manuel Alonso (Madrid: Consejo Superior de Investigaciones Científicas, 1943), 238.

deity,[25] and in this way, while shunning number in unity, they do not believe in a triune number of persons in the one essence of divinity, while I say that the beginning and end of all forms is ternary; and thus they do not receive the cause and origin and goal of all things that are formed; although confessing God with their lips, they do not know him in a profound way. These foolish ones, these inconstant ones, confess that there is a principle for change and for every difference, to wit one that is only binary in unity, namely the divine essence itself, and its life (*anima*). For this reason the Qur'an—by which name they call their law, and Qur'an, translated from Arabic, means a collection of precepts[26]—always introduces God speaking in the plural.

2. Furthermore, these blind ones deny that God the Creator is the Father,[27] because, according to them, no one becomes a father without sexual intercourse. And although they accept that Christ was conceived from a divine spirit, they do not believe that he is the Son of God nor, moreover, that he is God, but that he is a good, most truthful prophet,[28] free from all deceit and sin, the son of Mary,[29] begotten without a father;[30] he never died, because he did not deserve death—instead, although the Jews wanted to slay him, he slipped through their hands,[31] as-

25. Indeed, there are numerous statements in the Qur'an (e.g., suras 4.171; 5.73; and 5.116) that raise objections to a Trinitarian Godhead. Robert of Ketton's translation of Qur'an 5.173 quite explicitly condemns Christian dogma: "Sunt iterum increduli, firmantes deos tres esse: quia non est nisi Deus unus." ("Again they are unbelieving, affirming that there are three gods, because there is only one God.") Moreover, in his marginal glosses he adds that the text denies the Trinity *cum Sabellio haeretico*—with the heretic Sabellius. According to the numbering in Robert of Ketton's text, this is surah 12 (Bibliander, ed., p. 41; see http://www.wdl.org/en/item/9922/view/1/5/).

26. Robert of Ketton's translation begins: "Incipit lex Saracenorum, quam Alchoran vocant, id est, *Collectionem praeceptorum*" (Bibliander ed., p. 8; see http://www.wdl.org/en/item/9922/view/1/5/). My italics.

27. Qur'an 112.1–4 affirms that God neither begets nor is begotten. Therefore, God cannot be a father, nor can Jesus be the Son of God.

28. Cf. Qur'an 19.30.

29. For Peter's own views on Mary and the devotion the faithful owe to her, see esp. Bernard Billet, "Notes de mariologie. La devotion mariale de Pierre le Vénérable (1092–1156)," *Esprit et vie* 87.37 (1977): 465–72.

30. Cf. Qur'an 3.45–46.

31. Cf. Qur'an 4.157–59.

cended to the stars, and lives there now in the flesh in the presence of the Creator, until the advent of the Antichrist.[32] When the Antichrist comes, this same Christ will slay him himself with the sword of his virtue, and he will convert the remaining Jews to his law. Moreover, he will teach his law perfectly to the Christians, who a long time ago lost his law and Gospel owing, on the one hand, to his departure, and on the other hand owing to the death of the apostles and disciples, by which [law] all Christians at that time will be saved, just like his first disciples. Even Christ himself will die with them and with all creatures at one and the same time, when Seraphim—who they say is one archangel—sounds the trumpet; and afterward he will rise with the rest, and he will lead his disciples to judgment, and he will assist them and pray for them, but he will not himself judge them. Indeed, God alone will judge. The prophets and the individual messengers, however, will be present among them as their intercessors, and to assist them. Thus, to be sure, the most wretched and impious Mohammad has taught them, he who, denying all the sacraments of Christian piety by which men are especially saved, has condemned already nearly a third of the human race to the devil and to eternal death with the unheard-of foolishness of fables—by what judgment of God, we do not know.

3. It seems that one must speak about who he [Mohammad] was, and what he taught, for the sake of those who will read that book, so that they might better understand what they read, and come to know how detestable both his life and teaching were. For some think that he was that Nicholas who was one of the first seven deacons,[33] and that this law (*lex*) of the modern Saracens is the teaching of the Nicolaitans, who were named after him, which is denounced in the Apocalypse of John.[34] And

32. For the Antichrist, see Cyril Glassé, *The Concise Encyclopedia of Islam* (New York: Harper Collins, 1991), *s.v. ad Dajjāl*, p. 91.

33. Acts 6.5.

34. Cf. Rv 2.6, 15. For Peter's novel effort to link Mohammad and Islam with Nicholas of Antioch and Nicolaitism, see Alberto Ferreiro, "Simon Magus, Nicolas of Antioch, and Muhammad," *Church History* 72.1 (2003): 53–70. Since the early patristic era, Nicolaitism had been identified especially with sexual immorality. See idem, "Priscillian and Nicolaitism," *Vigiliae Christianae* 52.4 (1998): 382–92. Cf. also Alberto Ferreiro, *Simon Magus in Patristic, Medieval and Early*

others dream up other individuals and, as they are careless in
reading and unacquainted with the actual events, so here, just
as in other cases, they conjecture every manner of falsehood.

4. This one [Mohammad], however, as even the chronicle
translated from Greek into Latin by Anastasius the Librarian
of the Roman church clearly relates,[35] lived during the age of
the Emperor Heraclius,[36] a little after the time of the great Roman Pope, Gregory I,[37] almost 550 years ago;[38] he was one who

---

Modern Traditions (Leiden: Brill, 2005), 111–22 and 221–40. By the eleventh century, Christian moralists had extended this critique of Nicolaitism—increasingly defined as heresy—to include clerical marriage and concubinage, and sought
to deprive offending Christian priests of their benefices. See Uta-Renate Blumenthal, "Pope Gregory VII and the Prohibition of Nicolaitism," in *Medieval Purity and Piety: Essays on Medieval Clerical Celibacy and Religious Reform,* ed. Michael
Frassetto (New York: Garland Publishing, Inc., 1998): 239–67. Although Peter
the Venerable certainly wishes to identify Islam's origin with heretical teachers,
the next sentence makes clearer that he views the connection to Nicholas of
Antioch as spurious.

35. See *Chronographia et Anastasii Bibliothecarii Historia Ecclesiastica sive Chro-
nographia tripartita,* ed. Carl de Boor (Leipzig: G. Teubner, 1883–85; reprint,
Hildesheim: G. Olms, 1980), 1: 333, 2: 209. Anastasius the Librarian (Anastasius Bibliothecarius; d. ca. 878) translated works from Greek into Latin. His
Chronographia tripartita was compiled from the Greek histories of Theophanes,
Nicephorus, and Syncellus, and, as such, provided Latin Christians with access to Byzantine traditions concerning Mohammad and the origins of Islam.
For the importance of Byzantine sources in the medieval West's image of Islam, see Svetlana Luchitskaja, "The Image of Muhammad in Latin Chronography of the Twelfth and Thirteenth Centuries," *Journal of Medieval History*
26.2 (2000): 115–26.

36. Mohammad (570–632 CE) lived during the reign of the Byzantine
Emperor Heraclius (r. 610–41). Heraclius was well known for his campaign
against the Persians between 622–28, from whom he recaptured Jerusalem
and the provinces of Syria, Palestine, and Egypt. Among Arab chroniclers,
he was often praised for his piety and sagacity; according to Islamic tradition,
he acquainted himself with the Qur'an and acknowledged Mohammad's prophetic role. See Nadia Maria El-Cheikh, "Muḥammad and Heraclius: A Study
in Legitimacy," *Studia Islamica* 89 (1999): 5–21. Quite incorrectly Hugh of Flavigny's *Chronicon* (PL 154: 101), composed about 1112, reports that Mohammad was born in the fifth year of Heraclius's reign.

37. Gregory I ("the Great," ca. 540–604), reigned as pope from 590 until
his death in 604. Peter wrote this text in late 1143, or 553 years after Gregory
was elected pope and 539 years after his death.

38. Cf. *Contra Petrobrusianos* 161, p. 94: "almost all of the East and the Afri-

was of the Arab nation, of low birth, at first a worshiper of the
old idolatry—just as the other Arabs still were at that time[39]—
unlearned, nearly illiterate,[40] active in business affairs, and, being very shrewd, he advanced from low birth and from poverty
to riches and fame.[41] And here, increasing little by little, and by
frequently attacking neighbors and especially those related to
him by blood with ambushes, robberies, and incursions—killing by stealth those whom he could, and killing publicly those
whom he could—he increased fear of him, and because he often came out on top in these encounters, he began to aspire to
kingship over his race.

5. And when, with everyone equally resisting [him] and condemning his low birth, he saw that he could not pursue this
path for himself as he had hoped, he attempted to become
king under the cloak of religion and under the name of a divine prophet,[42] because he was unable to do so by the power
of the sword. And since he lived as a barbarian among barbarians, and as an idolater among idolaters, and among those who,

---

can region, having been deceived by the cursed Mohammad, have participat-
ed for almost 550 years in these and [other] superstitions beyond number ..."
For Peter's polemic against the Petrobrusians, see Jean Châtillon,"Pierre le
Vénérable et les Pétrobrusiens," in *Pierre Abélard—Pierre le Vénérable. Les courants philosophiques, littéraires et artistiques en Occident au milieu du XIIe siècle, Abbaye de Cluny 2 au 9 juillet 1972, Colloques internationaux du Centre National de la
Recherche Scientifique*, no. 546 (Paris: Éditions du Centre National de la Recherche Scientifique, 1975), 165–80.

39. Cf. Petrus Alfonsi, *Dialogue* 5, p. 151, which notes that when Mohammad was young he and the entire race of the Arabs worshiped idols.

40. Qur'an 7.157–58 identifies Mohammad as the "Unlettered Prophet."
Cf. Robert of Ketton, *Mistake-Laden and Ridiculous Chronicle of the Saracens
(Chronica mendosa et ridicula Sarracenorum)*, found in *The Pseudo-Historical Image
of the Prophet Mohammad*, 108 n. 59, which identifies the prophet Mohammad
as an illiterate layman (*laicus et illiteratus*). Cf. also *Rescriptum Christiani* cap. 37,
lns. 16–17, p. 65: "Cum Mahumet idiota et sine litteris esset ..."

41. Because Mohammad was born after his father's death and was, therefore, unable to inherit from him, he became the poor ward of his grandfather,
'Abd al-Muṭṭalib; when he was eight years old, his grandfather died, and he
was raised by his uncle and guardian, Abū Ṭālib. See Glassé, *The Concise Encyclopedia of Islam*, s.v. Muḥammad, 280.

42. Petrus Alfonsi remarks that Mohammad feared that the Arabs would
not accept him as their ruler, and so, "devising a path by which he could be
made king, he chose to fashion himself a prophet ..."; *Dialogue* 5, p. 151.

more than all races, were unacquainted with and ignorant of law both human and divine, he knew that they were easy to seduce, and he began to undertake the iniquitous task he had conceived. And since he had heard that God's prophets were great men, and saying that he is His prophet so as to pretend to be something good, he attempted to lead them partly away from idolatry, yet not to the true God but rather to his own false heresy, which he had already begun to bring forth.

6. Meanwhile, with the judgment of Him who is said to be "terrible in his counsels over the sons of men"[43] and who "has mercy on whomever he chooses, and hardens the heart of whomever he chooses,"[44] Satan bestowed success upon error, and he sent the monk Sergius,[45] a sectarian follower of the heretical Nestorius,[46] who had been expelled from the Church, to those parts of Arabia, and united the monk-heretic with the false prophet. Accordingly Sergius joined with Mohammad, supplied what he lacked and, explicating for him the Sacred Scriptures—of both the Old and the New Testament—in accord with the understanding of his master, Nestorius, who denied that our Savior is God, [and] partly in accord with his own

43. Ps 65 (66).5.

44. Rom 9.18; Ex 33.19.

45. The notion that Mohammad was instructed by a sectarian Christian monk, Sergius, can be traced back at least as far as Pseudo-al-Kindi's *Risālah (Apology);* see *Rescriptum Christiani,* cap. 38, p. 66. It became a staple of Christian apologetics. Petrus Alfonsi alludes to it as well, although he mistakenly identifies Sergius as an archdeacon of Antioch (*Dialogue* 5, p. 152). Richard of Cluny follows Peter the Venerable and identifies Sergius as a Nestorian monk who, having been expelled from his monastery, introduced Mohammad to his heretical teachings on Jesus ("A quodam tamen monacho nomine Sergio nestoriano, et ob hac de monasterio expulso, iuxta haeresim suam multa de Christo edoctus est"). For this excerpt, see *The Pseudo-Historical Image of the Prophet Mohammad,* 165. For a study of this tradition, see Barbara Roggema, *The Legend of Sergius Baḥīrā. Eastern Christian Apologetics and Apocalyptic in Response to Islam* (Leiden: Brill, 2009).

46. The heretical patriarch Nestorius (d. ca. 451) had been the bishop of Constantinople, until his views on the nature and person of Christ resulted in his condemnation at the Council of Ephesus in 431 and again at the Council of Chalcedon in 451. Nestorianism moved from the Roman to the Persian Empire, and a small Nestorian church survives today in Iraq, Iran, India, and elsewhere.

conception, and at the same time completely filling him up with fables from apocryphal books, he made him into a Nestorian Christian.

7. And, in order that the complete fullness of iniquity should coalesce in Mohammad, and so that nothing should be lacking for his damnation or for that of others, Jews were joined to the heretic, and lest he become a true Christian, the Jews whispered to Mohammad, shrewdly providing to the man who was eager for novelties not the truth of the Scriptures but their fables, which still today they have in abundance.[47] And in this way, taught by the best Jewish and heretical teachers, Mohammad created his Qur'an, and having confected it from both Jewish fables and the foolish nonsense of heretics,[48] he wove together that wicked scripture in his own barbarous fashion. Having created the lie that gradually this was conveyed to him in a book[49] by Gabriel,[50] whose name he knew already from

47. Petrus Alfonsi mentions two Jews of Arabia who influenced Mohammad and contributed to his heresy: Abdias and Chabalahabar. The names Abdias and Chabalahabar appear to be corruptions of Abdallah ibn-Salām (d. 663–664, a learned Medinan rabbi who converted to Islam) and Ka'b al-Ahbar, two Jews mentioned in the *Rescriptum Christiani* (cap. 12, p. 37; cap. 39, p. 67) as having influenced Mohammad. See *Dialogue*, p. 152, n. 27. The *De doctrina Mahumet* of Herman of Carinthia (or Dalmatia) also relates a tradition that four Jews came to Mohammad to test his knowledge of the Law. These were led by Abdia ('Abdallāh). At the end, he is so impressed with Mohammad's knowledge that he converts to Islam. For the texts, see *The Pseudo-Historical Image of the Prophet Mohammad*, pp. 116, 118.

48. The Jewish "fables" are likely drawn from rabbinic literature generally, and the Talmud in particular. In the chapter headings that he sent to Peter the Venerable, Peter of Poitiers notes that Mohammad's "heresy" can be traced especially to the Manichean heresy and to "that execrable book of the Jews, the Talmud." (See *infra*, p. 171.) Similarly, in his *Against the Inveterate Obduracy of the Jews*, Peter the Venerable condemns the Jew, who has deceived himself with Talmudic tales, for having inspired "his former disciple, Mohammad," with "similar dreamlike fables." See *Against the Inveterate Obduracy of the Jews* 5, p. 283.

49. "A book": *per thomos*, an unusual term (Gk. τόμος) that Peter uses again at *Against the Sect of the Saracens* 58.

50. Robert of Ketton reports that Gabriel delivered the Law (i.e., Qur'an) to Mohammad when the latter was forty years old. See his *Mistake-Laden and Ridiculous Chronicle of the Saracens* (*Chronica mendosa et ridicula Sarracenorum*), in *The Pseudo-Historical Image of the Prophet Mohammad*, 94. In his preface to his

Sacred Scripture, he poisoned a people that was ignorant of God with a lethal draught, and, in the manner of men such as this, coating the rim of the chalice with honey, with the deadly poison following after,[51] he destroyed—O woe!—the souls and bodies of that miserable race.

8. Clearly that impious man did so when, while commending both the Christian and the Jewish religion (*lex*), confirming that neither one ought to be embraced, he rejected them while proving himself reprobate. For this reason he confirms that Moses was the best prophet, that Christ the Lord was greater than all, proclaims that he [Christ] was born of a virgin,[52] confesses that he was the messenger of God, the word of God, the spirit of God,[53] yet he does not understand or confess [Christ as] the messenger, Word, or Spirit as we do. Actually, he ridicules [the Christian teaching] that he is said or believed to be the Son of God.[54] And, measuring the eternal birth of the Son of God in comparison to human generation, the bovine man[55]

---

translation of the Qur'an, Robert of Ketton identifies the Qur'an as a "'Collection of Precepts,' which the pseudo-prophet Mohammad feigned was sent to him from heaven by the angel Gabriel." See Ulisse Cecini, *Alcoranus latinus. Eine sprachliche und kulturwissenschaftliche Analyse der Koranübersetzungen von Robert von Ketton und Marcus von Toledo* (Berlin: Lit Verlag, 2012), 93.

51. Paulinus of Aquileia (d. ca. 804) condemns Elipandus of Toledo for attempting to make his heresy more palatable by concealing its bitter taste beneath something sweet, and by tempering a cup of poison with the taste of honey ("mos est haereticis, tristia laetis, dulcia permiscere amaris, veneni poculum mellis sapore temperare …"; *Libellus sacrosyllabus contra Elipandum*, PL 99: 153B). Vincent of Lérins (d. ca. 445), similarly, describes heretics who would make their doctrines more acceptable, just as one coats the rim of a cup with honey in order to encourage a child to drink a bitter medicine. *Tractatus Peregrini pro Catholicae fidei antiquitate et universitate adversus prophanas omnium haereticorum novitates* 25, PL 50: 672. Ultimately, this topos can be traced back to Lucretius (*De rerum natura* 1.936–42; 4.11–25), who explains that physicians often trick children into drinking a bitter medicine by first coating the rim of the cup with honey.

52. Cf. Qur'an 3.45–47.

53. Cf. Qur'an 4.171.

54. Robert of Ketton's prologue to the *Fabule Sarracenorum* notes that the Law (Qur'an) denies that Jesus is God and the Son of God (*Deum et filium Dei esse negat lex prava*). For the text, see *The Pseudo-Historical Image of the Prophet Mohammad*, 90.

55. "Bovine man": *vaccinus homo*. Peter uses a similar expression against the

denies and mocks with as much effort as he can that God could have either begotten or been begotten. With frequent repetition he affirms the resurrection of the flesh; he does not deny that there is a general judgment at the end of time, but it must be carried out not by Christ but by God.[56] He insanely affirms that Christ, as the greatest of all after God, will be present at that judgment and that he himself will be present to assist his people.

9. He describes the torments of hell such as it pleased him to do, and such as it was fitting for the great false prophet to invent. He painted a paradise that is not of the company of angels, nor of a vision of the divine, nor of that highest good that "no eye has seen, nor ear heard, nor has it entered into the human heart,"[57] but painted one such as truly flesh and blood desired, or rather the dregs of flesh and blood, and one which he desired to have prepared for himself. There, he promises to his followers a meal of meats and of every kind of fruit,[58] rivers of milk and honey,[59] and of sparkling waters; there he

---

Jews, whom he accuses of having a "bovine intellect." See *Against the Inveterate Obduracy of the Jews* 33, p. 103; and *Contra Petrobrusianos haereticos* 161, p. 94.

56. See Cyril Glassé, *The Concise Encyclopedia of Islam, s.v.* Resurrection, 334–35.

57. Is 64.4; 1 Cor 2.9.

58. Cf. Petrus Alfonsi, *Dialogue,* p. 150.

59. Qur'an 47.15 locates in paradise (*al-Jannah*) rivers of milk, wine, and honey, as well as an abundance of every fruit. Ibn Jarir al-Tabari (d. 923) notes that during Mohammad's ascent to the seventh heaven, he entered paradise, where there was a "river whiter than milk and sweeter than honey." See *The History of al-Tabari,* trans. W. Montgomery Watt and M. V. McDonald (Albany: SUNY Press, 1987), 6: 79. Among Latin authors, Anastasius the Librarian alleges that Mohammad preached that paradise would offer food for the body, drink, sexual intercourse, and a stream of wine, honey, and milk, as well as other delights. See *Historia ecclesiastica sive Chronographia tripertita* (Paris: e typographia regia, 1649), 104. Sigebert of Gembloux (d. 1112) describes this carnal paradise in similar terms; *Chronographia,* ed. L. Bethmann, MGH, SS 6 (Turnhout: Brepols Publishers, 2013), 323, ln. 16. Arnold of Lübeck (d. ca. 1211–1214) echoes Peter's description and alleges that the Saracens say that in paradise there are 4 rivers: namely, one of wine, a second of milk, a third of honey, and a fourth of water, and they say that every kind of fruit is borne there; they will eat there and drink as they will; and each one of them, every day, will have intercourse with nine virgins, in fulfillment of his desire. See

promises the embrace and sexual satisfaction of the most beautiful women and virgins,[60] in which the whole of his paradise is
defined. Vomiting up again among these nearly all of the dregs
of the ancient heresies, which he had absorbed from the devil's
instruction, he denies the Trinity with Sabellius,[61] rejects the
deity of Christ with his own Nestorius,[62] [and] repudiates the
death of the Lord along with Manichaeus,[63] although he does
not deny his return to the heavens.

10. Instructing the people in these and similar teachings not
for improvement but for damnation, he completely turned away

Chronica Slavorum 8.8, ed. J. M. Lappenberg, MGH, SS rer. Germ. 14 (Hannover: Hahn, 1868), 271.

60. This was a well-known feature of paradise for Muslims that Christians
derided. Cf. Petrus Alfonsi, *Dialogue,* p. 150. Most Christian polemicists simply
ridiculed this as a "carnal" conception of paradise, but some derived from it
certain theological questions. E.g., the Benedictine abbot Arnold of Lübeck
wonders, in his *Chronica Slavorum*—a continuation of Helmold of Bosau's
Chronica Slavorum, written before 1177—where all these virgins in paradise
will come from and what will happen to them after they have been deflow-
ered. See *Chronica Slavorum* 8.8, p. 271.

61. Sabellius was excommunicated ca. 220 CE. He is usually identified with
Monarchianism, that is, the teaching that there can be no permanent or enduring distinctions (such as Father, Son, and Holy Spirit) in the Godhead.
To allege Sabellianism was to impute heresy. This charge was also directed
against Peter Abelard, who, at the council of Soissons in 1121, was condemned
as a Sabellian heretic (*Sabellianus haereticus judicatus*). See F. Amboise, *Apologetica praefatio pro Petro Abaelardo* (PL 178: 89D). In 1140 Abelard (d. 1142) sought
refuge at Cluny, under the protection of its abbot, Peter the Venerable, and
the two may have influenced one another in their understanding of Islam.
See James Kritzeck, "De l'influence de Pierre Abélard sur Pierre le Vénérable
dans ses oeuvres sur l'Islam," in *Pierre Abélard—Pierre le Vénérable. Les courants
philosophiques, littéraires et artistiques en Occident au milieu du XIIe siècle, Abbaye de
Cluny 2 au 9 juillet 1972, Colloques internationaux du Centre National de la Recherche Scientifique,* no. 546 (Paris: Éditions du Centre National de la Recherche
Scientifique, 1975), 205–12. But Peter the Venerable did not, it seems, apply
the title "Sabellian" with any greater care.

62. See *supra,* n. 46, p. 39.

63. I.e., the Persian prophet Mani or Manes (216–277 CE), whose followers
are known as Manicheans. They rejected Jesus's Incarnation and interpreted
his death as purely symbolic. By the sixth century, they had become well established in Iraq, Persia, and North Africa. The Manichean movement attempted
to create a "school" within Islam. See Glassé, *The Concise Encyclopedia of Islam,*
s.v. Manicheism, pp. 252–57.

from God, and, lest a Gospel word besides could have a place among them—just as it does for those who know everything that pertains to the Gospel and Christ—he blocked entry to their hearts with the iron barrier of impiety. He decreed, moreover, that circumcision ought to be observed,[64] just as it had been adopted by Ishmael,[65] the father of that people; and, in addition to all these things, so that he could attract to himself more easily the carnal minds of men, he relaxed the reins on gluttony and libidinal pleasure; and, having himself eighteen wives at one and the same time,[66] and the wives of many others, committing adultery as if in response to divine command,[67] he joined a larger number of the damned to himself just as if by prophetic example. And lest he appear completely disgraceful,

64. It was a commonplace among Latin Christian authors to identify "Hagarenes" or "Saracens" with circumcision, a ritual practice that they also identified with Jews and which, they alleged, Christian baptism had replaced. The *Chronicon* attributed to Fredegar (d. 652) had long ago noted that "the Hagarenes, who are called the Saracens, [are] a circumcised race ..." (PL 71: 647A). In the first quarter of the twelfth century, Hugh of Flavigny echoed Fredegar's description in his *Chronicon* 1 (PL 154: 101C) as did Ekkehardus Uraugiensis (d. ca. 1126), in his *Chronicon universale* 5, ed. G. Waitz, MGH, SS 6 (Turnhout: Brepols Publishers, 2013; CD ROM), 153, ln. 35. In Peter Abelard's *Dialogue between a Philosopher, a Jew, and a Christian* (*Dialogus inter philosophum, Judaeum et Christianum*), the Jew seems to identify the Philosopher as a Muslim when he remarks that "you yourselves even today keep the practice in imitation of Ishmael your father when you receive circumcision at the age of twelve." See Peter Abelard, *Collationes* 39, ed. John Marenbon and Giovanni Orlandi (Oxford: Clarendon Press, 2001), 48; Abelard died in 1142, just a year before Peter the Venerable completed this text.

65. Ishmael, the son of Hagar, was circumcised at age thirteen at the same time as his father Abraham (Gn 17.25–26). Cf. also Gn 16.15–16.

66. Kritzeck remarked on this passage that "[t]he exact number of his wives is somewhat difficult to determine, but he certainly had at least eleven wives and six concubines" (*Peter the Venerable and Islam*, 137). Godfrey of Viterbo's late twelfth-century *Pantheon* follows verbatim the *Rescriptum Christiani* 25, 1.ff, pp. 52–53, and identifies by name seventeen wives of Mohammad (see *The Pseudo-Historical Image of the Prophet Mohammad*, 177). Perhaps 2 Chr 11.21—which notes that Rehoboam had 18 wives—suggested this number to Peter?

67. Cf. Petrus Alfonsi, who described Mohammad as "burning so much with the fire of lust that he did not blush to befoul another man's bed in adultery just as if the Lord were commanding it ..."; *Dialogue*, p. 154. Peter of Poitiers reiterates this claim in his *Capitula* 2.5 (*infra*, p. 168).

he commended a zeal for almsgiving and certain acts of mercy, he praised prayer, and in this way the utterly monstrous one joined "to a human head a horse's neck, and the feathers" of birds, as a certain one says.[68] Seeing that, at the persuasion of the monk already mentioned and the aforementioned Jews, he [Mohammad] completely abandoned idolatry, and persuaded those whom he could that it ought to be abandoned, and proclaimed that there is one God that ought to be worshiped, having abandoned a multiplicity of gods, he seemed to say what had not been heard before by those that are rude and unschooled.[69] And because, in the first place, this preaching was in harmony with their reason,[70] they believed him to be God's prophet.

11. From then, in the progress of time and of error, he was raised up by them to the kingship that he had desired. Thus, mixing good things with evil, confusing true things with false, he sowed the seeds of error, and, partly during his time and partly and especially in the time after him, he produced a nefarious harvest that should be burned up by an everlasting fire. Immediately thereafter, as the Roman Empire was declining or rather nearly ceased to exist, with the permission of Him "through whom kings reign,"[71] the dominion of the Arabs or the Saracens arose, infected with this plague, and, little by little occupying by force of arms the largest parts of Asia with the whole of Africa and part of Spain, just as it transferred its rule upon those subject to it, so too did it transfer error.

68. Horace, *Ars Poetica* 1: 1–2.

69. Cf. Hugh of Flavigny's *Chronicon* 1 (PL 154: 101B): "Tunc cepit praedicare Mahamet, ut derelinquerent idola manu facta et adorarent creatorem qui fecit quae sunt." ("Then Mohammad began to preach that they should turn away from the idols made by [human] hands and adore the Creator who made whatever exists.")

70. Peter seems to suggest that since belief in one God is grounded in reason, Mohammad's monotheism was acceptable to those who heard him. He does not imply, as does Petrus Alfonsi's interlocutor Moses, that Islam is "grounded on an unshakable foundation of reason" (*Dialogue*, p. 146). But he does acknowledge that the followers of Mohammad are "rational by nature." See *infra*, p. 79, *Against the Sect of the Saracens* 29.

71. Prv 8.15.

12. Although I would name them heretics because they believe some things with us, in most things they depart from us;
perhaps more correctly I should name them pagans or heathens, which is worse.[72] For although they say some things about
the Lord that are true, nonetheless they proclaim many others
that are false, and they participate neither in baptism, nor the
sacrifice [of the Mass], nor penance, nor any Christian sacra-
ment, which everyone other than these heretics has done.

13. The highest aspiration of this heresy is to have Christ the
Lord believed to be neither God, nor the Son of God, but, although a great man and beloved by God, nonetheless a mere
man, and certainly a wise man and a very great prophet. What
once, indeed, were conceived by the devil's device, first dissem-
inated by Arius[73] and then advanced by that Satan, namely Mo-

72. Peter fails to recognize Islam as a religion of independent origin; rather, he imagines that Muslims subscribe to a Christian heresy "because they
believe some things with us," and because they learned these beliefs from
heretical Christians like Sergius; possibly, he concedes, one should call them
pagans (*pagani*) or heathens (*ethnici*), however, because they do not share any
of the Christian sacraments, as other heretics do. But insofar as he regards
Muslims as heretics, he places them in a different category both from Jews
and from pagans. In his polemic *Against the Petrobrusians,* which Peter brought
to its final form in 1143 soon after his return from Spain, he remarked that
"in our day there exist chiefly four different types of sects in the world, i.e.,
Christians, Jews, Saracens, and pagans ..." (*Contra Petrobrusianos haereticos* 161,
p. 94). Both Jews and Muslims, however, will be subject to certain legal disabil-
ities—e.g., a prohibition against marriage to or even sexual relations with a
Christian.

Islam's late emergence also caused a problem. Indeed, Peter places in the
mouth of a Jew the question "How is it that when five hundred years after
Christ had passed, the Mohammedan heresy arose ... ?" (*Against the Inveterate
Obduracy of the Jews* 4, p. 190). Although Islam has spread through much of
the world, like a corrupt humor that has infected one member of the body,
Christianity, he proclaims, has spread everywhere to all peoples to restore the
body's health (ibid., 191–92). It remains for the medieval Church to combat
heresy, just as above (*Letter* [*to Bernard of Clairvaux*] *on His Translation* 3) he
exhorted Bernard of Clairvaux to take up the challenge to vanquish Mohammad's heresy, as the Fathers had opposed heresies in the early Church.

73. Arius (d. 336) was a Christian priest of Alexandria whose teaching gave
rise to Arianism. He was condemned at the First Ecumenical Council in Nicaea (325) for his unwillingness to confess that Jesus, the Son, and God the
Father are of the same essence or *ousia.*

hammad,[74] will be fulfilled completely according to diabolical design through the Antichrist. In fact, since the blessed Hilary[75] said that the origin of the Antichrist was in Arius,[76] then what he began, by denying that Christ is the true Son of God and by calling him a creature, the Antichrist will at last consummate by asserting that in no way was he God or the Son of God, but also that he was not a good man; this most impious Mohammad seems properly to be provided for and prepared by the devil as the mean between both of them,[77] as one who became in a certain sense both an extension of Arius and the greatest support for the Antichrist who will say worse things before the minds of the unbelievers.[78]

14. To be sure, nothing is so contrary to the Enemy of the human race as the faith of God Incarnate, by which we are particularly aroused to piety; and, renewed by the heavenly sacraments with the operative grace of the Holy Spirit, we hope to return again to that place from which he [the Enemy] took pride that we were cast out, namely, to the vision of the King

74. Robert of Ketton's *Mistake-Laden and Ridiculous Chronicle of the Saracens (Chronica mendosa et ridicula Sarracenorum)*, in *The Pseudo-Historical Image of the Prophet Mohammad*, 93), identifies Mohammad as the "son of the devil and the firstborn of Satan" ("Generatio Mahumet, filii diaboli et primogeniti Sathane").

75. Bishop of Poitiers; d. ca. 368.

76. Hilary of Poitiers, *De trinitate* 2.23, 6.43, and 6.46, ed. P. Smulders, CC SL 62 (Turnhout: Brepols, 1979).

77. A "mean" because, although he recognizes Jesus as a good man, he does not accept his divinity. Moreover, as John Tolan has pointed out, Peter seems to identify Mohammad as a principal actor in a long diabolical plot against the true faith that will be consummated with the advent of Antichrist. See John V. Tolan, *Saracens: Islam in the Medieval European Imagination*, 158. Cf. also Kevin R. Poole, "Beatus of Liébana: Medieval Spain and the Othering of Islam," in *End of Days: Essays on the Apocalypse from Antiquity to Modernity*, ed. Karolyn Kinane and Michael A. Ryan (Jefferson, NC: McFarland & Co., Publishers, 2009), 47–66.

78. Following the First Crusade, it became increasingly common to identify Muslims as Antichrist's attendants. See Robert the Monk's *Historia Iherosolomitana*, and Ralph of Caen's *Gesta Tancredi*, in *Recueil des historiens des croisades. Historiens Occidentaux*, 5 vols. (Paris: Academie des Inscriptions et Belles-Lettres, 1844–1895), 3: 695 and 828. Cf. Iogna-Prat, *Order and Exclusion*, chap. 11: "Islam and Antichrist."

and of our fatherland, with the King himself and the Creator God descending to our place of exile, recalling us to himself with mercy. From the beginning he endeavored to extinguish equally the faith and love of piety and of the divine dispensation in the hearts of men, and he attempted to eradicate this also at the beginning of the still nascent Church, if then it were permitted, by the most ingenious subtlety, and almost in the same way in which, later, he was permitted to seduce that most unhappy race.

15. To be sure, the blessed Augustine says that the philosopher Porphyry,[79] after he had wretchedly become an apostate from Christianity, reported this in his books that he produced against the Christians: to wit, that he consulted the oracles of the gods and asked, concerning Christ, what he was. The reply to him was, actually, from the demons, that Christ was indeed a good man, but that his disciples had sinned gravely when, ascribing divinity to him, they invented something that he had never said about himself.[80] This opinion is very often found among those fables [of the Saracens], almost in the same words. How great was this subtlety of the devil that he said something good about Christ, when he knew that if he spoke only evil of him, in no way would one believe him, not caring what Christ was thought to be so long as divinity, which especially saves men, was not believed to be in him; if anyone wishes to understand more fully, let him read the eighteenth book and the nineteenth book of *The City of God* by this same father Augustine, and the first [book] of *The Harmony of the Evangelists*.[81] In fact therein, if one has a good and studious talent, he should be able to surmise with certainty both what the devil planned

79. Porphyry (d. ca. 305) was a Neoplatonic philosopher who polemicized against Christianity in his no longer extant *Against the Christians*. It was the fifth-century church historian Socrates Scholasticus that claimed that Porphyry was an apostate Christian (*Historia ecclesiastica* 3.23); Augustine described him as the bitterest enemy of the Christian faith, but a very noble philosopher. See Augustine, *Sermo* 241 (PL 38: 1137); *De civ. Dei* 19.22, ed. Bernard Dombart and Alfons Kalb, CC SL 48 (Turnhout: Brepols, 1955).

80. Cf. Augustine, *De civ. Dei* 19.23, p. 688.

81. Cf. Augustine, *De consensu evangelistarum* 1.15, ed. Franz Weihrich, CSEL 43 (Vienna: F. Tempsky, 1904), 22.

to do then but was not allowed to do, and what at length he did in this single most wretched race, with a hidden judgment allowing it, once he was unleashed.

16. In no way, in fact, could any mortal have invented such fables as the written ones that are singled out here, unless by the assistance of the devil's presence, through which [fables], after many ridiculous and insane absurdities, Satan planned particularly and in every way to bring it to pass that Christ would not be believed to be Lord, the Son of God and True God, the Creator and Redeemer of the human race. And in reality this is what he wanted to introduce persuasively at that time through Porphyry, but through God's mercy he was blown away from the Church, which at that time was burning still with the first fruits of the Holy Spirit; [but] at length, [he] used that most wretched man Mohammad (and as it is reported by many, one who is possessed by an evil spirit and by epilepsy)[82] as an instrument and implement, as it were, most suited to him; alas, he plunged into eternal damnation, along with himself, a very large race and one which at present can be reckoned as nearly a half part of the world. Why this was permitted to him He alone knows to whom no one can say, "Why do you do this?" and who said, "Even from among the many that are called, few are chosen."[83]

17. For this reason I, choosing to tremble all over rather than debate, have briefly noted down these things so that the

---

82. For the claim that Mohammad suffered from epilepsy, see Anastasius the Librarian, *Historia ecclesiastica sive Chronographia tripertita* (Paris: e typographia regia, 1649), 103; accessed at https://books.google.com/books?id=-bj SEbLhrAIC&pg=PP11&lpg=PP11&dq=Chronographia++et+Anastasii+ Bibliothecarii+Historia+Ecclesiastica+sive+Chronographia++tripartita,&source =bl&ots=qbl6IP4Ehv&sig=6eyJNEOkxPnZAk8KwyTZoIH39Bg&hl=en&sa=X &ei=5Ae9VKK5HIODNvuVgfgK&ved=0CCAQ6AEwAA#v=snippet&q= Mahomet&f=true. This became a topos in medieval Latin polemics in the twelfth century (and after). Cf. Hugh of Fleury, *Historia ecclesiastica II*, in *The Pseudo-Historical Image of the Prophet Mohammad*, 73; Sigebert of Gembloux (d. 1112), *Chronographia*, ed. L. Bethmann, MGH, SS 6 (Turnhout: Brepols Publishers, 2013), 323, ln. 13; Ekkehardus Uraugiensis (d. ca. 1126), *Chronicon universale* 5, ed. G. Waitz, MGH, SS 6 (Turnhout: Brepols Publishers, 2013), 153, ln. 22.

83. Mt 20.16, 22.14.

one who reads them will understand, and if there is such a one
as wishes to and can write against this entire heresy, he will
know with what kind of enemy he will do battle. Perhaps there
yet will be one whose spirit the Lord will awaken, in order to
free the Church of God from the great disgrace that it suffers
therefrom, because although up until our own time, you may
be sure, it has confounded all heresies—both ancient and modern—by responding to them, not only has it not replied at all
to this one alone, which, beyond all others, has caused the un-
bounded destruction of the human race, both in bodies and in
souls, but neither has it attempted to inquire—even a little or
inadequately—how great a plague it is or whence it came.

18. It was for this entire reason that I, Peter, humble abbot
of the holy church of Cluny, when I tarried in Spain for the
visitation of our properties that exist there,[84] had translated
from Arabic into Latin, with great effort and at great expense,
that entire impious doctrine and the accursed life of its terrible inventor,[85] and, once it was laid bare, I had it come to our
acquaintance, so that one would know how foul and frivolous
a heresy it is, and so that some servant of God, with the Holy
Spirit enkindling him, would be spurred on to refute it with a
written composition. O shame! that there is no one who will do
this, because with nearly all ardor for these efforts of the saints
everywhere grown cool already in the Church, I actually have
waited a long time, and [because] there was no one who would
open [his] mouth and move the pen and growl with the zeal of
holy Christianity, I myself, at all events, proposed for some time
to undertake this, if my extensive occupations permitted, with
the Lord assisting. Nonetheless, I would always prefer that this
be done better by someone else, rather than worse by me.

84. In 1142, Peter traveled to Spain with a large entourage for the inspec-
tion of Cluniac monasteries and properties there. See esp. Charles Julian Bishko, "Peter the Venerable's Journey to Spain," in *Petrus Venerabilis 1156–1956:
Studies and Texts Commemorating the Eighth Centenary of His Death,* ed. Giles Constable and James Kritzeck, Studia Anselmiana 40 (Rome: Herder, 1956), 163–
75.

85. A reference to the texts translated as the Toledan Collection. See Introduction, pp. 18–19, 21–24.

AGAINST THE SECT OF
THE SARACENS

(*Contra sectam Saracenorum*)

Prologue

IRST AND FOREMOST, I call upon the omnipotent Spirit of God to take action against the nefarious doctrine of the impious Mohammad, so that the One that has failed no one nor failed his Church when acting against his enemies, also would not fail to dispose me to act against the worst adversaries of both. He "has spoken through the prophets,"[86] enkindled the apostles, inspired the entire world with overflowing gifts, and flowed down "like the precious ointment on the head [...] that ran down to the hem of the garment."[87] Let his ever-abundant largesse, I pray, support me, the least of his [servants], and may he who "holding all things together, knows the voice"[88] fill the heart with knowledge, fill the mouth with a voice and with an appropriate word, in order to accomplish in a useful fashion the task upon which I enter. I hope that he will make himself present to one calling upon him, because he is benevolent—"For the spirit of wisdom is benevolent";[89] in fact—and this is something greater—I do not doubt this, because I belong to that Church to which the Savior promised: "And I will ask my Father, and he will give you another Paraclete, to be with you forever."[90] But perhaps one inquires

---

86. Nicene Creed; cf. Lk 1.55, 70; Heb 1.1.
87. Ps 132 (133).2. 88. Sir 1.7.
89. Sir 1.6.
90. Jn 14.16. Peter seems unaware that Muslim theologians understood references to the coming of the Paraclete in the Gospel of John (e.g., Jn 15.26) to foretell the coming of the prophet Mohammad. See Sidney H. Griffith, "Ar-

about the reason for writing. That must be presented, lest as a
writer I appear to be unnecessary.

2. Clearly this was the reason that I had to write here, which
reason existed for many people and for the great Fathers. They
were unable to suffer any harm or even a small loss to the Christian faith, nor would they tolerate the madness of diverse heresies raging against sound teaching. They avoided remaining silent when one had to speak out, heeding those that know most
fully that they must deliver themselves in the presence of God
to the delicate balance-scale of judgment no less for a fruitless
or, what is greater, a damnable silence than for an idle or inju-
rious word. For this reason, with letters, books, and diverse and
robust treatises, they stopped up "the mouth [...] of them that
speak wicked things"[91] and—according to the Apostle—with the
spirit of God that was speaking through them they laid low, they
trod down, they destroyed "every height" of Satan, "that raised
itself up against the knowledge of God."[92]

3. I pass over the ancient and, for their very antiquity, less
famous heretics: Basilides,[93] Apelis,[94] Marcion,[95] Hermogenes,[96]

---

guing from Scripture: The Bible in the Christian/Muslim Encounter in the
Middle Ages," in *Scripture and Pluralism: Reading the Bible in the Religiously Plural
Worlds of the Middle Ages and Renaissance,* ed. Thomas Heffernan and Thomas
Burman (Leiden: Brill, 2005), 29–59, esp. 36–45.

91. Ps 62.12.

92. 2 Cor 10.5.

93. Basilides was a second-century gnostic scholar and teacher in Alexandria, whose followers were known as Basilidians. In addition to commentaries
that he composed on the canonical Gospels, he compiled a not-extant "gospel" of his own, which was meant to reveal a secret tradition. Clement of Alexandria (among others) polemicized against the Basilidians.

94. Apelis/Apelles was a disciple of the second-century figure Marcion.
Tertullian remarks that Marcion denied both Christ's nativity and that he had
a real body; his disciple Apelles later abandoned his teaching and sought other interpretations. See *De carne Christi* 1, ed. E. Kroymann, CC SL 2 (Turnhout: Brepols, 1954; CD ROM).

95. Marcion was a Christian heretic active during the second century. His
teachings are known principally from the polemics of his opponents, e.g., Tertullian's *Adversus Marcionem (Against Marcion).* Chief among these was his rejection of the Old Testament, and his reception only of New Testament texts that
could be traced to Paul.

96. A second-century Christian heretic who taught, among other things,

the Cataphrygians,[97] Encratites,[98] Montanus[99] with the insane women Prisca and Maximilla,[100] Novatian,[101] Eunomius,[102] and many other monsters nominally Christian.[103] Having encoun-

that God had not created the world out of nothing (*ex nihilo*) but out of previously existing, uncreated matter. Tertullian wrote in response his *Adversus Hermogenem* (ed. E. Kroymann, CC SL 1 [Turnhout: Brepols, 1954]).

97. The "Cataphrygians" were members of the Montanist sect, which followed the teachings of "the Phrygians," i.e., Montanus, Maximilla, and Priscilla. Later the term Cataphrygians ("after the Phrygians") became more common; see William Tabbernee, *Fake Prophecy and Polluted Sacraments. Ecclesiastical and Imperial Reactions to Montanism* (Leiden: Brill, 2007), xxx. Augustine uses the term "Cataphrygians" and explains that it stems from the fact that Montanus and his early followers lived in Phrygia. See Augustine, *De haeresibus* 25, ed. R. Vander Plaetse and C. Beukers, CC SL 46 (Turnhout: Brepols, 1969; CD ROM). Since Peter lists the Cataphrygians separately from Montanus, Priscilla, and Maximilla, he may have had only a vague notion of who the Cataphrygians were.

98. The Encratites were second-century ascetics. Early heresiologists identified Tatian as the founder of the movement that, Augustine remarks, condemned the institution of marriage and refused to eat meat. See his *De haeresibus* 25.

99. Montanus was a pagan priest who was baptized as a Christian, ca. 155. Later he declared that he was filled with the Holy Spirit and began to prophesy. He was soon joined by two prophetesses, Prisca/Priscilla and Maximilla. Together they claimed to have received a new revelation, which stood in continuity with the New Testament but was ethically more rigorous, demanded frequent fasts, and condemned marriage; cf. Tertullian, *De ieiunio aduersus psychicos*, ed. A. Reifferscheid and G. Wissowa, CC SL 2 (Turnhout: Brepols, 1954; CD ROM), 1274. They promoted an imminent eschatological expectation and claimed that after them the world would come to an end. The New Jerusalem of the New Kingdom would be established, it was thought, in Phrygia.

100. Prisca (or Priscilla) and Maximilla were two prophetesses associated with Montanus and Montanism (see *supra*, n. 99).

101. Novatian was a Roman priest. After Pope Fabian died in 250 during the Decian persecution, a schism appeared in the Roman church between those who would follow Cornelius and those who would follow the more rigorous Novatian, who emerged as an anti-pope for his unwillingness to accept the reconciliation of those who had sinned gravely or had lapsed during the period of persecution.

102. Eunomius (d. ca. 394) was Bishop of Cyzicus and a defender of Arianism. He was opposed by the Cappadocian Basil of Caesarea, who composed a work *Against Eunomius;* see trans. by Mark DelCogliano and Andrew Radde-Gallwitz, FOTC 122 (Washington, DC: The Catholic University of America Press, 2011). Eunomius was condemned by the Second Ecumenical Council at Constantinople in 381.

103. Peter's list of heretics was a common rhetorical device. Cf. the fourth-

tered them, the great and learned men of their time, Agrip-
pa,[104] the philosopher and martyr Justin,[105] Theophilus the
Bishop of Antioch,[106] the Bishop Apollinaris of Hierapolis,[107]
Philip the Bishop of Crete,[108] Musanus,[109] Modestus,[110] Irenae-
us the famous martyr-bishop of Lyons of our [province of]
Gaul,[111] Rhodon of Asia,[112] Miltiades,[113] Apollonius,[114] Serapi-

---

century *Physiologus Latinus* (recension B) 11.29, which warns the reader to flee
from Sabellius, Marcion, Manicheus, to beware of Novatian, Montanus, Val-
entinus, Basilides, and Macedonius ("fuge igitur Sabellium, Marcionem, Man-
ichaeum, caue Nouatianum, Montanum, Ualentinum, Basilidem, Macedoni-
um"), ed. F. J. Carmody (Paris: Librairie E. Droz, 1939), 24.

104. Agrippa Castor, a Christian apologist from the first half of the second
century who polemicized especially against Basilides and Gnosticism. See Jerome, *De viris ill.* 21 (PL 23: 639B).

105. Justin Martyr (d. ca. 165), a second-century Christian apologist and
author of a first and second *Apology,* the *Dialogue with Trypho,* and other works
that are not extant. Cf. Jerome, *De viris ill.* 23 (PL 23: 641B–C).

106. Theophilus of Antioch died in the second half of the second century.
His three books to *Autolycus* are extant. According to Jerome, he also composed a treatise against Marcion and another against the heresy of Hermogenes. See *De viris ill.* 25 (PL 23: 643B–C).

107. Apollinaris, Bishop of Hierapolis in the second half of the second century, was the author of *Against the Greeks; Concerning Truth; Against the Jews;* and
Against the Heresy of the Phrygians. Cf. Jerome, *De viris ill.* 26 (PL 23: 645A); Eusebius, *Hist. eccles.* 4.27, p. 389.

108. According to Jerome, Philip was Bishop of the city of Gortina of Crete
(during the second half of the second century), and the author of a treatise
Against Marcion. See Jerome, *De viris ill.* 30 (PL 23: 647A).

109. Musanus, whose dates remain uncertain, wrote against the Encratites.
Eusebius placed him in the reign of Marcus Aurelius (d. 180). Cf. Eusebius,
Hist. eccles. 4.28, p. 389; Jerome, *De viris ill.* 31 (PL 23: 647A).

110. According to Jerome, Modestus wrote a treatise against Marcion ca.
180. Cf. *De viris ill.* 32 (PL 23: 647B).

111. Irenaeus (d. ca. 200/203) was Bishop of Lyons and composed a very
popular *Against Heresies* (*Adversus haereses*) in five books, which included a
lengthy refutation of Gnosticism. Cf. Jerome, *De viris ill.* 35 (PL 23: 649A).

112. Rhodon of Asia (fl. 165–175), a student of Tatian, composed a polemic
against Marcion, *Solutions,* and a commentary on the creation story in Genesis. See Jerome, *De viris ill.* 37 (PL 23: 651B).

113. A Christian author of the second half of the second century. Eusebius
(*Hist. eccles.* 5.28, p. 501) mentions him alongside Justin Martyr, Tatian, and
Clement of Alexandria. According to Jerome, he composed works against the
Montanists. See Jerome, *De viris ill.* 39 (PL 23: 655A).

114. Apollonius wrote against the Montanists near the end of the second
century. See Jerome, *De viris ill.* 40 (PL 23: 655A).

on,[115] Hippolytus,[116] Victorinus,[117] Reticius of the Aedui,[118] and many others not known to us, opposed their madness. And I pass over them. I turn to the chief plagues of diabolical impiety with which Satan has especially attempted to afflict the Church of God and to overthrow it as if with the strongest battering rams. I am referring, indeed, to the Manicheans, the Arians, Macedonians, Sabellians, Donatists, Pelagians, and, last of all, the Nestorians and Eutychians.

4. The first among these, the Manicheans,[119] casting aside all of the texts of the Old Testament, rejecting the prophets, and receiving part of the Gospels while condemning part, established two principles of good and evil. [They held] that God fought with the people of darkness; in order not to be vanquished, he mixed part of himself into fruits, meat (*carnibus*),[120] plants, trees, and all things of this sort, in order to be liberated gradually, after eating such things, by human belching. These unnatural people, lost among the most foolish tales, rave that the death of the Lord is a ghostly fantasy, that the resurrection

115. Serapion was Bishop of Antioch ca. 190–203. He wrote against Montanism as well as against the influence of Gnosticism. See Jerome, *De viris ill.* 41 (PL 23: 655C–657A).

116. Hippolytus (d. 235) was a priest in Rome ca. 189–98; it seems that he became anti-pope in Rome from 217, in opposition to Pope Callixtus. His most important work was his *Refutation of the Heresies* or *Philosophoumena*, in ten books; books 2–3 did not survive. He also wrote numerous works of theology and biblical commentary. See Jerome, *De viris ill.* 61 (PL 23: 671A–673A).

117. Victorinus (d. ca. 304), Bishop of Pettau, died as a martyr during the Diocletian persecution. He wrote a number of biblical commentaries, including a *Commentary on the Apocalypse*, as well as a treatise *On the Creation of the World*. Jerome also attributes to him a work *Against all Heresies*. See Jerome, *De viris ill.* 74 (PL 23: 683B–C).

118. Jerome describes Reticius as from the Aedui, a Gallic people, and identifies him as the Bishop of Autun during the reign of Constantine the Great (d. 337). He attributes to him a commentary on the Song of Songs, as well as a large treatise *Against Novatian*. See Jerome, *De viris ill.* 82 (PL 23: 689B–691A).

119. For the Manicheans, followers of the Persian prophet Mani (216–ca. 276), see *supra*, n. 63, p. 43. Peter's account of their teaching here is largely correct.

120. Faustus the Manichean maintains that he abstains from eating all meat. See Augustine, *Contra Faustum* 4.1, ed. Joseph Zycha, CSEL 25.1 (Vienna: Tempsky, 1891), p. 268.

is a falsehood,[121] and many other such things that should not be mentioned but about which one should remain silent. The Arians,[122] a crop of the devil more fertile than others, "setting their mouth against heaven and with their tongue passing through the earth,"[123] willfully treat with contempt the divinity of the one true and highest God—of the Father, Son, and Holy Spirit. They attribute Godhead only to the Father, and number among created things the Son and the Holy Spirit. They said that the Son was the greatest among created things, [and] that the Holy Spirit was inferior to the Son but was greater than other created things. And the Macedonians,[124] who are also insane, split in half the heresy with the Arians and confess that the Son is true God and co-essential with the Father, while separating the Holy Spirit from the Godhead of both. The Sabellians,[125] ridding

121. For Faustus's repudiation of Christ's death and resurrection, see Augustine, *Contra Faustum* 11.3, CSEL 25.1, p. 317.

122. Arius (d. 336), a priest of Alexandria, was condemned as a heretic at the First Ecumenical Council at Nicaea (325 CE) for professing that the Word or the Son is not of the same substance or essence as God the Father, and that the Word (as well as the Holy Spirit) is a creature and therefore not eternal. He was sent into exile; subsequently, after accepting a theological compromise, he was promised readmission to the Church, but Arius died before he was reconciled. Arianism was equally condemned, but it survived in some form in the West especially among the Germanic tribes (e.g., Goths, Ostrogoths, Visigoths, et al.) that acquired political control there after the collapse of Roman imperial administration in the second half of the fifth century. Although in Visigothic Spain the Arian king Reccared I (d. 601) converted to Catholic Christianity in 589, traces of the heresy endured even as late as the arrival of the Muslims in 711.

123. Cf. Ps 72 (73).9.

124. The Macedonians, even though they accepted the divinity of Christ the Son, were judged to be enemies of the Holy Spirit (and thus called Pneumatomachians) because they did not extend divinity to the Spirit but insisted, instead, that the Spirit was created by the Son and subordinate to both the Son and the Father. They were condemned at the Alexandrine Synod of 362 CE.

125. The Sabellians are named after Sabellius, who lived in Rome ca. 215 and was condemned by Pope Calixtus I. Sabellius is associated with the teaching that the Father, Son, and Spirit constituted a single monad, and are distinguished only by their respective operations (creation, redemption, and sanctification). That is, there exists no enduring and permanent distinction of three Persons. Despite the condemnation of Sabellius, the heresy revived in the early 4th C., when Arians often applied this label to the defenders of

themselves of the entire question of the Trinity as something too troublesome, thought that there was only one person of the Deity that should be understood under three names. The Donatists,[126] having understood that the whole of the world had been rejected for salvation owing to the holy books that were surrendered to persecutors during the time of persecution, asserted that the Church can exist only in Africa, in contradiction to Christ, who says: "it was necessary that Christ suffer, and rise again from the dead on the third day, and that penance and remission of sins should be preached in his name, unto *all* nations, beginning at Jerusalem."[127] The Pelagians,[128] the proud and the very worst enemies of God's grace, by which alone we are saved, more shrewdly than other heresies "sharpened their tongues like serpents," and "with the venom of asps concealed

---

Nicene orthodoxy, and yet again toward the end of the 4th C. See also *supra*, n. 61, p. 43.

126. The Donatists, named after Donatus, became an important force during and after the Diocletian persecution (303–305 CE). Imperial edicts had demanded that Christians surrender all copies of their holy books and Scriptures to Roman authorities. Some bishops and communities chose to do so, to escape death and persecution. But the Donatists were rigorists who praised martyrdom instead, and viewed the surrender of these books as tantamount to apostasy. As such, clerics who handed over the books (so-called *traditores*) were viewed by the Donatists as lacking genuine clerical authority, rendering their sacraments invalid. Augustine spent years battling the Donatists, who were a significant presence in N. Africa, and composed numerous attacks upon Donatism, including a work entitled *Against the Donatists (Contra Donatistas)*, ed. Michael Petschenig, CSEL 53 (Vienna: F. Tempsky, 1910). Nevertheless, Donatism survived still in N. Africa when Islam spread to the region in the later 7th C.

127. Lk 24.46–47. My italics.

128. As Augustine (the "doctor of grace") spent many years fighting the Donatists, so too he spent the last years of his life fighting the Pelagian heresy, so named after the monk Pelagius. Pelagius was active in Rome in the first decade of the fifth century, before going to Palestine, where he found himself opposed by no less an authority than Jerome. Pelagianism, which denied that Adam's sin had irreparably corrupted us and which affirmed that through our own moral struggle we train free will in order to live without sin, was first condemned by a series of African synods, and finally was condemned throughout the Church at the Council of Ephesus in 431. For Augustine's anti-Pelagian writings, see esp. Augustine, *Four Anti-Pelagian Writings*, trans. John A. Mourant and William J. Collinge, FOTC 86 (Washington, DC: The Catholic University of America Press, 1992).

under their lips"[129] claimed, among many blasphemies on this matter, that the human substance certainly comes from God, [but] that human goods exist from men themselves, moreover, because of free will. Second to last among these, the Nestorians[130] removed the godhead from Christ, both God and man, denying that he was God and proclaiming that he was merely a man. The Eutychians,[131] the last among those listed above, although they oppose the Nestorians, are not for that reason any less impious—unlike them in their judgment, they are equal to them in perfidy—and just as the latter deny that Christ is true God, the former deny that he is true man. For Nestorius said, "Christ is only man"; Eutyches said, "Christ is only God."

5. And now, following the same order in which the heresies were presented, let us present also the destroyers of heresies; Archelaus, the Bishop of Mesopotamia, acted first or almost first, having brought forth a book of disputation against the Manicheans.[132] After him Serapion, himself a bishop, composed

129. Ps 139 (140).4.

130. Nestorius (d. 451), the Patriarch of Constantinople from 428–431, having scandalized his church by asserting that it was inappropriate to refer to the Virgin Mary by the title *theotokos* ("god-bearer") but acceptable only to call her *christotokos* ("bearer of the Christ"), was condemned at the Council of Ephesus in 431, allegedly for having separated in reality the nature of Christ's divinity from the nature of his humanity, just as in his language he sought to separate the two—according to his principal rival, Cyril of Alexandria— with reference to Mary. Peter's account is a gross oversimplification. Although Nestorius was condemned, Nestorianism survived beyond the borders of the Roman Empire, in Persia, and it endures still in small pockets today in Iraq, India, Syria, Lebanon, and elsewhere.

131. Eutyches (d. 454), from whom Eutychianism derives its name, was an archimandrite in the church of Constantinople. As an ardent supporter of the Alexandrian Christology and an opponent of Nestorius, he emphasized the *one* nature of the Word after the Incarnation, and is associated with Monophysitism, which suggests that Christ's human nature was subsumed in a single essence. Eutyches was condemned for heresy at a Constantinopolitan synod in 448, but the following year he was exonerated by the Second Council of Ephesus (the so-called "Robber Council"). The Fourth Ecumenical Council at Chalcedon (451) condemned Eutyches with finality.

132. Cf. Jerome, *De viris ill.* 72 (PL 23: 683A). Jerome indicates that Archelaus was active during the reign of the Emperor Probus (r. 276–282) and that he composed a polemic against the Manicheans in Syriac, which then was translated into Greek. An account of his public debate with Mani appears in

and published an excellent book.[133] The great Augustine—who came after these men, was younger than they but greater in understanding and far more eloquent—in like manner assailed and vanquished cursed heresy in powerful books that he produced against both Faustus[134] and Fortunatus, the chief figures among the Manicheans. Against the Arians, as far as pertains to what has been written, I read that Eustathius,[135] Bishop of Antioch, proceeded first to battle, armed with faith and eloquence. Who, after he had written many works against the Arian tenets, having been made an exile from see and country at the command of the emperor Constantine, endowed his own place of exile with honor, dying with a glorious and unchanging confession. After him, I read also that Marcellus,[136] Bishop of Ancyra, composed numerous volumes against these same ones. I read also of Athanasius of Alexandria[137] driving against the Arians

---

the *Acta Archelai,* which exists in a complete version in a Latin text from the late 4th C., attributed to Hegemonius (or Ps. Hegemonius). The critical edition can be found at https://archive.org/details/hegemoniusactaao1beesgoog.

133. Serapion Scholasticus, Bishop of Thmuis in Egypt in the mid-4th C., who, Jerome notes, composed a book *Against the Manicheans,* as well as commentaries on biblical texts. Cf. *De viris ill.* 99 (PL 23: 699A).

134. Augustine (d. 430), Bishop of Hippo in N. Africa, composed several works against the Manicheans in the last decade of the fourth century. Among these is an extensive work against Faustus the Manichean, *Against Faustus (Contra Faustum),* and another *Against Fortunatus (Contra Fortunatum).* Both have been edited by Joseph Zycha in CSEL 25.1 (Vienna: Tempsky, 1891).

135. Eustathius (d. ca. 337) was an opponent of the Arian doctrine at the First Ecumenical Council in Nicaea (325). Jerome notes that he composed a treatise *Adversus Arianos,* and that he was later exiled to Thrace by the Emperor Constantine the Great. Cf. *De viris ill.* 85 (PL 23: 691B).

136. Marcellus of Ancyra (d. 374) was Bishop of Ancyra. He was an aggressive opponent of the Arians at the First Ecumenical Council (325) and, according to Jerome, wrote many texts to include one written specifically *Against the Arians.* Unfortunately, he was also suspected of supporting the teaching of Paul of Samosata, Bishop of Antioch ca. 260, and Marcellus was therefore deposed and banished in 336.

137. Athanasius (d. 373), Bishop of Alexandria, was a chief defender of Nicene Orthodoxy. He composed numerous works against Arianism, including three *Orations against the Arians (Orationes contra Arianos)* as well as a *Defense against the Arians (Apologia contra Arianos).* According to Jerome, he also wrote a treatise in one book specifically against the bishops Valens and Ursacius, who were committed Arians and became close advisors to the Emperor Constantius II (d. 361). See *De viris ill.* 87 (PL 23: 693A–B).

not only with efforts, not only with words, but also with writings, and writing an entire book against Valens and Ursacius, the protectors of the Arians. And who does not know that Hilary of Aquitaine,[138] a truly holy man and learned in every science, composed twelve books against the Arians? From whom is it hidden that he wrote one book of his to the Arian emperor Constantius,[139] which he presented to him while still alive, and another addressed to him, which he wrote after Constantius's death? There is also another that he published against the already mentioned Valens and Ursacius. Also the famous rhetorician Victorinus wrote books in a dialectical fashion against Arius, the master of the Arians.[140] Didymus of Alexandria did likewise against these same ones in two books.[141] The philosopher and Bishop Maximus[142] offered a brilliant book *On the Faith*, against the Arians, to the Emperor Gratian[143] in Milan.

138. Hilary, Bishop of Poitiers (d. ca. 368), was an ardent opponent of Arianism and composed numerous works, including a polemic *Against Ursacius and Valens* (see above), a text against the Arians intended for the Emperor Constantius (*Liber in Constantium imperatorem*), and a treatise in twelve books *Against the Arians,* which became one component of his larger work, *De Trinitate.* Cf. Jerome, *De viris ill.* 100 (PL 23: 699B). See further Daniel H. Williams, "The Anti-Arian Campaigns of Hilary of Poitiers and the 'Liber contra Auxentium,'" *Church History* 61.1 (1992): 7–22.

139. I.e., Emperor Constantius II (d. 361).

140. According to Jerome, [Marius] Victorinus taught rhetoric in Rome during the reign of the Emperor Constantius II. Best known as a translator of Aristotle's *Categories* and *De interpretatione* and Porphyry's *Isagoge*, Victorinus converted to Christianity ca. 355, and composed books, in a dialectical fashion (*more dialectico*), *Against the Arians.* Cf. Jerome, *De viris ill.* 101 (PL 23: 701A).

141. Didymus of Alexandria (Didymus the Blind, d. 398). According to Jerome, although blind from childhood, Didymus became renowned for his mastery of dialectics and geometry, and composed two books *Against the Arians* (not extant), as well as a treatise *On the Holy Spirit* that Jerome translated into Latin. Cf. Jerome, *De viris ill.* 109 (PL 23: 705A).

142. Our Maximus was a native of Alexandria, from which he was banished by Emperor Valens in 374. Later he was consecrated Bishop of Constantinople, and he presented to Emperor Gratian a work entitled *De fide* that polemicized against the Arians. Cf. Jerome, *De viris ill.* 127 (PL 23: 713A). The appellation "the Philosopher" points instead to another Maximus, a friend and teacher of Emperor Julian ("the Apostate," d. 363) who was executed by Emperor Valens ca. 371.

143. Gratian was emperor from 375–383; he resided in Milan during 382–383.

6. The books published against the Arians, indicated above, are sufficient also against the Macedonians.[144] For they praise the deity of the Holy Spirit as well as that of the Father and the Son, both in majesty and in substance, which the Macedonians deny. The already mentioned Didymus wrote one book *On the Holy Spirit* in order for their error to be refuted by books specifically dedicated to it.[145] And Basil of Caesarea, a Bishop of Cappadocia, composed a volume on the same topic, *On the Holy Spirit*.[146] Also Gregory Nazianzen published another book on the same subject matter.[147] So too Ephrem, a deacon of the church of Edessa, published another volume in the Syriac language on the same topic, the Holy Spirit.[148]

7. Although I did not find works specifically against Sabellius,[149] nevertheless whoever resists the Arians, whoever struggles against the Macedonians, in like manner contradicts the Sabellians as well. What is more, I say that not only do Catholics take action against them, but heretics too resist the Sabellians. For Sabellius says that there exists one person of the Trinity; the Catholic denies this, the Arian denies this, the Macedonian denies this. The consensus, then, of both Catholics and here-

144. On the Macedonians or Pneumatomachians, see *supra,* n. 124.

145. See *supra,* n. 141.

146. Basil of Caesarea ("the Great"; d. 379), was Bishop of Caesarea and Metropolitan of Cappadocia. In addition to his work *Against Eunomius* (see *supra,* n. 102), he composed a work *On the Holy Spirit* against the Macedonians. Cf. Jerome, *De viris ill.* 116 (PL 23: 707C).

147. Gregory Nazianzen (d. 391) was a principal support for Basil of Caesarea and an ardent defender of Nicene orthodoxy. He opposed both the Arians and the Pneumatomachians in his five *Theological Orations.* Cf. Jerome, *De viris ill.* 117 (PL 23: 709A).

148. Ephrem the Syrian (ca. 306–373) was a theologian of the fourth century. He wrote in Syriac, and some of his works were translated into Greek, Coptic, Armenian, and other languages. In addition to Ephrem's hundreds of hymns—including *Hymns against Heresies*—Jerome mentions having read a work of his on the Holy Spirit. Cf. Jerome, *De viris ill.* 115 (PL 23: 707B). Ephrem's eighty-seven *Hymns on Faith,* which develop his defense of Nicene Orthodoxy, have been translated by Jeffrey Wickes, FOTC 130 (Washington, DC: The Catholic University of America Press, 2015).

149. Peter would have been more successful in his search for works specifically refuting the Sabellians were he able to read Greek texts, e.g., Ps. Athanasius's *Contra Sabellianos* (PG 28: 96–121), or Basil of Caesarea's *Contra Sabellianos et Arium et Anomoeos* (PG 31: 600–17).

tics suffices for the condemnation of the Sabellians. The entire world cries out as one against the Donatists, whose enemies
they are, but the African Optatus, Bishop of Mileve, wrote six
books specifically against them.[150] In a final battle our Augustine of Hippo, truly one of ours, vanquished them in both word
and writing.[151] The greatest and highest doctor of the Latins,
Augustine, the same one as mentioned above, dedicated almost
the last years of his life to writing distinguished books against
the Pelagians and their authorities Pelagius, Caelestius, and Julian of Campania.[152] The second council of Ephesus[153] was convened against the Nestorians and their authority Nestorius, at
which the Nestorian heresy was condemned and Nestorius, its
authority, was determined to be a heretic and was expelled from
the Constantinopolitan episcopate.[154] The holy pope Leo,[155] the
first of this name, a man great in faith, wisdom, and eloquence,

150. Optatus of Mileve (or Milevis; d. ca. 370) wrote a spirited attack upon
the Donatist Bishop of Carthage, Parmenian. Jerome mentions that Optatus
composed a work *Against the Donatists*, in six books. Cf. Jerome, *De viris ill.* 110
(PL 23: 705B). A seventh book was added later. The text is available in English
translation as *Optatus: Against the Donatists*, trans. Mark Edwards (Liverpool:
Liverpool University Press, 1997).

151. Augustine wrote numerous works against the Donatists in the early
fifth century, to include *Ad catholicos de secta Donatistarum, Breuiculus collationis
cum Donatistis*, and the *Contra Donatistas*. See also *supra*, n. 126.

152. See *supra*, n. 128. Caelestius/Coelestius was the most famous disciple
of Pelagius, and, after Pelagius took up residence in the Holy Land, Caelestius
became Augustine's principal opponent and representative for Pelagianism.
Julian of Campania, i.e., Bishop Julian of Eclanum (d. 454)—Eclanum being
near Benevento in Campania—was a defender of Pelagianism, for which he
was deposed and exiled in 418. Augustine responded in a work entitled *Contra
Julianum Pelagianum*.

153. Peter errs here. It was the first Council of Ephesus (431 CE)—the
Third Ecumenical Council—that condemned Nestorius, and not Second
Ephesus, also known as the "Robber Council" (449 CE). For the "Robber
Council" see *supra*, n. 131.

154. For Nestorius, see *supra*, n. 130.

155. Pope Leo I ("the Great") ruled from 440–461. In the theological
controversy aroused by Eutyches, Leo sent to Flavian, Patriarch of Constantinople, an epistle known as Leo's *Tome*, which states that Eutyches was correctly condemned at the Synod of Constantinople in 448. See *supra*, n. 131.
Although Eutyches was exonerated at the "Robber Council" in 449, in part
because Dioscorus of Alexandria had prevented a reading of Leo's *Tome* at the

wrote memorable letters, renowned both for their insight and style, against Eutyches and against the Eutychian heresy named after him. Because of his pastoral zeal, the almost six hundred bishops gathered at Chalcedon[156] cut off from the body of Christ—that is, from his Church—Nestorius and his disciples, [and] Eutyches and his disciples, and they delivered them to perpetual anathema unless those that remained should recover their senses. The priest Jerome, a man of consummate knowledge, published, as was his custom, volumes distinguished by eloquent speech against Jovinian, who equated marriage and virginity, against Helvidius, who denied the perpetual virginity of the Mother of the Lord, [and] against Vigilantius, who condemned the relics or bodies of the dead saints; and [Jerome] revealed how much one ought to despise them.[157] These indeed preceded Nestorius in time, but they were unable to produce a sect (*secta*) bearing their name.[158]

8. God's Church has always done this and does so now; it roots out, with the zealous hand of its gardeners, the "briars and thorns"[159] so much at variance with those belonging to the Lord. At no time has the indefatigable strength of the saints shrunk from hostile darts, but rather it has protected its disciples from the furor of enemies, vanquishing hostile forces with virtue, cunning with wisdom and with the "shield of faith,"[160]

---

council, a new council was convened in 451, the Council of Chalcedon, which condemned Eutyches and his disciples with finality.

156. Leo I declared that 600 bishops were in attendance, but this is surely an exaggeration, unless one includes the proxies for Western bishops who were themselves unable to appear. Nonetheless, a very large number of prelates attended.

157. Between 383 CE and 406 CE Jerome (d. 420) composed works against Helvidius (*Aduersus Heluidium de Mariae uirginitate perpetua*), Jovinian (*Aduersus Iouinianum*), and Vigilantius (*Contra Vigilantium*). Jerome was a Latin Christian priest and a prolific writer, polemicist, and translator. In opposition to Helvidius, Jerome elevated the state of virginity over the married condition, and in attacking Vigilantius he defended the cult of relics, voluntary poverty, and clerical celibacy. His renown earned him the title Doctor of the Church.

158. The Latin *secta* need not imply a sectarian community; it can simply indicate a doctrinal position or teaching. Here, however, Peter seems to draw a contrast to Nestorius, whose followers did create a separate Nestorian church.

159. Is 5.6; 9.18.

160. Eph 6.16.

and, with a vigorous effort, it has launched sharp thunderbolts
for their destruction. It has not been able to suffer the whispers
of the poisonous serpent to prevail over heavenly oracles, nor
for the pathway of right faith that leads to eternal blessedness
to be turned back to hell by the perverse steps of error. This,
I say, this clearly was the entire and the sole cause for these
saints to write, for which cause they inveighed against the enemies of Christian salvation not only with words and with books,
and neither did they spare their disciples nor themselves nor,
in the end, their own life. It is the same for me. Although I am
far inferior to them and unequal to them, I should not be less
zealous than they on behalf of the Church of God, the bride of
Christ, since there has been or there is but "one faith, one baptism, one God"[161] for me as well as for them, one eternal life,
which they already attain and to which we aspire.

9. But should one resist some errors, perhaps, but remain
silent concerning others? The Fathers did not hold this opinion. The Bishop Hippolytus revealed this,[162] writing, among his
many other works, *On the Pasch against all Heresies*. Also, in times
past the distinguished Bardesanes[163] demonstrated this in various writings among his disciples in Mesopotamia. He, blazing
with cleverness and vigorous in disputation, wrote texts beyond
number against nearly all the heretics that emerged in his era.
The most distinguished and the most powerful book among
them is one to which Jerome pays witness, which [Bardesanes]
delivered to Marcus Aurelius. Victorinus—not the one I men-

---

161. Eph 4.5–6.

162. On Hippolytus, see Jerome, *De viris ill.* 61 (PL 23: 671A–B), and *supra,*
n. 116. Jerome mentions, among other works of Hippolytus, *De Pascha* and *Adversus omnes haereses*. Peter seems to have understood these two to constitute
but a single text.

163. I.e., the Syriac Christian philosopher and theologian Bardaisan of
Edessa (ca. 154–222). According to Eusebius, he wrote dialogues in Syriac
against Marcionism, as well as a treatise *On Fate*. See Eusebius, *Hist. eccles.*
4.30.1–3, p. 393. It is Jerome, whose description Peter follows, who identifies
Bardesanes as having written an endless number of texts against almost every
heresy. The text presented to a certain Antoninus is the treatise *On Fate (De
fato)*. Jerome writes that Bardesanes delivered this treatise to *M. Antonino;* see
Jerome, *De viris ill.* 33 (PL 23: 647B). Peter's text expands that to read *Marcus
Antoninus,* presumably the Roman emperor, Marcus Aurelius (d. 180).

tioned earlier, but rather the martyr and bishop of Pettau—affirmed the same thing.[164] He, who was well instructed in both the Greek and the Latin language,[165] wrote against all the heresies of earlier times or of his own time, and, writing against all, he showed that one should neglect none. Let the reader observe whether those that follow him ought to imitate him when writing, not only for the doctrine but also in the martyrdom that he suffered unto death for the faith that he defended. The holy and famous Epiphanius,[166] Bishop of Salamis on the island of Cyprus, affirmed this, writing nonetheless books against all heresies and handing them down to the churches of all the world to be read. No heresy therefore may be neglected, as these examples from among the saints teach; none ought to be passed over in silence, according to the instruction of so many teachers. Every error ought to be refuted, every wrong against the understanding of the faith ought to be reproved and, if it can be done, corrected. The Church must be presented without stain or wrinkle to Christ by those to whom he committed it, so that it can hear from him: "You are fair, O my love, and there is no spot in you."[167]

10. If, then, no heresy that has arisen at any time whatsoever could be exempt from "the sword of the spirit which is the word of God,"[168] will the error of Mohammad be safe from it? Or perhaps Christian speech will pass it by as something insignificant or trifling? Or perhaps it will spare it as something harmless or less than harmful? And what heresy, O reader, has ever harmed the Church of God to such an extent? What error has ever damaged the Christian community so? What has wrought so much damage against its borders? What has increased the

---

164. See *supra*, n. 117. For the other Victorinus (Marius Victorinus), mentioned earlier, see *supra*, n. 140.

165. Actually, Jerome says that Bishop Victorinus did not know Latin and Greek equally well (*non aeque Latine ut Graece noverat*). *De viris ill.* 74 (PL 23: 683B).

166. Epiphanius (ca. 305–403), Bishop of Salamis and Metropolitan of Cyprus. The text against heresies is his *Panarion*, composed between 374–77, which treats some 80 heresies. Cf. Jerome, *De viris ill.* 114 (PL 23: 707B).

167. Song 4.7.

168. Eph 6.17.

number of those damned for hell by such a large multitude? The Arian plague, the greatest of the aforementioned heresies, occupied certain parts of the earth for some time, and infected them with a lethal draught administered by Satan. It added certain Gothic kings[169] to its wickedness, and, what is worse, it corrupted two emperors of the Roman world, Constantius[170] and Valens.[171] It crossed from foreign soil to Pannonia,[172] and from there it spread to Italy. Driven out from there, it invaded the southern part of Gaul, I mean Aquitaine, but, fleeing from King Clovis of the Franks,[173] finally it settled in a Spain that was overcome by military power. There, after barely a hundred years had passed, it collapsed, once the king of the Goths, who ruled over a heretical race, was converted to the Catholic faith by the agency of the Spirit of God.

11. The Mohammedan madness, which took its beginning among the Ishmaelite Arabs, corrupted the Persians, Medes, Syrians, Armenians, Ethiopians, Indians, and the rest of the kingdoms of the East, and almost the whole of Asia itself, which is largest among the three parts of the world, and either by turning them away from Christianity or by converting them from any of the ancient errors to the teaching of that lost man, it drew them away from Christ; it surrendered them to the devil. Thereafter, not by gentle reason but by violent incursion, once almost the entire East was overcome by arms, as was said, it subjected Egypt, Libya, and all of Africa to the impious religion, and having thus seized two parts of the world, it did not leave the third part, which is called Europe, entirely to Christ or his

169. Arianism had spread among the Visigoths, Ostrogoths, Vandals, Lombards, Burgundians, and others. Over the course of the sixth century, most of the other kings in the West also abandoned Arianism and embraced Catholic Christianity, although pockets of Arian influence endured until Islam arrived in Spain in 711. See *supra*, n. 122.

170. Emperor Constantius II (d. 361).

171. Emperor Valens (d. 378).

172. Roman Pannonia encompassed Hungary and E. Austria, as well as portions of the Balkan states.

173. In 496 CE, Clovis, King of the Franks, adopted Catholic Christianity and opposed Arianism. In Visigothic Spain the Arian king Reccared I (d. 601) converted to Catholic Christianity in 589.

Christians, having spread throughout Spain.[174] And what more shall I say? If you counted all the heresies that have been incited by a diabolical spirit throughout the eleven hundred years from the time of Christ, and simultaneously weighed them as if assembled together on a balance scale, they could not equal this one, nor will you find that all of them have, to the same extent, cast so much material on the eternal fires. Will Christian speech, which has left no heresy or even a small heresy intact, then, pass over this one, the greatest error of all errors, dumb and mute?

12. But perhaps one will say or think: "The Church responded to those heresies in the past which, as the Apostle John says, 'went out from us, but were not of us.'[175] But this error did not go out from us, nor was it of us. Indeed, the aforementioned Fathers responded by dragging or drawing Christians away from every error concerning the Church (that is, the body of Christ), and condemned those foreign errors circulating beyond the Church with silence. Among those can be numbered this error, which, as is said, did not go forth from the Church, and it shows that what did not go forth from the Church, like other heresies of error, does not really deserve the name 'heresy.' In fact, it is not called heresy unless it issues from the Church and acts against the Church."[176]

13. To this I say: I concede this, even I say that Christians stubbornly taking action against any part of the right faith already were called, by a name already in ancient usage, heretics,

174. Peter discusses the geographical expansion of the "Mohammedan error" (*Mahumeticus error*) as well in his *Against the Inveterate Obduracy of the Jews* 4, p. 191; there, however, he contrasts the more limited regional expansion of Islam to the worldwide expansion of Christianity that had been prophesied. Muslim armies arrived in Spain in 711; additional expeditions crossed the Pyrenees into France, where they were defeated in a famous battle near Poitiers by Charles Martel in 732.

175. 1 Jn 2.19.

176. Peter attempts here to address the argument of those who would say that Islam is not a Christian heresy because it does not stem from Christianity, but rather that it is a pagan or heathen religion. He addressed this issue earlier in *A Summary of the Entire Heresy of the Saracens* 12. See also *supra*, n. 72, p. 46. Peter himself seems to vacillate, even though the titles or *incipits* of his two polemics refer to the *heresy* of the Saracens.

and that that which they think or confess perversely is called a
heresy. But whether the error of Mohammad ought to be called
heresy, and whether his followers should be called heretics or
heathens, I do not fully settle. Indeed, I see that they receive
certain things from the Christian faith in the manner of heretics, and reject other things, equally to do or to teach according
to pagan rite what no heresy is ever written to have done. For,
along with certain heretics—and Mohammad wrote in this way
in his own faithless Qur'an—they say that Christ was born of
the Virgin Mary, that he is greater than every man and even
than Mohammad himself; they affirm that he lived without sin,
that he proclaimed truths, that he performed wonders; they
confess that he was the spirit of God, the word of God[177]—but
not the Spirit of God or the Word as we understand or express
them[178]—[but] they insanely propose with the Manicheans not
only that the passion or death of Christ was mere appearance
(*phantastica*), but that actually it never occurred at all.[179]

14. They think these things and others like them along with
the heretics. Along with pagans, moreover, they reject baptism,
spit out the Christian sacrifice, and mock penance and all the
remaining sacraments of the Church. Choose then what you
like! Either call them heretics owing to the heretical understanding according to which they agree with the Church in
part and in part disagree, or call them pagans owing to the ex-
ceeding impiety, since they surpass the errors of all the heresies

177. See Qur'an 4.171 and Robert of Ketton's Latin translation of the text
(which is the one Peter knew), ed. Bibliander (Basel, 1543), p. 37, lns. 35–36:
*Iesus Mariae filius, Dei nuncius, suusque spiritus, & verbum Mariae coelitus missum
existit.*

178. Similarly, in his *Against the Petrobrusians*, Peter remarks that the Saracens "confess that Christ lived in a holy fashion, born from a virgin, from a
divine breath [*flatus*], as they say, that he taught truths, that he performed miracles ..." but they do not participate in his sacrifice (the Eucharist) or receive
his precepts (*Contra Petrobrusianos* 161, p. 94). For Jesus and Christology in Muslim tradition, see "'īsā," *Encyclopedia of Islam*, 30 January 2015; http://reference
works.brillonline.com/entries/encyclopaedia-of-islam-2/i-sa-COM_0378.

179. Cf. Qur'an 4.156–57. In his *Confessions*, Augustine criticizes his own
former belief as a Manichean, asking how Jesus could deliver him from sin if
his death on the cross were a mere phantasm (*phantasma*) and if his death in
a fleshly body were unreal. See *Confessiones* 5.9, ln. 6–7, ed. Luc Verheijen, CC
SL 27 (Turnhout: Brepols, 1981; CD ROM).

by an ungodly profession. If you have called them heretics, it has been demonstrated that one should oppose them over and above all the heretics or heresies. If you call them pagans, on the authority of the Fathers I prove and I show that one ought not oppose them any less.

15. To affirm this, let there come back before us the afore-mentioned philosopher and martyr, Justin.[180] This one

labored much for the defense of the Christian religion, so much so that he presented a book written against the pagans (*gentes*) to the emperor Antoninus [Pius] and his sons and to the Senate, and he did not blush at the ignominy of the Cross, and he presented another book to the successors of this same Antoninus—Marcus Antoninus Verus and Lucius Aurelius Commodus.[181] There is another volume of his against the pagans, where he also debates the nature of demons. Likewise, he has a fourth book against the pagans to which he gave the title "Elenchos." And there is a dialogue against the Jews, which he had against Trypho, a leader of the Jews.[182]

To establish this further, let Apollinaris, the Bishop of the city of Hierapolis[183] (which is in Asia), follow him; he not only pre-sented to the emperor Marcus Antoninus Verus a remarkable volume on behalf of the Christian faith, but he also wrote five other books against the pagans. Irenaeus of Lyons[184] also pub-lished a volume against the pagans. Miltiades,[185] too, wrote oth-er books against the pagans and against the Jews. Also Apollo-nius,[186] a senator of Rome under the emperor Commodus <and

180. For Justin Martyr, see *supra*, n. 105.

181. I.e., the emperors Marcus Aurelius (r. 161–80) and Lucius Verus (r. 161–69). The two texts indicated here are evidently Justin's *First Apology* and *Second Apology*.

182. Peter follows verbatim Jerome's *De vir. ill.* 23 (PL 23: 641B–C), and Jerome followed Eusebius's *Hist. eccles.* 4.18.2–6. Eusebius attributed the fol-lowing works to Justin: (1) an *Apology* to Antoninus Pius (138–61), his sons, and the Senate (composed ca. 150–55); (2) an *Apology* to the successor of An-toninus Pius, Marcus Aurelius (161–80), and his adopted brother and co-ruler Lucius Verus (161–69); (3) a *Liber adversum paganos*, which, according to Euse-bius, treated the nature of demons; (4) a *Liber adversum paganos*, the *Elenchos* or *Confutatio* (according to Rufinus); (5) the *Dialogue with Trypho*.

183. See *supra*, n. 107.   184. See *supra*, n. 111.

185. See *supra*, n. 113.

186. Cf. Jerome, *De viris ill.* 42 (PL 23: 657A–B); Eusebius, *Hist. eccles.* 5.21.1–5, p. 485. Apollonius was martyred under the Emperor Commodus (r. 180–92).

Severus>,[187] composed an extraordinary volume against the pagans (*contra paganos*), which he read in the Senate, providing an argument for his faith, and after his reading, by the judgment of the Senate, he was beheaded for the sake of Christ.

16. The rhetor Arnobius succeeded them,[188] and under the Emperor Diocletian[189] he wrote *Against the Pagans,* which was read publicly during that era. Also Methodius,[190] Bishop of Tyre, composed books against the pagan philosopher Porphyry.[191] The Bishop of Laodicea, Apollinaris,[192] sharpened the pen and composed thirty books against this same one. Athanasius the Great,[193] Bishop of Alexandria, who was named above and often ought to be named, was not absent on behalf of this contention. This one not only wrote against the Arians, his special enemies, but even published two books *Against the Pagans.*[194] And let Eusebius, Bishop of Emesa,[195] a man of rhetorical and

187. The addition "and Severus" may reflect Jerome's contention that he had been denounced by his slave, Severus, or it may refer to the successor to Commodus, Emperor Septimius Severus (r. 193–211).

188. Arnobius of Sicca (d. ca. 330). At *De viris ill.* 79 (PL 23: 687A), Jerome claims he wrote a work entitled *Adversus gentes.* This is likely the *Adversus nationes,* written in seven books.

189. Diocletian reigned 284–305 CE.

190. Jerome claims that Methodius was Bishop of Olympos in Lycia and then later became Bishop of Tyre. But there is no other support for the claim that he was bishop in Tyre, and it has been generally rejected. He also states that he wrote a work against the philosopher Porphyry, which is no longer extant, and adds that he suffered martyrdom at the "end of the last persecution" (311 CE?), although Jerome also expresses some uncertainty over just when he died. See Jerome, *De viris ill.* 83 (PL 23: 691A–B).

191. For Porphyry, see *supra,* n. 79, p. 48.

192. This Apollinaris (d. 390), not to be confused with Apollinaris of Hierapolis, was Bishop of Laodicea in Syria. Although a fierce opponent of Arius and Arianism, his own Christology became a subject of debate, and for it he was condemned at the Second Ecumenical Council, at Constantinople (381 CE). Peter's notion that he wrote 30 books against Porphyry likely depends upon Jerome, *De viris ill.* 104 (PL 23: 701B); cf. Jerome's *Epist.* 70, in which he claims Eusebius wrote 25 books, and Apollinaris 30. See *Epistulae* 70.3, ed. Isidore Hilberg, CSEL 54 (Vienna: F. Tempsky, 1910; CD ROM), p. 703.

193. See *supra,* n. 137.

194. I.e., *Adversus gentes libri duo.* See Jerome, *De viris ill.* 87 (PL 23: 693B).

195. Eusebius (d. ca. 360), Bishop of Emesa (today, Homs, Syria) from ca. 339, was a student of Eusebius of Caesarea and was himself a semi-Arian. Peter

stylistic genius, follow after him. This man, as one reads, composed books beyond number, among which the chief ones were against the Jews and against the pagans. Augustine followed after all of them, inferior in doctrine to none of the aforementioned but rather perhaps superior to them, and, with the publication of the very well-known *City of God* in twenty-two books, he taught what ought to be done in word and in writing not only against the heretics, who went forth out of the Church, but also against the pagans and the Jews, who never were in the Church, and against every error whatsoever, at the appropriate time.[196]

17. Therefore, regardless of whether the Mohammedan error should be soiled with a heretical name, or whether it should be disgraced with a heathen (*gentilis*) or pagan one, one must take action against it, one must write against it. But because the Latins and especially the moderns, with the ancient zeal suffering decline—according to the word of the Jews, who, in the past, were surprised by the diverse languages of the apostles[197]—knew only their own language "to which they were born,"[198] they were unable to know to which sort this great error belongs, nor could they oppose, shall I say, so great an error. Therefore, "my heart grew hot within me, and in my meditation a fire was kindled."[199] I was angry that the Latins were unaware of the cause of such great destruction and, because of that ignorance, they could not be aroused to oppose it. In fact,

---

follows Jerome nearly verbatim. See *De viris ill.* 91 (PL 23: 695A). As Kritzeck suggests (*Peter the Venerable and Islam*, 40 n. 133), since we do not have evidence that Eusebius of Emesa composed polemics against Jews and pagans, Peter seems to have confused him with Eusebius of Caesarea, who did compose such works.

196. On Augustine, see *supra*, nn. 128, 134, and 151. Although Augustine writes against the pagans in *The City of God*, which he composed between ca. 414–425 CE, the work is not directed specifically against the Jews. For some treatment of his discussion of Jews in *The City of God*, see Jeremy Cohen, *Living Letters of the Law: Ideas of the Jew in Medieval Christianity* (Berkeley: University of California Press, 1999), 30–33.

197. Peter refers here to the Pentecost event, when the apostles, filled with the Holy Spirit, "began to speak with other tongues" (Acts 2.4).

198. Acts 2.8.

199. Ps 38 (39).4. The Vulg. reads *exardescet:* "will be kindled."

there was no one who might respond, because there was no one who might understand it. Therefore, I betook myself to those with expert knowledge of the Arabic language, out of which proceeds the lethal virus that has infected more than half the world. I persuaded them, both by entreaty and with money, to translate from the Arabic language into Latin the damned man's origin, life, teaching, and the law itself, which is called the Qur'an.[200] And so that no one will lack complete faith in the translation, and so that nothing could be removed from notice by some deceit of our own, I added a Saracen, moreover, to our Christian translators. The names of the Christian translators [are]: Robert of Ketton, Herman of Dalmatia, [and] Peter of Toledo. Mohammad[201] was the name of the Saracen. These men, after searching through the most secret libraries of that barbarous race, have published a not very small volume for Latin readers from the aforementioned material. It was done in that year when I went to Spain and had a meeting with Lord Alfonso, the victorious emperor of Spain.[202] This was in the year 1141 after the Incarnation of the Lord.[203]

18. But perhaps someone still [asks]: "What will it profit to bring food to those that refuse it, what will it profit to convey a sound for 'the deaf adder that stops its ears,'[204] with a complicated disputation? For the men against whom you are disposed to act are foreigners, they are barbarians, not only in customs

200. Peter refers often to the great expense he incurred to produce translations of the texts that form the Toledan Collection. See *supra*, n. 65, p. 18, and n. 13, p. 34. The "damned man," *perditus homo*, is the prophet Mohammad himself.

201. Nothing more is known of this Muslim co-translator. Kritzeck (*Peter the Venerable and Islam*, 69) acknowledges the risks he took, "since Islamic law ruled that the Koran should be withheld from the hands of unbelievers." Nor is it entirely clear what role he played, since the Christians mentioned were practiced translators of Arabic. Kritzeck speculates that his role may have been to comment on the precise meaning of Arabic words and to provide general background on Islamic thought and traditions.

202. Emperor Alfonso VII (d. 1157). For more on this journey, see the Introduction, p. 19.

203. In fact, Peter's journey to Spain occurred in 1142–43. See Charles Julian Bishko, "Peter the Venerable's Journey to Spain," in *Petrus Venerabilis 1156–1956*, pp. 163–75.

204. Ps 57 (58).5.

but also in their language, manifesting nothing that is common to them and to the Latins. How, then, will the Arab hear, to say nothing of understand, the Latin; how will the Persian [understand] the Roman; the Ethiopian or the Egyptian, the Frenchman? One must consider this so that effort is not expended in vain; one must take care so as not to leave a useful task behind, so that time is not wasted on one that is unnecessary."

19. To which I say: It can happen that the book will be translated into their language; the Christian truth can be put into Arabic letters or any others, just as, by my effort, the deplorable error could cross over to the notice of the Latins. Thus the Latin work, when translated into a foreign language, may possibly profit some others whom grace, which leads to life, wills to win over to God. In this way, from the Hebrew letters the Old Testament, [and] in this way from the Greek (except for the Gospel of Matthew)[205] the New Testament, having been translated into all the languages of the whole world, made the world subject to God, recalling it from hell, and has restored it to heaven by the Christian faith. In this way both the Latin has transferred many other works of the Fathers from Greek, and the Greek has received [many] from Latin. Nor, among the many other languages of the world unknown to us, has there been lacking this reciprocal transfer of words one to another, concerning which it could almost be said, as of the apostles, "There are no speeches nor languages, where their voices are not heard."[206]

20. If, perhaps, this written work with which one is concerned either did not have translators, or once it was translated, did not prove useful, at least the Christian armory will have arms also by which it may defend itself against those enemies,

205. According to ecclesiastical tradition, the Gospel of Matthew was written in the Hebrew language rather than in Greek. See, for example, Eusebius, *Hist. eccles.* 3.39.16, p. 293. This tradition was transmitted to the Middle Ages. E.g., an anonymous Irish text of the early Middle Ages declares that although the other Gospels were written in Greek, Matthew was written in Hebrew ("De lingua in qua scripta sunt iiii evangelia: Matheus in hebraica lingua, Marchus, Lucas, Iohannes in greca lingua scripserunt"). *In Evangelia excerpta,* 10, in *Scriptores Hiberniae Minores,* CCSL 108B.1 (Turnhout: Brepols, 1973), p. 214. Peter the Venerable would surely have received this same tradition.

206. Ps 18 (19).4.

or by which it may stab the enemies, if perhaps it has come to battle. The published volume will likely counteract our private thoughts, by which they can be brought to stumble by thinking that some piety exists among those impious ones, and by believing that some truth exists among the ministers of lies.[207] No small authority is joined to this argument that even if in law one ought to lead in such things, no obstacle should exist if one should follow the argument in the matter proposed.

21. Those already presented and many others about whom I have kept silent have written various, extensive, and wondrous works against heretics, Jews, or heathens; nonetheless, those writing did not choose or know beforehand whom they could benefit. And although they did not choose nor did they know beforehand whose particular efforts should serve salvation, they did not on that account allow the mind to rest from striving, or the tongue from speaking, or the hand from writing. The Greek writer did not take into account the fact that Greek could not profit the Latin, nor did the Latin think that the Greek would read Latin in vain, nor did any one, no matter how foreign, consider that the Catholic taking action against whatever errors assumes that he is undertaking the labor of writing in vain because his work could only benefit men having a foreign language once it was translated into various languages. They knew, they were certain, that "the Holy Spirit breathes where he wills,"[208] but they could not know on whom, when, or how much he breathes. They knew that "neither the one who plants nor the one who waters is anything, but only God who gives the growth."[209] Therefore by watering [and] planting like good servants they completed what was his, they remitted to the Lord what belonged to God. He who wished to follow them, I think, or rather I affirm, will not err. If I have done it myself, I am certain that I will not err. Clearly I will not err, if I have acted with the artless eye that belongs to me, and I have preserved for God what is his, as I said. It will not be possible, certainly it will not

207. Peter seems to acknowledge here that some Christians are attracted to Islam, at least in their "private thoughts."

208. Jn 3.8.

209. 1 Cor 3.7.

be possible for a work that has been undertaken for God's cause to pass completely without fruit, if either it has been useful to gain converts, or to resist enemies, or to defend those at home, or if at the least the "peace" promised to "men of good will"[210] will not be wanting for the writer of these [pages].

22. Let, then, the commencement of a long-delayed work follow, in the name of the Lord.

In conclusion, I add that I knew that, and I am certain that, by the unusual length of the prologue I have exceeded by a little the customary limits in such matters. But in order that the reader may excuse me, let him know that this has occurred because of the irksome objections of those engaged in the debate, for which, lest I seem too brief, I have been (I hope rightfully) more verbose than others.

Book One[211]

23. In the name of the Father and the Son and the Holy Spirit, of the one omnipotent and true God, a certain Peter, a Frenchman by nationality, a Christian by faith, an abbot by profession of those that are called monks, to the Arabs, the sons of Ishmael, who observe the law of the one who is called Mohammad.

24. It seems strange, and perhaps it really is, that I, a man so very distant from you in location, speaking a different language, having a state of life separate from yours, a stranger to your customs and life, write from the far parts of the West to men who inhabit the lands of the East and South, and that in speaking I attack those whom I have never seen, whom I shall perhaps never see. But I do not attack you by arms, as some of us often do, but by words; not by force, but by reason; not in hatred, but in love.[212] With such love, nonetheless, of a kind that ought to exist

---

210. Lk 2.14.

211. The *incipit* reads: *The First Book begins of the Lord Abbot Peter of Cluny Against the Accursed Heresy or Teaching (sectam) of the Saracens.*

212. This well-known passage has often been cited to demonstrate Peter's irenic approach to the Muslim world, and in order to contrast it with the military assaults of the Crusaders. Cf. Jean Leclerq, "Pierre le Vénérable et l'invitation au salut," *Bulletin des Missions* 20 (1946): 145–56. But it must be placed in

between worshipers of Christ and those who have been turned away from Christ, of such a kind as existed between our apostles and the pagans of their time, whom they invited to the law of Christ, of such a kind as between God the very Creator and director of all things and those whom, while they still served a creature and not the Creator, he, through his own followers, turned away from the worship of images and demons. Plainly he himself loved them, before they would love him;[213] he knew them before they would know him; he called them while they still would condemn him. He conferred good upon those doing evil; he had mercy by grace alone upon those who were perishing; and in this way he snatched them away from everlasting misery. The Church of the Christians has this from him, so that like him, as our Christ says, it "makes his sun rise on the evil and on the good, and sends rain on the righteous and on the unrighteous,"[214] and in this way and in him it loves friends, and on account of him it loves enemies.

25. A clear argument follows this Christian proof-text, according to which "every animal," as a certain one says, "loves its own kind."[215] From this it is proved that, although under this genus, that is, animal, all the quadrupeds, flyers, or species of every such kind are contained, every animal is more familiar to

context: Peter introduces these "good wishes" in a work intended to lead Muslims to Christian conversion, whereas his earlier *Summary of the Complete Heresy and of the Diabolical Teaching of the Saracens or Ishmaelites,* which Peter composed for a Christian audience soon after his return from Spain in 1143, harshly depicted Mohammad and his followers as engaged in a diabolical conspiracy with Antichrist to destroy the Church.

213. Cf. 1 Jn 4.19.

214. Mt 5.45.

215. Eccl 13.19. Peter does not include the rest of the passage—"so also every man loves what is nearest to himself"—although his readers could be expected to complete it. The biblical text is echoed in Scholastic discussions of animals. Cf. Albertus Magnus, *Quaestiones super de animalibus,* 8, q. 14: "Quare equus maxime diligit suam speciem" ("Why the horse particularly loves its own kind"), in *Opera omnia Alberti Magni,* ed. E. Filthaut, 12 (Monasterii Westf.: Aschendorff, 1955), 192–94. This text appears in translation in Albert the Great, *Questions Concerning Aristotle's* On Animals, trans. Irven M. Resnick and Kenneth F. Kitchell, Jr., FOTC, MC 9 (Washington, DC: The Catholic University of America Press, 2008), 279–83.

its like in its own species than in the universal genus. This is apparent in domestic animals, and it is well known in wild beasts, which either always or almost always abhor those which nature has set apart from them, and which follow those that they perceive to be like themselves or formed like them. If, as is wont to occur, they fight with one another for any reason from the movement of bile,[216] they will quickly return to a peaceful state once the motion has been calmed, and they cannot forget that they have been created [the same species] for a longer period of time. And since man also exists among the infinite number of species which, as it is said, is contained under [the genus] animal, and since, furnished with reason, he has what no other species of animal has, he is induced, moreover, to love one like himself by the persuasion of reason far more than he is by the force of nature.

26. These are the reasons why the Christian ought to love you, why he ought to choose salvation for you. One of them is divine, the other is human. In the former he is obedient to divine instruction; in the latter, he satisfies his own nature. In the same way I, the most insignificant among those beyond number and the most insignificant among the numberless servants of Christ, love you; loving, I write to you; writing, I invite you to salvation—not to the salvation of the sons of men, in whom, according to David's words, "there is no salvation"[217] because, according to the same one, "vain is the salvation of man,"[218] but to that [salvation] concerning which the same one says: "But the salvation of the just is from the Lord, and he is their protector in the time of trouble."[219] I propose these words of the Psalms to you for this reason, because I hear from your Mohammad that the Psalms were given to David by God.[220] For, speaking

216. Perhaps Peter depends on Petrus Alfonsi here, since Alfonsi claims that anger results from the movement of red choler or bile. See *Dialogue*, p. 66.

217. Ps 145 (146).3.   218. Ps 59 (60).3.

219. Ps 36 (37).39.

220. For the Psalms as revelation given to David, see Qur'an 17.55 and 4.163. Cf. J. Horovitz and R. Firestone, "Zabūr," in the *Encyclopedia of Islam*. University of Tennessee at Chattanooga. 03 February 2015, http://reference works.brillonline.com/entries/encyclopaedia-of-islam-2/zabu-r-SIM_8061.

to the Jew Abdia,[221] he said so: "One, indeed, is God;[222] two are Adam and Eve; three, indeed, are Gabriel, Michael, and Seraphael;[223] four are the Law of Moses, the Psalms of David, the Gospel, and Al-Furqān."[224] Again, "For the word of God did not come upon me all at once, as the Law was given all at once to Moses, the Psalms to David, and the Gospel to Christ."[225]

27. I invite you to a salvation that does not pass away but that will endure, not one that comes to an end with a brief life but that will endure in life eternal. It was given to mortals to pursue this, to enjoy this, at the time prescribed by God, but only for those who perceive of God what he is, not what he is not, who worship him not in accord with the phantasms of their heart,[226] but just as he himself wills and commands that he be worshiped.

221. The name Abdia recalls Petrus Alfonsi's claim that Abdias and Chabalahabar were two Jews "among the heretics of Arabia" that joined Mohammad and offered him instruction. See *Dialogue* 5, p. 152. Abdias and Chabalahabar appear to be corruptions of 'Abd Allāh b.Salām and Ka'b al-Aḥbar, two Jews mentioned in Ps.-al-Kindi's *Apology* as having influenced Mohammad. See the *Rescriptum Christiani* cap. 12, ln. 11, and cap 39, ln. 5, pp. 37, 67. Abdia Ibensalon is also one of the Jews appearing in *De doctrina Mahumet,* translated by Herman of Dalmatia, who comes to Mohammad to ask him 100 questions based on the Law of the Jews; ultimately, he converts to Islam. For an excerpt of this text, see *The Pseudo-Historical Image of the Prophet Mohammad,* 116–18. For other traditions regarding 'Abd Allāh b.Salām, see *s.v.* in the *Encyclopedia of Islam.* University of Tennessee at Chattanooga. 03 February 2015.

222. Absolute monotheism is a basic principle of Islam. See Qur'an 112.1.

223. In rabbinic tradition, both Michael and Seraphiel/Seraphael are rulers of the seraphim. See Rosemary Ellen Guiley, *The Encyclopedia of Angels,* 2d ed. (New York: Facts on File/Checkmark Books, 2004), 138–40; 243–45; 325–26. In Islamic angelology, Seraphiel was the Prophet's companion for three years (*s.v.* "Isrāfil," in the *Encyclopedia of Islam*); the angel Gabriel dictates the Qur'an to the prophet Mohammad. This latter claim was well known to Christian polemicists, who sought to undermine it: e.g., Hugh of Flavigny's *Chronicon* contends that Gabriel when he appeared to Mohammad was in reality the devil in disguise (PL 154: 101B).

224. Al-Furqān has many meanings, but is a synonym for the Qur'an. See R. Paret, "Furkān," in the *Encyclopedia of Islam.* University of Tennessee at Chattanooga. 03 February 2015.

225. For the progressive revelation of the Qur'an, see Qur'an 17.106.

226. William of St. Thierry (d. 1148), a Benedictine abbot who later entered a Cistercian foundation, equates the "phantasms of the heart" to idols. See

28. To these [things] you [say]: "Far be it for our understanding to perceive otherwise; far be it for our profession to express itself otherwise! We have not idly imagined anything about Him, we have certainly not fabricated anything. Not according to the phantasms of our heart do we think about Him, do we confess about Him, but according to what our Prophet, sent to us by Him, has handed down to us. Since he is last among the prophets in order and is just like 'the seal of all the prophets'[227] and is not the author but the bearer of the divine law, not God but a messenger, he received the content of the heavenly commandments—neither more nor less—sent to him by God through Gabriel, and he handed down those that were received to our fathers and to us to be safeguarded. These we serve, these we guard; we have dedicated our souls to them, we have dedicated our bodies to them, we have dedicated our life to them, and our death."

29. And, O men—men, I say, rational not only by nature but rational even by ingenuity and art[228]—would that you would of-

---

Meditationes deuotissimae (Meditatiuae orationes) 2.14, ed. P. Verdeyen, CC CM 89 (Turnhout: Brepols, 2005; CD ROM), 12.

227. Qur'an 33.40. In contrast, as Glei points out (p. 272, n. 268), in his polemic against Judaism Tertullian identifies Jesus as the "seal of the prophets" ("christus est signaculum omnium prophetarum"); see *Adversus Iudaeos* 8 and 11, ed. E. Kroymann, CC SL 2 (Turnhout: Brepols, 1954; CD ROM).

228. Peter alludes to the elevated reputation that Arabic science and philosophy enjoyed in the high Middle Ages. It was precisely this reputation that encouraged Latin translators in Spain to translate hundreds of Arabic texts—especially scientific and philosophical texts. Petrus Alfonsi thought of himself principally as a transmitter of Arabic science (especially astrology and astronomy), and it was this knowledge more than any other that enabled him to establish a place for himself in England. See Charles Burnett, *The Introduction of Arabic Learning into England,* The Panizzi Lectures, 1996 (London: The British Library, 1997), esp. 39–40. Robert of Ketton, as already indicated, noted that he had to put aside his customary study of (Arabic) astronomy and geometry in order to accept Peter the Venerable's commission to translate the Qur'an (see *supra,* n. 12, p. 30). Finally, it has been argued that Peter Abelard's "Philosopher," in his *Dialogue among a Philosopher, a Jew, and a Christian,* is modeled after the Andalusian Muslim philosopher Avempace (ibn Bâjja) and represents in general the tradition of Islamic philosophy. Indeed, the "Jew" acknowledges that the "Philosopher" has been circumcised, like the descendants of Ishmael. See Petrus Abaelardus, *Dialogus inter Philosophum, Iudaeum,*

fer me here the intellectual "ears" of your hearts; would that, having removed the stubbornness of superstition, you would listen to what I am preparing to introduce. I say "you would listen" because I have heard what is very surprising, if nonetheless it is true, that you do not want to hear anything contrary to the custom to which you are habituated, that you do not want to hear anyone intending to do anything contrary to your fathers' laws, that you do not want to hear anyone seeking to engage in debate over the rituals handed down to you by the one that, above, I called your prophet. And not only have I understood that you do not wish to hear this from any one, but also that, with a renown that has spread from your East to our West, he declares that you have been commanded by law to prevent the very beginnings of a discussion with stones or swords or some other kind of death.

30. Consider, therefore, you men who are skilled in terms of worldly science, consider, I say, and after having removed the barrier of a stubborn will, consider subtly whether the practice is plausible, whether it can be supported by any argument. For clearly no man who is rational, rational not only by nature but rational also from a vigorous mental acuity, wishes to be deceived in temporal things; he does not wish to accept as certain what is uncertain, or to accept as uncertain what is certain, so that, like one who is deluded by a cleverness of some kind or by negligence, he thinks that what is true is false, or reckons that what is false is true. He does not yield in this respect to any compulsion, nor on these matters should he acquiesce to one dearest to him, not to friends, not to those joined to him by affinity of blood, nor can he calmly allow himself to be deceived knowingly by spouses, those to whom he is joined by a stronger bond of love. And although very often a great many and even the greatest burdens of flesh or spirit are borne patiently by friends for the sake of friends, nonetheless nature endows a man with this—not to permit himself to be deceived in any way

---

et Christianum, ed. Rudolf Thomas (Stuttgart-Bad Cannstatt: Friedrich Frommann Verlag, 1970), 68, 731. For the identification with Avempace, see Jean Jolivet, "Abélard et le philosophe (occident et Islam au XIIe siècle)," *Revue de l'histoire des religions* 164 (1963): 181–89.

by anyone, no matter how closely related to him, or by a friend. Examine carefully all the functions of mortals and the liberal arts themselves, or even those that are called servile;[229] observe whether any of the studious lovers of worldly science wants to be deceived about such things or in such things, rather than accept their true and certain knowledge from instructors or from teachers.

31. This is shown especially by the pursuit of earthly wisdom itself. When those who are called "philosophers" in Greek and "lovers of wisdom" in Latin were seeking with the greatest effort to obtain this wisdom, and when various of them made various judgments about it according to the diversity of their intellects, they gave free rein to their discourses; and, bringing forward in proportion to their greater or lesser powers of reason, and with copious argumentation, the judgments which they had made, they labored to reach the truth about the matters at issue in the questions put forward. They did not shut the mouths of those whom they believed to be devoted to investigating the truth; rather more, by debating opposing hypotheses, they bestirred themselves and others to the praiseworthy study of every kind of assertion. This was always the practice proposed by wise men among the Greeks, among the Latins, among the Persians, among the Indians, and among other peoples, with the result that they always insist one has to investigate the truth of things, and they invigorated with frequent conversations those striving to inquire after, to examine, to define the same thing. Who may count their prodigious multitude, who may count those who were especially distinguished among the rest in investigating the truth of things? Renowned and well-established among us is the fame of those who handed down to the men of their own time as well as to posterity the truth and virtue of created things, not by being silent nor by shutting the mouths of men to silence them; instead, by discussion and de-

229. The seven liberal arts (grammar, rhetoric, dialectic, arithmetic, geometry, astronomy, and music) teach one how to live, and train the faculties in order to achieve human perfection and true freedom; the servile or utilitarian arts, on the other hand, enable one to be a servant—to another person, to the state, or to some other institution.

bate they unveiled the hidden things of nature and discovered those that are indubitably certain and true.

32. Since every rational mind, then, desires to know the truth of created things and wishes to turn to its advantage a knowledge of that truth, and it is unable to pursue that by remaining silent, it wants to pursue it by inquiry and debate; then should the true knowledge of *uncreated*[230] reality ever be neglected, and must it not be investigated, debated, and examined until the one who does not grasp it will understand? Should not the human mind be goaded with much sharper spurs in order to know the uncreated essence, than to investigate created nature? It seems that it gives more weight to the one of these two that may better serve human advantage. It seems to do so, I say, so that later the human mind will acknowledge which inquiry it ought to pursue more. Clearly, I want to know the power or virtue of visible things now, so that in some way they may support me while here in this mortal life, so that they may bring help or advantage in some way to my transitory sojourn. Why do I seek to know uncreated reality, however, and in addition to know the One who creates all things and rules all things that are created, unless so that he provide suitable supports for living this life in the present, and so as to assure a life blessed and eternal after this death? What is this nature, actually, what is this substance or essence? Is it not that which by the common usage of all races, according to the proper term in each language, is believed to be God, is called God? That nature, therefore, is the God who alone is uncreated, who alone is the Creator, who alone is the master of all things, who alone is the author and dispenser of goods present and eternal.

33. Consider then, you, consider then, I say, you to whom I write, and, according to the Psalm of David (which I believe you do not discredit), "Judge justly, sons of men,"[231] consider whether one should enter a debate over creation and remain silent concerning the Creator, whether the faculty of free speech should be accorded to one seeking base and fleeting goods, and whether the mouth of one seeking after and pursu-

230. Italics are mine.
231. Ps 57 (58).2.

ing the highest and eternal good should be stopped up. Will I be able to have a free discussion about everything when I want to speak of all things created, and as soon as I want to treat their Creator, will the Mohammedan law shut my mouth, or, if perhaps I should say something opposed to it, hardly after the first words have escaped, will it cut off [my] head? Does this pertain to any law other than yours? Does this pertain to any race other than yours? Does this pertain to any doctrine other than yours? Truly it pertains to no other, it clearly pertains to no other. Direct your eyes hither and thither, and scrutinize the laws, rites, and customs of all races from the rising of the sun to its setting, from the South so far as the North, and if you can find anywhere the like of what you stipulate or hand down, bring it forward. The Christian Law is not like this (I will be silent for the time being concerning the others); the Christian Law is not like this, and this is not what it commands the great apostles of Christ: "Be ready," it says, "to make your defense to anyone who demands from you an accounting for the faith and hope that are in you."[232] Surely what, what does a practice like yours indicate, what does a law such as this want for itself, such a law, I say, which prohibits listening to one who engages in debate with you, which cannot allow for reason to lead the way against the errors, as one believes them to be, that you commit? Does this not appear to you to be completely shameful, do you not perceive this to be crammed with every kind of dishonor? Truth always has a free appearance; it does not seek corners, it disdains concealment, it flees darkness, and it seeks a clear openness for everything. Only falsehood fears to be known, is afraid of being discussed, rejoices in hiding places, trembles like death to be disclosed in public.

34. Why is this? Why do I say that truth longs for the light, while falsehood longs for darkness? Clearly this is the cause; it is this, and there is no other cause except the one that our Christ revealed in his Gospel (which your Mohammad said and wrote was given to him), for those acting properly and for those doing evil: "For all," he said, "who do evil hate the light and do

232. 1 Pt 3.15.

not come to the light, so that their deeds may not be exposed. But those who do what is true come to the light, so that it may be clearly seen that their deeds have been done in God."[233] Surely these words are words of the Truth. Clearly these are the words of one that your Mohammad (about whom I wrote a little earlier) exalts with boundless praise, whom, in various places in his Qur'an, he confesses to be a messenger of God, the word of God, the spirit of God, who, he does not deny, lived without sin, is greater than every man, even greater than he. Who, if he lived on earth without sin—according to him—then he is certainly not a liar. For if he had not avoided the mark of a liar, certainly he would not have been a small sinner but a great one. His are the words I set down before: "For all who do evil hate the light, and those who do what is true come to the light." Why is that? [Evil] shuts off access and a hearing to those who, according to reason, want to debate with it, with a spurious practice, with an unheard-of law, which does not want to permit what is permitted to all. If that practice, if that law belongs to truth, why does it fear to come to the light in order to make plain that its deeds are in God or of God? But why should I take the long way round, in vain, concerning a matter that is known to all? Therefore plainly, indubitably, that practice, that oft-named law hates the light, loves the darkness, does not put up with one who unveils it, does not allow one to contradict it, lest its falseness be made known, lest its wickedness, cloaked by a deceitful silence, become known throughout the entire world.

35. Pay attention to the things above, and consider again the words of the one that you regard as your prophet; consider how frivolous they are, how weak, how much they lack all the strength of truth and reason. While presenting God as the one speaking to him, he says: "'So if anyone wants to dispute with you, say that you and those that follow him have surrendered[234] to God,'[235] by doing which both those knowledgeable in the law and those who are unschooled in the law will follow a good law.[236] If not, howev-

---

233. 1 Jn 3.21.
234. Lit., "turned the face toward ..."
235. Qur'an 3.18–19.
236. As Glei points out (p. 79), "those knowledgeable in the law" and "those

er, you are only responsible for revealing my precepts to the people." And again, "If anyone has wanted to engage you in debate concerning the law, say to him anathema, and tell him that only God's wrath threatens such as these."[237] And again: "Do not dispute with those that have the law."[238] "It is better for you to kill, than to argue."[239]

36. I ask you, what kind of words are these? What kind of commandments are these? Should the rational soul be buried, then, beneath so much asinine stupidity, to bear patiently any burdens imposed upon it, no matter how great, in the manner of that brute animal, and not dare to make a judgment concerning them, nor presume to inquire whether they are good or evil, whether they are useful or harmful? If I concede this, then necessarily I will be carried off by every wind of doctrine and, like a reed, disturbed by every breeze, bent in one direction and another, to submit to every error, to acquiesce to every kind of falsehood, to hold nothing as certain, to confuse as indistinguishable goods and evils, truths and falsehoods. If I concede this, what will separate man from beast? What difference will exist between the human soul and a brutish spirit? Clearly none so far as concerns stupid obedience, but then again a great deal so far as concerns a different nature. Indeed, then man will not be comparable to draught animals, but rightly will

who are unschooled in the law" correspond to "those to whom the Book has been revealed" and "those without a Book" in Qur'an 3.19. These two expressions indicate generally the Peoples of the Book (e.g., Jews and Christians), on the one hand, and heathens on the other (Glei, pp. 272–73, n. 276). Peter's source—Robert of Ketton's Latin translation of the Qur'an—confuses the sense of the passage; Peter cites this passage, moreover, in his *Against the Inveterate Obduracy of the Jews* (4, p. 193), in order to demonstrate that Islam took hold among the Saracens without the support of reason. Later in this text he acknowledges that "those that have the law" refers to Jews and Christians. See *infra,* section 40, p. 88.

237. Qur'an 3.61.
238. Qur'an 29.45.
239. Qur'an 2.187, 214. Peter cites all of these passages in his *Against the Inveterate Obduracy of the Jews* (4, p. 193), with one significant change; in that text, this passage reads: "It is better for you to yield (*cedes*), than to argue," whereas in this text it reads *caedes*—to kill or cut down. Either the vowel disappeared in the manuscript tradition of *Against the Inveterate Obduracy of the Jews,* or it has intruded here.

be judged as even more obtuse than a beast. For a beast, because it lacks a rational soul, does not contradict any command
whatsoever, while the rational soul acquiesces even when the
judgment of reason contradicts. Because judgment is not given
to the beast, it yields to all commands indiscriminately. One for
whom it is natural to discern the difference between good and
evil, between true and false, who obeys even those commands
that he judges ought to be condemned, has become worth less
than a beast.[240] I am amazed, nor do I cease to be amazed, at
how this could have been wrested away by any sort of cleverness
from skilled and learned men so that they would believe that
the words that I presented above were produced by God, when
either a careless or a studious reader would find in them nothing that is not stupid, cruel, or absurd.

37. For why is this so: "If anyone wants to dispute with you,
say that you and those that follow him have surrendered to
God"?[241] So if—and I would address you yourself, O Mohammad—if surely you would have no answer for me (as one that
wishes to debate with you whether your law is just or unjust)
other than "you and those that follow him have surrendered
to God," should I believe that you have spoken the truth? Shall
I believe that you were a true prophet of God? Shall I believe

240. Peter introduced a similar discussion in his *Against the Inveterate Obduracy of the Jews* (5, p. 211), where he concluded that, having introduced rational arguments in defense of Christianity, the Jew who rejects those arguments
must be deficient in reason and, consequently, something less than human.
He declared there: "if I have satisfied every human being, then I have satisfied
you too, if, nonetheless, you are human. In fact, I do not dare avow that you
are human, lest perhaps I lie, because I recognize that that rational faculty
that separates a human from the other animals or wild beasts and gives pre-
cedence over them is extinct or, rather, buried in you." In his polemic against
the Saracens, he again argues that they seem to have lost their reason completely, becoming more like beasts.

241. Qur'an 3.18–19. Lit., "say that you have turned your face and the followers of his face to God." In Peter's *Against the Inveterate Obduracy of the Jews,*
written about a decade before *Against the Sect of the Saracens,* Peter cites these
passages in order to show that it was not reasoned debate that persuaded Mohammad's followers of the truth of Islam; rather, Mohammad's deceitful authority, and the power and worldly pleasures he promised, seduced them. See
Against the Inveterate Obduracy of the Jews 4, pp. 193–94.

that the law that you delivered to your race was delivered to you by God? If I assent, then in reality I am worse than an ass; if I agree, then truly I am worse than a brute beast. If you claim that you have surrendered yourself to God, or have turned away from God, how do you make me believe in the slightest way that you have spoken anything truthfully? But that is monstrous which you add that God said to you, I maintain: "that by doing so, both those knowledgeable in the law and those who are unschooled in the law will follow a good law." By doing what? If you say that you have surrendered yourself to God, is it the case on account of this, then, that both those who are knowledgeable in the law and those who are uneducated will follow your law, which you call good? But why should I follow something so clearly ridiculous?

38. And another verse follows the one cited above. Indeed, you write that God added: "If not, however, you are only responsible for revealing my precepts to the nations." What does this mean? You had said that God said that if you speak those words which were just set forth, "both those knowledgeable in the law and those who are unschooled in the law will follow a good law." Then why did you add: "But if not, however, you are only responsible for revealing my precepts to the nations"? First you make God speak in a declarative way, and now you introduce words of doubt? He spoke in a declarative way when he said that those who are knowledgeable in the law and even those who are uneducated will follow a good law; but he introduced some doubt when he said: "If not." But if he said that in a declarative way, why is it that not all, both of those who are knowledgeable and of those who are unschooled, follow your law? If he doubted that they would believe you, why did he say that everyone would follow your law?

39. But another chapter follows that I have already introduced: "If anyone has wanted to engage you in debate concerning the law, say to him anathema, and tell him that only God's wrath threatens such as these." And for whom should this not be allowed? Clearly, for whom among men would this not be very easy? I am not prevented from saying to you the very same thing that you commanded them to say to me: just as it is easy for

you to pronounce anathema upon me for wishing to engage in a debate concerning your law, so too it is perfectly easy for me to pronounce anathema upon you, if you are unwilling to agree to discuss my law with me. If it is easy for you to threaten me with God's wrath unless I believe you, so too it is easy for me or for anyone at all to threaten you in the same way and to call down upon you God's wrath unless you agree with me. Is it just, then, is it reasonable, when I am not presented with any authority or with a rational argument already set forth, that I should believe you, that I should give assent to your law, if you have said nothing to me more than anathema, if you have done nothing but threaten me with God's wrath? But because it is clear even to brute beasts that your words have this sort of consequence, I proceed.

40. "Do not," he says, "dispute with those that have the law. It is better for you to kill, than to argue." And who does not see that this is infernal advice? "Do not," he says, "dispute with those that have the law." Who are those that have the law? So far as we can understand that man's obscurities, the ones that have the law are none other than Jews or Christians. For having turned the sharp gaze of my eyes hither and thither, I see that no others existed in the world who possessed the law when he said these words, or exist even now, except those I have already mentioned: namely, Jews or Christians. Clearly they and no others had accepted the law previously, and once having accepted it they bound themselves to it according to their own free will or understanding: the Jews, who were given the Law by Moses, and the Christians, who were given the Law by Christ. For neither the pagans nor the Saracens of your race who came before your Mohammad could be said to have accepted the law earlier. For no one had given any law to the pagans, whom error alone poisoned with the false opinions of men that should not even be mentioned, nor to the Saracens, because the already-mentioned bearer (let me not say "author") of your law had not yet come.

41. If anyone perhaps has objected that some legal statutes were delivered to the Greeks, or to the Latins, or to any other races, such as the laws of Solon[242] were to the Greeks at one time,

242. Solon (d. ca. 558 BCE) was an Athenian lawmaker, sometimes credited with having introduced democratic reforms to Athens. The laws "of certain

or those of certain wise Latins were to the Romans, I reply that it was not stipulated or handed down among these laws what they should believe about God, or with what ritual or in what manner they should worship him, but it was only provided—not by divine command but according to human counsel—how each and every nation should rule its own state, and according to what order it should carry on its life during time of peace or war, so that they would not venture to live in a bestial manner were they without the boundary of any fixed law whatsoever, nor confuse evil with good by commingling just with unjust indiscriminately, and neither they nor their state could endure very long in such greatly disturbed conditions.

42. But in fact there is no discussion among them of things divine, except one that is devoid of any authority and reason, or one that draws its origin from ridiculous myths or from foolish human imaginings or from fraudulent demonic oracular sayings, which does not lead people to true knowledge or to worship of the Godhead, but turns them aside from it entirely and altogether most wretchedly in order to worship idols or whatever created things have been set in place of the Creator. For this reason, one should not say that people of this sort have a law, for they have not received a law from God, but instead that they fashioned for themselves ceremonies for living or for worshiping God, just as they pleased. Therefore, only the Jews or Christians before Mohammad or his age should be said to have a Law that was not invented by them but which they received as handed down from God. It seems to me, then, that his statement refers to them: "Do not dispute with those that have the law."

43. Why did he make this statement, why did he command

---

wise Latins … to the Romans" likely refers to the Twelve Tables (ca. 450 BCE), the earliest effort to produce a Roman law code. Peter distinguishes these laws produced by human legislators from those that have a divine origin. Augustine claimed that the Romans borrowed from the Athenians Solon's laws, but amended them, and therefore their laws too were without divine origin. See *De civ. Dei* 2.16, ed. Bernard Dombart and Alfons Kalb, CC SL 47 (Turnhout: Brepols, 1955; CD ROM). The Carolingian Freculphus of Lisieux (d. 851/52) adds that it was the laws that the Romans took from Solon that were written down in the Twelve Tables. *Historiarum libri XII* 1.4.10, ed. Michael I. Allen, CC CM 169A (Turnhout: Brepols, 2002; CD ROM), 224.

them not to enter into debate with those that have the law? If
he was confident in the truth of his law, why did he prohibit
his followers from entering into debate? If he was lacking confidence, why did he write down things that his followers could
not defend? But either he knew, or (with all due respect) the
one who spoke through him, Satan,[243] knew, that the firmness
of the Jewish or Christian Law is so great, its foundation so
stable, that I would say that it cannot be overcome by human
words or arguments, and neither can it be shaken even a little by warlike force, nor by clamor of arms, nor by the most
dire torments, even if struck by every kind of death. From the
constancy of that first Law during the time of the Jews under
the Maccabees,[244] from the endurance of the martyrs during
the days of evangelical grace, he had learned that human arguments could not prevail over eternal wisdom, that the weak
and feeble attempts of mortals could not resist the power that
cannot be conquered. For this reason, how could he who per-

---

243. The assertion that it is not God but Satan that is the source for the
Qur'an parallels Peter's contention in *Against the Inveterate Obduracy of the Jews*
that Satan is the one who whispered false teachings to the Jews—the "syna-
gogue of Satan" (3, p.121)—and that the Jews have been deluded by "phantasms of Satan" (4, p. 141; 201). This Satanic influence does not undermine the
truth of the Old Testament for Peter, but rather it enables him to dismiss Jewish
biblical exegesis and to contend that Satan, the "father of lies" (3, p. 122), is
the source for the post-biblical, rabbinic myths or fables that are recorded in
the Jews' Talmud (5, p. 229). Above, in his *Summary of the Entire Heresy of the
Saracens,* he traced the origin of Mohammad's doctrine, in part, to the Jews'
rabbinic traditions, insisting that "the Jews whispered to Mohammad, shrewdly
providing to the man who was eager for novelties not the truth of the Scriptures but their fables, which still today they have in abundance"; *Summary* 7,
pp. 40–41. In this way he creates a chain of transmission: Satan whispered his
lies to the Jews, and the Jews whispered them to Mohammad. Kritzeck's claim
(*Peter the Venerable and Islam,* 170) that by "placing the blame upon Satan" Peter
"partially exonerates Mohammad" seems to ignore the fact that above he refers
to Mohammad as "that Satan" (*Summary* 13, p. 46); moreover, it neglects the
"chain of transmission" mentioned above. The link to Satan becomes a staple
of the polemic against Islam and Mohammad. Robert of Ketton's *Mistake-Laden
and Ridiculous Chronicle of the Saracens* (*Chronica mendosa et ridicula Sarracenorum*)
identifies Mohammad as "the son of the devil, and the firstborn of Satan" ("filii
diaboli et primogeniti Sathane"; *The Pseudo-Historical Image of the Prophet Mohammad,* 93).

244. Cf. 2 Mc 7.1–42.

ceived that worldly wisdom, that human power had already surrendered to divine laws, flatter himself concerning a promised
victory for his side in a debate, or even endure the first blows of
disputation? Devoid of all support for resistance, therefore, he
took refuge in flight, and the one who could neither propose
nor object anything in a reasonable fashion, chose silence.

44. But in order not to appear to yield entirely to the opposing
faction, he took up arms instead of reason, and after the fashion
of those who are given to madness, he turned to rocks, clubs,
or swords, giving no response to one asking questions. Armed
in this way, he attacks any one that acts against him; or rather,
almost before he begins to act, rushing upon him suddenly just
like a cruel, wild animal, he kills him. Your prophet Mohammad
puts just such an end—so just and so rational!—to disputations,
O Hagarenes;[245] he distinguishes between factions that oppose
him with precisely that impartial judgment; the praiseworthy ar-
biter offers such a judgment, never heard before, to his own century, or to yours. But, as I mentioned, these are his words.

45. In fact, after he said, "Do not dispute with those that have
the law," he added: "It is better for you to kill, than to argue."
And what shall I say? Words fail for refuting such absurdity, such
bestial cruelty, such detestable wickedness. In reality it was Satan, a beast greedy for human blood, who invented this; he ex-
haled it through him [Mohammad] just as if through an instrument well suited to him; having employed his tongue just like a
quill or reed pen, he spoke and wrote down such an inhuman
and monstrous outrage. He knew that a teaching so incredible
and so foolish (as will be demonstrated later in its proper place)
otherwise could not last very long; he was not ignorant of the
fact that such an error-filled dogma could be torn apart with little difficulty, just like a spider's web, if free access were granted
to those who want to oppose it, if it were permitted to preachers
of the divine Word to debate it in time-honored fashion.

46. Nor was he unmindful of the fact that in the past "their
sound went out to all the earth, and their words went forth to
the ends of the world";[246] those sent by Christ spread the word

---

245. For the term Hagarenes, see *supra,* n. 24, p. 34.
246. Ps 18 (19).5; Rom 10.18.

of eternal life everywhere, and conducted almost the entire
world to a knowledge of Truth. He knew that not one of those
that believed through them could have believed if first he did
not hear what he should believe, and he could not hear that
if there were no preacher. For just as a certain individual, our
great Apostle, said: "Faith comes from hearing; and hearing by
the word of Christ";[247] but Christian faith could not have arisen
in the minds of men if it were not heard preached, nor could
preaching be heard apart from a preacher. And because the
subtle fallen angel knew that he would be defrauded of his
greatest profit to deceive and destroy—just as it pained him
that he had been defrauded in the past—if one were given access to hear the word of God, and he did not doubt that he
would be expelled from the hearts of those who were deceived
if that [word] were allowed to enter, he established then an
iron barrier which he drew up from the depths of his wicked
counsel, which no one could pass through. He did this in order
to hold his entry hall (which is already very large—O sorrow,
alas!) even more secure, safeguarding its tranquility, so that
one who could have been saved by hearing the word of salvation would perish there for eternity once that hearing was removed by such a stratagem.

47. On account of all these things, your [Mohammad], so
oft-named already, proclaimed that statement that is so solemn-
ly worthy of condemnation: "It is better for you to kill, than to
argue." Indeed, the Christian law also condemns quarrelsome
debate, such that our aforementioned Apostle teaches: "A servant of God," he said, "must not enter into dispute."[248] In fact,
he condemns the spirited quarrels of debates such as those
which do not arise for the sake of finding the truth, but for
the sake of defending one's own opinion in an insolent pursuit. Clearly Christian moderation, as I said, condemns proud
and fierce debates, and teaches the disciple wisely and modest-
ly either to declare what ought to be declared or to contradict
what ought to be contradicted. It does not recommend, nonetheless, as your prophet does, that you kill, nor does it say, "It

247. Rom 10.17.
248. 2 Tm 2.24.

is better for you to kill, than to argue." It teaches that both of these are evil, and it does not remain silent concerning the fact that both are worthy of condemnation. But although each of these is rejected by its judgment, nevertheless it condemns one of these more. It does not say either that "it is better for you to kill, than to argue," or that "it is better for you to argue, than to kill," because it admits no comparison between something that is altogether evil added to something that is altogether good, or conversely. In fact, a comparison can be made between two that are good or two that are evil, but not when one is good and the other an evil, or when one is evil and the other a good. Therefore, as was already mentioned, our Apostle did not say what your Mohammad claimed, namely that killing is better than debate or debate better than killing, but rather that killing is far worse than debate.

48. And what sort of mind that is even a little (I will not say very) rational will not see that this is true? Investigate the judgments of all peoples, and wherever the sun shines upon the earth determine whether human laws, which differ in many other respects, do not agree in this one, that the crime of unjust murder receives a far greater punishment than the transgression of a harmful argument. It is surprising if even your laws, which we know are discerning according to the flesh, do not agree on this cause that is so very just, such that nature herself also preaches with silent words that the greater injury ought to receive the greater punishment, and the greater damage ought to be sentenced to pay a greater retribution. If this is the case, then it is false that it is better to kill than to argue. While it is true that quarrelsome argument is evil, killing is much worse than an argument. If perhaps his understanding of what he said—"do not dispute with those that have the law"—does not exclude the ancient pagan founders of whatever laws, yet what he wrote is more monstrous and untrustworthy when he has not dared even to debate with those whose laws had emerged unsupported by divine authority, unsupported by the power of truth. What then remains? Put aside such infamy, and do not allow yourselves to be branded with such a foul mark thereafter, since one imagines that you so distrust your own doctrine,

which is so devoid of the strength of every argument, that you do not dare (I do not say willingly) to appear even when challenged publicly, or to join hands in debate with any or even the slightest opponent.

49. And how will it become known to us or to the world whether there can be any truth or justice on your side? How will the light of Christian faith illuminate you and yours if you do not set forth your teachings, of whatever sort they may be, and do not hear our teachings from us? And although we are not ignorant of the fact that yours seem to suffice for you, that you believe that you have complete knowledge of the Godhead, that you consider that both we and everyone else who follow religions (*leges*) that are different or strange err, except for you, nevertheless listen respectfully to what should be set forth, and do not be the only ones to depart in this respect from the custom of all peoples or religions (*leges*), especially since you are entirely free, once all the arguments and allegations have come to an end, either to approve or condemn or accept or reject anything that was said. And it is not because you were so far distant and so unknown to us that I was compelled to write these things, but instead the cause of your salvation and the love that I have toward you—not as toward Christians but as toward heathens—have not allowed me to remain silent; you should, then, at least repay me for my own love such that, even if you do not want to agree to the things that must be said, at least you will not refuse to listen. Nor was there absent that persistent memory of those who hear or read your [laws], so that, because, in matters subject to doubt, what is true cannot be known unless what is false is first destroyed, I will be obliged to speak out against your legislator and against his legislation with words that are suited to the matter, because no small injury will be done to truth if the proponent should spare falsehood either in his judgments or in his statements, contrary to justice.

50. Do not be immediately disturbed, therefore; do not immediately succumb to rage, so to speak, and run to take up stones or swords, as I mentioned above. Imitate us, at least in this respect, those of us who, since they often engage with the Jews in conversation, of whom the greater number among them lives

subject [to Christians], hear from them many things, almost all
of them contrary to Christian faith, who are not roused to fury
as if against blasphemers nor incited to slaughter them, but listen to them patiently, [and] reply wisely; neither do they destroy
them immediately as enemies of their own salvation but instead
wait calmly should they at some time, perhaps, be converted.[249]
They retain this same attitude even toward the countless captives
of your race and of your law whom they were often accustomed
to take in battle, and although the ability to return to their own
land has been taken away, they do not take freedom of speech
away from them.[250] And, just as if taking your side, we will raise
an objection for us which, because perhaps you are not aware of
it, you could not raise against us yourselves: one reads in the Law
of the Jews—which is also the Law of the Christians, although
we have understood it as it ought to be understood—that God
commanded that blasphemers be killed who dare to cast dishon-
or, either with words or impious deeds, upon whatever pertains

249. Peter's defense here is disingenuous, to say the least, and stands in
contrast to the harshness he expresses in *Against the Inveterate Obduracy of the
Jews,* and elsewhere.

250. Peter's claim that Christians treated Muslim captives in a humane fashion seems, once more, disingenuous. Certainly he would have been aware that,
both before and after his sojourn in Spain in 1142–1143, Christian efforts to
conquer Muslim regions in Spain had resulted in the utter destruction of some
Muslim towns. According to the *Chronica Adefonsi Imperatoris,* Alfonso VII's army
set fire to the land around Seville, destroyed mosques, put Muslim teachers to
the sword, and burned their sacred books. Cf. *Chronica Adefonsi Imperatoris* 35–
36, ed. Emma Falque, Juan Gil, Antonio Maya, CC CM 71 (Turnhout: Brepols,
1990; CD ROM). Muslim treatment of Christian captives was not necessarily
any better; *Chronica* 59 reports that the Bishop of Lescar was taken captive and
Muslims tortured him, circumcised him, and forced him to abjure his religion.
Cf. Ludwig Vones, "Zwischen Kulturaustausch und religiöser Polemik. Von den
Möglichkeiten und Grenzen christlich-muslimischer Verständigung zur Zeit
des Petrus Venerabilis," in *Wissen über Grenzen. Arabisches Wissen und lateinisches
Mittelalter,* ed. Andreas Speer and Lydia Wegener, Miscellanea Mediaevalia 33
(Berlin: Walter de Gruyter, 2006), 217–37, esp. 217–20. It has been argued,
moreover, that Peter of Poitiers was in fact the author of the *Chronica Adefonsi
Imperatoris,* although authorship remains controversial; see Angel Ferrari, "El
cluniacense Pedro de Poitiers y la 'Chronica Adefonsi Imperatoris' y Poema de
Almeria," *Boletin de la real Academia de la Historia* 158 (1963): 153–204. Certainly,
if Peter of Poitiers composed these two works, then we have all the more reason
to suppose that Peter the Venerable was acquainted with them.

to God.[251] But this does not help your side even in the slightest, because no one now living in the world—except for a few pagans[252]—doubts that the author of this Law is the true God, whereas except for you the race of all peoples under heaven affirms that your teaching does not come from God. Therefore, it is just that you put off killing, meanwhile, those you believe to be blasphemers, until one should know by the indubitable test of truth that your prophet was sent by God, that your law was given by God, in the same way that the true God, who commanded that blasphemers be slain, is proved to exist.

51. In just this fashion, with just such consideration—not roused to rage but solicitous, not headstrong but modest—all the peoples of the whole earth, kings and princes, have received the messengers of Christ, have listened to those they received, and, although they struggled to resist a great deal and for a long time, finally they ceased to resist reason, clear truth, and even the light-giving Spirit of God. I want to offer you as an example from among them (putting aside those beyond number, lest I go too far) a certain kingdom in the most distant part of the West, situated almost beyond the world, and a king by the name of Ethelbert,[253] who lived almost at the same time as your Mohammad.

52. That kingdom was first called Britain by the ancient Britons, but now it is called England (*Anglia*), which name is derived from the race of the Angles. That race migrated almost five hundred years ago from the region of the Saxons and by

251. Lv 24.16.

252. In his *Against the Petrobrusians* Peter alleges that few pagans remain in the world, and those that still live are found only in the extreme northern regions, near the marshes of Meotidis, i.e., near the North Sea. See *Contra Petrobrusianos haereticos* 161, p. 95.

253. Ethelbert of Kent (d. 616 CE), who received Augustine of Canterbury (sent to evangelize Britain by Pope Gregory I), would become the first Christian king in Britain. For Peter's discussion of Ethelbert, drawn from Bede's *Ecclesiastical History of the English People,* and its function within this polemic, see Max Lejbowicz, "Développement autochtone assumé et acculturation dissimulée," in *Les relations culturelles entre chrétiens et musulmans au moyen âge: Quelles leçons en tirer de nos jours?* Colloque organisé à la Fondation Singer-Polignac le mercredi 20 octobre 2004 par Rencontres médiévales européennes, ed. Max Lejbowicz (Turnhout: Brepols, 2005): 57–81, esp. 57–70.

military force acquired large parts of that island (for it is an
island surrounded by a great sea, the Ocean), and on it established a kingdom for themselves. This race was still ensnared in
the ancient errors of idolatry and, bestowing the worship of the
Creator upon something created, was far removed from him.
At length, the benevolent Creator had compassion for the race
given to error, and thanks to the supreme teacher of the Christians—I mean the Roman pontiff—who was called Gregory,[254]
he snatched them away from death and brought them to eternal life. Actually, inspired by the divine spirit, he dispatched
chosen disciples to proclaim the Gospel of Christ to that race.
The leader among them was a certain holy man by the name
of Augustine.[255] By their words and remarkable acts the king
was converted with his entire people to the faith of Christ and
surely was added to the number of Christians. But listen now to
the manner in which he received the messengers sent to him,
and how he replied to them after the purpose for their visit was
disclosed, what he did, how he was disposed to them, because
it pertains to the purpose for which much—or rather everything—is done. In fact, these very passages have been excerpted from an ancient history of the Angles:[256]

53. At that time, Ethelbert was the very powerful king in Kent, who
had extended his dominion as far as the boundary formed by the river Humber, at which the southern English people divide their borders from the northerners. On the eastern shore of Kent is the not
very small island of Thanet,[257] of a size, according to the English way

254. For Pope Gregory the Great, or Gregory I, see *Summary* 4, and n. 37,
p. 37.

255. St. Augustine of Canterbury (d. ca. 604) was a Benedictine monk
sent, with approximately 40 monks, to evangelize the peoples of Britain. He
established both the monastic foundation of Saints Peter and Paul and the
cathedral of Christ Church at Canterbury; after having received the episcopal
pallium from Rome in 601, he consecrated 12 bishops for England.

256. I.e., the history of the Venerable Bede (d. 735), an English monk in Jar-
row. His *Historia ecclesiastica gentis Anglorum,* dedicated to King Ceolwulf of Nor-
thumbria, was completed in 731. For the complete text, see the Latin-French
Histoire ecclésiastique du peuple anglais, ed. André Crépin, Michel Lapidge, Pierre
Monat, and Phillipe Robin, SC 489–491 (Paris: Éditions du Cerf, 2005).

257. Although in the past this area was separated from the mainland by
the river Wantsum (or the Wantsum Channel), today it is no longer an island
but has been rejoined to the mainland as rather flat marshland.

of reckoning, for six hundred families. The river Wantsum divides it from the mainland; the river is about three furlongs (*stadia*) wide, and can be crossed only in two places. At each end it extends to the sea. The servant of the Lord, Augustine, arrived on this island, then, along with his companions, almost forty men in number, as they report. By order of the blessed Pope Gregory, they obtained <one hundred> interpreters from the race of the Franks, and they confided to the king that they had come from Rome and carried a very important message, which without any doubt promised to those who were obedient to it eternal joy in heaven and a kingdom without end with the living and true God. When he [Ethelbert] heard this, he commanded them to remain on that island where they had landed, and that they be provided with the necessities, until he should see what to do with them. <...>[258] Days later the king came to the island, therefore, and, sitting in the open air, he ordered Augustine to come there with his companions for a discussion with him. In fact, he had taken the precaution that they not enter into any dwelling to approach him lest, at their coming, if they practiced anything of the art of sorcery, they would overcome him by a deception, according to an ancient prediction of the discipline. But they came to him endowed not with a demonic power but with divine power, carrying a silver cross as a banner and with an image of the Lord Savior painted on a board and,[259] chanting litanies, they offered up prayers to the eternal Lord for salvation for themselves and, at the same time, for those for whose sake they had come.

54. When they sat down in accord with the king's command, they preached to him and to all of his attendants who were present there the Word of life; he replied, saying: "Your statements and the promises that you bear are indeed excellent, but because they are novel and uncertain, I cannot offer assent to them, to abandon those that I have safeguarded for so long with the whole of the English people. But in truth because you have come here as strangers from far away and, as I seem to have discerned for myself, you also desire to share with us those things that you believed to be true and important, we do not want you to be troubled, but rather we want you to receive hospitality courteously, and we will take care to supply you with the provisions necessary for you. Nor do we prohibit you from preaching in order to gain as many as you can to the faith of your religion." He gave them, therefore, a dwelling in the city of Canterbury,[260] which was the me-

258. Peter omits the next passage in Bede's account, which describes Ethelbert's Christian wife, Bertha, and her chaplain Liudhard.

259. On the panel paintings that Augustine and his companions brought from Rome, see esp. Paul Meyvaert, "Bede and the Church Paintings at Wearmouth-Jarrow," *Anglo-Saxon England* 8 (1979): 63–77.

260. Bede (and Peter) uses the Roman name for the town, *Dorubernis*.

tropolis of his entire kingdom, and, as he had promised, along with
supplying worldly provisions, he did not take away from them the li-
cense to preach.[261]

In this way this king, in this way other kings of other nations
beyond number, received the messengers of Christ, and once
they received them they treated them with all humanity and
with honor. It is fitting for you to do the same thing or, if you
are not inclined to imitate them fully, at least it is fitting to hear
and to consider whether what they bring is something for your
advantage or salvation.

55. Now let the discourse move quickly toward the main point,
and, assisted first and foremost by the Spirit of God, let it be
girded for battle against the worst enemy of God. But before an
argument that is accustomed to doing battle urges close combat hand-to-hand, I pass over what should be passed over, and
inquire into what should be inquired into. Since several years
ago the Mohammedan law was translated by my effort from the
Arabic language into [my] native one, that is, Latin,[262] I do not
cease to be amazed, nor can I be amazed enough at the reason why that prophet of yours mixed together in his Qur'an
some things selected from the Jewish religion[263] and some from
the Christian religion and, since he showed himself with all his
might to be a great enemy to both peoples, why he confirms, as
though he were a Jew or a Christian, many things that he writes
based on the authority of their Law. Now if he believes in those
things that are ours, certainly insofar as he believes, he agrees
with us rationally, with no resistance. If he agrees with us in
part, why does he not give assent to everything that we believe?
If he is content with the Jewish or Christian writings in part, why
is he not content with the whole? Why does he reveal himself as
monstrous by taking from our writings what he wants, and by
rejecting what he does not want? Now, I read that he introduces

261. Peter's long citation is drawn from Bede's *Histoire ecclésiastique du peuple anglais/ Historia ecclesiastica gentis Anglorum* 1.25.1–2, SC 489:198–200.

262. Peter refers to the translation of the Qur'an that he commissioned
Robert of Ketton to prepare. See *supra,* n. 8, pp. 29–30.

263. "from the Jewish religion": *de Hebraica ... lege.* The Lat. *lex* can be
translated as either "law" or "religion," depending on the context.

to that book of his the names or deeds of individuals whom the Hebrew texts celebrate; I understand that he names those that the Christian scriptures mention. I see that these were selected, as it were, from among the former: Noah,[264] Abraham,[265] Lot,[266] Jacob,[267] Joseph,[268] Moses,[269] Pharaoh,[270] David,[271] and certain others. Among the latter: Zachariah,[272] Elizabeth,[273] John the son of Zachariah,[274] Mary,[275] Jesus or Christ the son of Mary,[276]

264. See Qur'an 71 (*Noah*); Qur'an 11.26–48; 37.75–81; and 54.9–17.

265. Qur'an 51.24–37; 37.83–114; 26.69–87 and 88–104; 15.51–77; 19.41–50; 21.51–73; 11.69–76; 29.16–27 and 31–32; 6.74–86; 2.124–34. Cf. R. Paret, "Ibrāhīm," *Encyclopedia of Islam*, 11 February 2015. http://referenceworks.brillon line.com/entries/encyclopaedia-of-islam-2/ibra-hi-m-SIM_3430.

266. Qur'an 11.77–83; 15.51–77; 26.160–75.

267. Qur'an 2.132–40; 3.84; 11.71; 19.49; 21.72; 29.27; 38.45. Cf. R. Firestone, "Ya'ḳūb," *Encyclopedia of Islam*, 11 February 2015. http://referenceworks .brillonline.com/entries/encyclopaedia-of-islam-2/ya-k-u-b-SIM_7965.

268. Qur'an 12 (*Yūsuf*). Cf. "Yūsuf," *Encyclopedia of Islam*, 11 February 2015. http://referenceworks.brillonline.com/entries/encyclopaedia-of-islam-2/yu -suf-COM_1369.

269. Qur'an 7.103–62; 20.9–98; 28.7–51; 40.23–37. Cf. "Mūsā," *Encyclopedia of Islam*, 11 February 2015. http://referenceworks.brillonline.com/entries/ encyclopaedia-of-islam-2/mu-sa-COM_0803.

270. See the passages related to Moses, in the note above. Also see Cyril Glassé, *The Concise Encyclopedia of Islam* (New York: Harper Collins, 1991), *s.v.* "Pharaoh," 308–9.

271. Qur'an 2.251; 4.163; 5.78; 6.84; 17.55; 21.71–80; 27.15–16; 34.10–11, 13; 38.17–26. Cf. R. Paret, "Dāwūd," *Encyclopedia of Islam*, 11 February 2015. http://referenceworks.brillonline.com/entries/encyclopaedia-of-islam-2/da -wu-d-SIM_1754.

272. Qur'an 3.37–38; 19.2, 7; 21.89. Cf. B. Heller and A. Rippin, "Zakariyyā'," *Encyclopedia of Islam*, 11 February 2015. http://referenceworks.brillonline .com/entries/encyclopaedia-of-islam-2/zakariyya-SIM_8093. Also cf. *infra*, n. 274, on John the son of Zachariah.

273. Elizabeth is not, in fact, mentioned by name in the Qur'an.

274. That is, John the Baptist. See Qur'an 6.85; 19.7. Cf. A. Rippin, "Yaḥyā b. Zakariyyā'," *Encyclopedia of Islam*, 11 February 2015. http://referenceworks.bril lonline.com/entries/encyclopaedia-of-islam-2/yah-ya-b-zakariyya-SIM_7956.

275. Qur'an 3.23–57; 4.157–59; 5.110–15; 18.17–22; 43.58–64. Cf. "Maryam," *Encyclopedia of Islam*, 11 February 2015. http://referenceworks.brillonline.com/ entries/encyclopaedia-of-islam-2/maryam-COM_0692.

276. Qur'an 2.87, 253; 3.45, 84; 4.157, 171; 5.46, 71, 110, 112, 114, 116; 19.34; 33.7; 57.27; 61.6, 14. Cf. "ʿĪsā," *Encyclopedia of Islam*, 11 February 2015. http://referenceworks.brillonline.com/entries/encyclopaedia-of-islam-2/i-sa -COM_0378.

Gabriel speaking to Zachariah or Mary,[277] the origin of John,[278] the birth of Christ from a virgin,[279] and certain others.

56. Since, therefore, as I said, he has excerpted certain things from the already mentioned scriptures, why did he not become either a Jew by receiving all the Jewish books, or a Christian by completely giving approval to the Christian books? Why did he call the Jewish Law good, which he does not follow; why does he preach the Christian Gospel, which he disparages? Either these scriptures are wrong and ought to be rejected, or they are true and ought to be proclaimed. For a law comprised of divine words differs from one comprised of human words, and the basis for divine law differs from the basis for human tradition. For if among the laws of any people some have been decreed justly, it often happens nevertheless that some of them, or perhaps many of them, have been established in contradiction to the rule of equity. But this is not the case, this is really not so for the heavenly law, it is not the case for heavenly prophecies, whenever and to whomever they were given. For although some truths are provided in a rational manner by human ingenuity, using reason, because they are humans it can happen that they err, sometimes rarely and sometimes often. Thus in the Psalms, which your already-mentioned prophet affirms were handed down to David, one reads: "Everyone is a liar."[280]

57. Just as light cannot be changed into darkness, however, that eternal majesty that is God—from whom stems all truth, rather who is essentially truth itself—does not know how to lie,[281] either when speaking to rational creatures by an audible sound or when by an inspiration of the intellect. From this, it happens that all that he gave to mortals and ordered through

277. Not explicitly identified as speaking to Mary or Zachariah in the Qur'an.

278. This reference to the origin of John (*Iohannis exortum*) is uncertain. Perhaps Peter has in mind Lk 1.13.

279. See n. 275, p. 100.

280. Ps 115.2 (116.11). For the claim that the Psalms were revealed to David, see *supra*, n. 220.

281. See Anselm, *Cur Deus Homo* 1.12, in *S. Anselmi Cantuariensis Archiepiscopi Opera Omnia*, ed. F. S. Schmitt, (Rome and Edinburgh: Thomas Nelson and Sons, 1946), 2:70.

mortals in scripture is true, certain, and beyond doubt. And
one gathers from these things that if the Jewish or Christian
texts—or rather, to speak more truthfully, their meaning—has
proceeded from God to men, and has been handed down to
them from him, the texts ought to be respected, they ought to
be received completely and not in part as true, as your prophet
does, and just like a river that derives from the font of truth.
Why, then, has your legislator approved these scriptures in
part, condemned them in part, received them in part, and rejected them in part? For, just as was said, if they are divine, they
ought to be received not in part but completely. If they are not
divine, they ought to be condemned not just in part but entirely. Therefore, either let him receive these scriptures as divine,
as he guards his Qur'an, or, if he has denied that they are divine, let him remove from his Qur'an what he took from them;
or rather, having accepted more just counsel, when removing
the untruths that he had taken from the false scriptures, at the
same time let him deem as false his entire Qur'an and take it
away because of them.

58. Some one of you [will reply] to this: "I do not deny that
the Jewish or Christian books were divine, but they were divine
just as they were written down by their first authors. But over
the recent course of time, from various mishaps, those first
books perished; and later the Jewish books were restored by
certain Jews, and the Christian ones were restored by certain
Christians. Those who were ignorant of the original truth of
the first books reconstructed the books that Jews or Christians
possess now, both out of the variant accounts of what went before and out of the conjectures of their own hearts, just as they
wished; and, mixing true with false and false with true, they
stripped them of all of truth's immutability. For this reason, I
do not have confidence in books of the sort that either of these
peoples uses at the present time; for this reason, I maintain
that they were falsified or corrupted. Nonetheless, it was certainly the case that what was chosen by God and given to our
prophet and added by him to the scripture of our law was true.
Through him, our legislator, God distinguished between the
true and the false, by sending to him in a volume those that

(according to you) than your

celebrated Qur'an. For that is what you affirm was sent by God
from the heavens and delivered by Gabriel to your prophet, not
all at once but little by little and in parts during the month that
you call Ramadan.[283] Therefore, read over that book, I say, read
over the whole of the book of your supreme law, from its very
beginning—which says, "In the name of the Lord, the holy and
the merciful. This book, without the addition of falsehood or
error, is truthful,"[284] until its end, in which again it says, "In the

282. See Justinian's *Institutiones* 2, tit. 20, 4: "quia semper necessitas proban-
di incumbit illi qui agit." Cf. *The Institutes of Justinian,* trans. Thomas Collett
Sandars, 1st American ed. (Chicago: Callaghan & Company, 1876), p. 299; accessed February 13, 2015 at https://archive.org/stream/institutesjustioohamm
goog#page/n364/mode/2up.

283. Ramadan, the ninth month in the Islamic calendar, is the month
during which the Qur'an was revealed to the prophet Mohammad. See Qur'an
2.185.

284. Qur'an 2.2. In Robert of Ketton's translation, Qur'an 1 is not counted;

name of the Lord, the holy and the merciful. Rise up continually and in supplication before the Lord, the king of all, God of all, who sanctifies you above all peoples"[285] —and if you can elicit from it anything that has been said either by God or by your prophet concerning falsified Jewish and Christian books, place it before me.[286]

61. Examine also the other books, though of far inferior authority, which you read or possess, and propose to us briefly one word, or at least one iota, signifying that the aforesaid scriptures have been corrupted by anyone at any time. But we are not so unacquainted or so unfamiliar with your texts, nor could the Arabic language distance itself to such an extent from the Latin understanding, that it could hide from us something from among those that relate to the cause that has been taken up, and so that we could remain in ignorance over whether your texts contain in some part of them [the claim] that ours have been falsified. For our race has many who are skilled in both languages, who have solicitously drawn out of your writings not only those things that pertain to religion or to your religious observances, but have also entered the nooks and crannies of your libraries for whatever refers to your humanistic and scientific studies. And as much on the basis of the texts already translated into Latin as on the basis of the Arabic texts themselves, we know that neither your Qur'an, nor the book of Abdias the Jew,[287] nor the geneal-

---

Qur'an 2.1–141 forms the first surah; 2.142–202 constitutes the second; 2.203–52 forms a third; and 2.253–86 forms a fourth. See Glei, p. xvi.

285. Qur'an 114.1–3.

286. Peter evidently had not read Qur'an 2.75, where this theme is introduced. This claim of the corruption of Jewish and Christian scriptures (*taḥrīf*) became important for Islamic theologians. See Jean-Marie Gandeul and Robert Caspar, "Textes de la tradition musulmane concernant le taḥrīf (falsification) des écritures," *Islamochristiana* 6 (1980): 61–104; Sandra Toenies Keating, "Revisiting the Charge of Taḥrīf: The Question of Supersessionism in Early Islam and the Qur'an," in *Nicholas of Cusa and Islam. Polemics and Dialogue in the Late Middle Ages,* 202–17; and W. M. Watt, *Muslim-Christian Encounters: Perceptions and Misperceptions* (London: Routledge, 1991), chap. 3.

287. For Abdias, see *supra,* n. 221. Here the book mentioned refers to the *Doctrina Mahumet,* translated by Herman of Dalmatia from the *Masā'il 'Absillāh ibn-Salām,* i.e., the "questions" of 'Abdallāh ibn-Salām. For further description, see Kritzeck, *Peter the Venerable and Islam,* 89–96.

ogy of Mohammad,[288] nor any other volumes giving expression to your law or your legislator, mention that the Hebrew or Christian scriptures were falsified at any time or in any respect or in the slightest way.

62. Since these things appear to be so, since nowhere do your books contain the claim (as is often said) that our books or those of the Jews have ever been falsified, then where do you get this idea? Where does this rumor come from? Based on what authority has a tradition so false, or rather so empty, arisen? It is astonishing, and it is astonishing beyond what I can say, that men who are so prudent in temporal and human matters, as I wrote above, are so obtuse in matters eternal and divine that they are unable to perceive that one ought not place credence in any tradition without having examined it, that one ought not acquiesce to vulgar rumor without an authority that is sure and that deserves confidence. Actually, it is stupid to accede to a doubtful authority, but it is even beyond a brute animal to embrace an empty, common rumor of such a foolish and stupid people without the name of any authority. In fact, this alone seems to be left: that altogether absurdly or rather imprudently you opine that the divine books were lost in an earlier mishap, and that later, after falsehood was mixed with truth, they were reconstructed in a fashion that pleased the new writers.

63. But now let that infamous tradition appear before us and show, with a true statement that is beyond doubt, in what mishaps the oft-named books were lost. And let it declare first, having guarded an appropriate order, how the Jews lost the Law given them by God along with the books of the prophets and others attached to them. For it is well known to the world that the Jewish volumes preceded the Christian ones by a long time, whereas the evangelical or apostolic books were transcribed much later by the evangelists and the apostles. It is proper to prove, therefore, that they have been falsified, that they perished, in the order in which they perished, in the order in which they are said to be false.

288. I.e., *Liber generationis Mahumet,* translated by Herman of Dalmatia, based upon the *Kitāb Nasāb Rasūl Allāh* by Saʿīd ibn-ʿUmar. See Kritzeck, *Peter the Venerable and Islam,* 84–88.

64. "When the Jews were released," they say, "from the Babylonian captivity by the indulgence of the king of the Persians, and were permitted to return to their Palestine, they placed the divine books (which they had kept with them while they were captives) on an ass,[289] and in this way they began a journey with an indiscriminate multitude.[290] And because, as is the custom of a multitude going on a journey, some went faster, some more slowly, and, distracted by the various needs for many things on the journey, they were occupied first with this and then with that, they watched the ass carrying the divine Law inattentively. And since they marched along carelessly, with the first divided from the last over a long stretch of road, that brute animal, now lacking a guide and being frisky, as is common with those animals, left the path of the journey. Proceeding little by little and at one point running across plains and at another point climbing mountains, separated from its own, it disappeared; and since no one followed it, it perished in some mishap, together with the Law of God which it carried."

65. What is this rumor, O men, what is this tradition that assures you that the Jewish Law has been lost, that the prophetic books have been lost? And how, how, I ask, could circumspect men be persuaded that the Jews, when returning from the already mentioned captivity, could have been so incautious, so indolent, so inattentive toward their sacred [books] that alone had survived when everything else had been lost to them? Already seventy years earlier, when they were taken captive,[291] once the city was destroyed, the Temple burned, the Ark of

---

289. Cf. Qur'an 62.4–5, which compares Jews carrying the Torah to a donkey carrying heavy books.

290. Cf. Ezr 2.64–67.

291. The prophet Jeremiah proclaimed that the Babylonian exile would last 70 years (Jer 25.12 and 29.10), and this number is confirmed in 2 Chr 36.21. In 538 BCE Cyrus decreed that the Jews in Babylonia could return to Jerusalem. The beginning of the exile can be variously dated: from before King Jehoiakim's rebellion, crushed by Nebuchadnezzar (598–597 BCE); from the surrender of Jerusalem (597 BCE); or from the Temple's destruction (587–586 BCE). "Seventy years," then, is an approximate number (cf. "Exile, Babylonian," in *Encyclopedia Judaica* [Jerusalem: Keter, 1971], 6:1036–41). But "seventy years" was accepted by medieval Christian authors—e.g., Petrus Alfonsi, *Dialogue* 2, p. 104.

God lost,[292] after the gold, silver, and bronze vessels of great
weight that had been consecrated to God were conveyed with
the captive people to Babylonia,[293] none of their sacred things
remained for those returning except the Law and the vessels
restored to them by royal gift. How, then, can it appear true
or likely that men who were hastening to their fatherland with
the most ardent spirits, impassioned in all their labor for the
religion (religio) bestowed upon them, so neglected the Law of
God, on which all their hope depended and because of which
they, alone among all the other peoples of the world, near
or far, were glorified, [and] in that way placed it on the most
worthless animal, in that way left it uncared for, not just for
one mile but for at least many miles that followed? And where
were the ministers when they had turned aside, where were the
Levites,[294] where were the priests who returned from captivity?
And if there was a mixed, scattered multitude of nobles and
commoners marching along, upon whom the responsibility for
guarding the Law had not been imposed, that followed or preceded the Law-bearing ass, not paying attention to it when it
strayed, does it seem logical that all those chosen for it turned
away to other things all at the same time; rather, as I would say,
that they abandoned their entire hope, that there was not even
one among the large number of guardians to safeguard the
Law? Now, does anyone neglect his own horse so readily, or any
beast of burden whatsoever, with no concern for its protection?

66. But let it be so. Let what was not so, be so: the ass wandered, and following along the path disappeared; when the ass
wandered the stupid and idle people lost the Law, it lost in this

292. According to most traditions, the Ark of God (or Ark of the Covenant)
was lost to the Philistines (1 Sm 4.10–11), but then restored to Israel; King David had it brought to Jerusalem (2 Sm 6), and King Solomon had it installed in
the First Temple (2 Sm 7; 1 Kgs 6.19, 8.1–11). It is hardly mentioned thereafter,
until in 2 Chr 35.1–3 King Josiah (d. 609 BCE) directs the Levites to place
it in the Temple. As Petrus Alfonsi correctly notes (Dialogue 9, pp. 217–18)
the Ark was not used in the Second Temple that the returnees built in Jerusalem.

293. 2 Chr 36.18.

294. King David had given the Levites sole responsibility for carrying the
Ark. Cf. 1 Chr 15.2.

mishap, rather in such a great misfortune, the sacred volumes which the already mentioned animal then carried; was there no other volume of the same Law that remained somewhere in the entire world, either in the possession of Jews or in the possession of some others? Was there among so many thousands of Jews, either those who returned from Chaldea to Syria,[295] or those who were made captive or had fled to the many and various parts of the world, was there no one who had that same Law transcribed in another volume? And if you do not refuse to believe in either the divine or the other true histories, before that captivity that was created for the Jews by the king of the Chaldeans, who was called Nebuchadnezzar,[296] the kings of the Assyrians transferred ten of the Jewish tribes among the Medes, the Persians, and other eastern peoples.[297] Did so large a race, rather so numerous a people that shared that Law of God, not carry any books of such a renowned Law with them when they were transferred?

67. And what people, living by any written law, has been satisfied with one and only one copy (*volumen*)? How could only one volume of their Law suffice for a people beyond number who lived scattered throughout many cities, villages, towns, [and] farms, and who filled a large part of the earth? Would not all peoples everywhere, not only in separate cities but even in separate and modest villages, keep their own individual volume, or perhaps many volumes, of the Law to which they had dedicated themselves? Do not the Jews, whose Law is being considered, who live under the Christians throughout all of Eu-

295. I.e., the province the Romans called Syria-Palestine.

296. Nebuchadnezzar II (d. 562 BCE) was the ruler of Babylon; in 586 BCE he captured Jerusalem, destroyed the Temple, and carried Judean captives into exile. See *supra*, n. 291.

297. These ten "lost" tribes of Israel disappear from biblical memory following the Assyrian conquest of the northern kingdom of Israel in 721–722 BCE (cf. 2 Kgs 17.6). Apocryphal texts, like 2 Esdras 2.39–41, anticipated their return in the future. The return of the ten lost tribes became a feature of medieval eschatology, especially in vernacular literature. See Andrew Colin Gow, *The Red Jews: Antisemitism in an Apocalyptic Age 1200–1600* (Leiden, New York, Cologne: E. J. Brill, 1995). Also useful will be the contributions to *Prester John, the Mongols and the Ten Lost Tribes,* ed. Charles F. Beckingham and Bernard Hamilton (London: Variorum, 1996).

rope and in other parts of the world—not only a thousand or a hundred, but even sixty or fifty dwelling in one place at one and the same time—daily show us, offer us, and furnish to us and our own in their synagogues the entire Law, all the prophets, and other books of the Hebrew language?[298] Clearly there are hardly twenty Jews living together among us who are found without books of this kind. Is it not the same among you, too? Look about you in those parts in which you have made them subject to your dominion, and you will discover, I think, that I do not utter falsehoods.

68. It was even their custom, before they were held captive by various pagan kings, while they still dwelled in certain parts of Syria[299] granted to them by God along with their own capital city, Jerusalem, to retain volumes of the Law as well as volumes of other books, not only in that city in which alone it was permitted to them to offer sacrifice to God,[300] but also in all their other cities, and in almost all the fortified places and towns in their jurisdiction. In no other way, as well-considered reason declares, could a people so especially numerous learn or entrust to memory the teaching of a Law so profuse, unless a multitude of books was present in the many and diverse places remaining, and the knowledge of many teachers was not lacking. It could not happen that that entire people that gathered together only three times each year in the principal city[301] for the purpose of prayer and sacrifice, according to God's command, could be instructed in and could be fully taught God's Law during the few days it tarried there, by however many teachers, as the insis-

298. The nature of the "other books" remains vague. Although in his *Against the Inveterate Obduracy of the Jews* (5, p. 212), Peter had inveighed against the Talmud, which the Jews prefer, he claims, to the books of the prophets, he likely refers here to the Hebrew apocrypha.

299. "Syria": see *supra*, n. 295.

300. Over time, sacrifices in ancient Israel were confined to the Jerusalem Temple (cf. Dt 12.4–14). After the destruction of the Second Temple by the Romans in 70 CE, the sacrificial cult became impossible, at least for the present.

301. Peter refers here to the three pilgrimage festivals commanded in Torah and observed in Jerusalem: Sukkot (the Feast of Tabernacles), Passover (the Feast of Unleavened Bread), and Shavuot (the Feast of Weeks). Cf. Ex 23.14–17; Ex 34.18–26; Dt 16.16.

tent press of time would prevent it. They had many places then, and the many people dwelling in various places had the entire corpus of the divine Law and of other volumes, and so the Law of God, having been distributed in the parts of Syria as well as in other regions throughout the world, having been preserved by those beyond number, could not have perished.

69. But why do I say of the Hebrews, why do I say of other peoples, that they do not keep the laws by which they live—whether handed down by God or invented by themselves—together in only one place, but rather that they distribute them throughout the locations either over which they have dominion, or in which they abide? I address you, I ask you. Does Mecca alone contain your Qur'an that was handed down by God to your Mohammad (so you say), as the only city in which it is situated? Is there no other city of Arabia, of Egypt, of Africa, are there no cities in the East that are subject to you, is there no camp, no village, except Mecca that possesses the Qur'an? I believe, unless you choose to be monstrously pertinacious and reject a well-known truth, that, based on your example and the example of all peoples, you will concede that the Jews were never satisfied with a single copy of their scriptures, and that the Law of God could not have been lost during the return of the Jews from Babylon because of the mythical, fictitious wandering of a—or rather of any—brute animal. Actually, it streamed from various parts of the world, whereby there was no lack of opportunity to take it up again, and whereby it could be recopied from numerous exemplars.

70. Because this cannot reasonably be denied, let the discussion proceed to what follows, and let it show that after their return from Babylonia the Jews did not lack the books of the divine Law. Indeed, one reads in the book of Ezra, which belongs among the number of Jewish books: "And all the people were gathered together as one on the street which is before the water gate, and they spoke to Ezra the scribe, to bring the book of the Law of Moses, which the Lord had commanded to Israel. Then Ezra the priest brought the Law before the entire multitude of men and women, and all those that could understand, on the first day of the seventh month. And he read it

in the street that was before the water gate, from the morning until midday, before the men and the women and all those that could understand. And the ears of all the people were attentive to the book."[302] And, after an intervening verse: "And Ezra opened the book before the entire people ... and Ezra blessed the Lord God in a mighty voice. And the entire people replied: 'Amen.'"[303]

71. Was not Ezra among the number of captives by whose carelessness the Law of God, according to your opinion, perished, as has been said? Did Ezra create a fake Law so quickly? And since in that same volume he is himself proclaimed to be a man just and wise, and there was then no hope either for him or for the people except in God, what person of sane mind dares suppose that he corrupted the Law of God, and that the corrupted Law was brought out to be read in view of the entire people? But because one should not tarry long over things that are so clearly false, either let sure evidence be produced that proves that the book of the divine Law was falsified either by Ezra or by anyone else, or let that opinion be condemned as absurd and senseless, proceeding from the "Father of lies."[304]

72. But again and again I am moved to wonder, and I cannot be more astonished at such wonders, how through the cleverness of Satan it is possible that men with full use of their reason can be persuaded, so that either they believe or think that books that are true according to the testimony of so many centuries, and which were diffused everywhere in the world for more than two thousand years, could have been corrupted by the art of any falsifier whatsoever. Why? Even if it should happen, in accord with your suspicion, that some falsifiers counterfeited them, would it follow that the world received them without any investigation into their truth? At any time was human understanding so eclipsed, was reason so buried that it would not judge what it received, but rather (what is far more amazing) that all languages and peoples except yours would

302. Neh 8.1–3.
303. Neh 8.5–6.
304. I.e., Satan. See Jn 8.44; see also *Against the Inveterate Obduracy of the Jews*, pp. 122, 207–8.

give assent to such a great falsehood? How is it that for almost
a thousand years that Law of God still remained uncorrupted,
as you believe, that it was received by none but the Jews, and
then, having been counterfeited, it was diffused among all peoples to the ends of the world? But what falsehood can be discovered in these volumes? In which of its parts, in which verses
does the first book of that Law, which is called Genesis, appear
to be corrupted, having been turned away from truth, [and]
mixed with falsehood? In which does Exodus? In which does
Leviticus? In which does the book of Numbers? In which does
Deuteronomy? For the highest part of the Jewish Law is in these
five. In which do the books of Joshua, Judges, and Ruth appear
falsified, which, when added to the prior five books, are called
by the Greek word *Heptateuch*?[305] Perhaps in the historical narrative? Or in the legislation?

73. If there is a question about the history (that is, about
the events) from the very creation of heaven and earth, up to
the end of these same books, does not Mohammad, imagining
that God is speaking to him in his Qur'an, grant nearly everything just as one reads it there? On the creation of heaven and
earth,[306] on Adam and Eve,[307] on paradise,[308] on the wood of
paradise, on the forbidden tree[309] and the serpent,[310] on the
expulsion of Adam and Eve from paradise,[311] on Cain and
Abel,[312] on Noah and the ark,[313] on the flood, on Abraham and

305. The term Heptateuch refers to the first *seven* books of the Hebrew
Bible, Genesis through Judges. The addition of Ruth, which follows Judges in
the Latin Vulgate, produces eight, known as the Octateuch.

306. Cf. Qur'an 2.164; 3.189–90; 7.54; 10.6; 11.7; 14.32; 40.64.

307. Cf. Qur'an 2.35. In fact, Eve's name does not appear in the Qur'an;
she is identified only as Adam's wife. See "ādam," *Encyclopedia of Islam,* 17 February 2015. http://referenceworks.brillonline.com/entries/encyclopaedia-of
-islam-2/a-dam-SIM_0295; ibid., "Ḥawwāʾ," http://referenceworks.brillonline
.com/entries/encyclopaedia-of-islam-2/h-awwa-SIM_2821.

308. Cf. Qur'an 11.108; 18.107; 23.11.

309. Cf. Qur'an 2.35; 7.19.   310. Cf. Qur'an 20.117, 120–21.

311. Cf. Qur'an 2.36.

312. Cf. Qur'an 5.27–30. The Qur'an does not identify these two sons of
Adam by name, however. See "Hābīl wa Kābīl," *Encyclopedia of Islam,* 17 February 2015. http://referenceworks.brillonline.com/entries/encyclopaedia-of
-islam-2/ha-bi-l-wa-k-a-bi-l-SIM_2581.

313. See Qur'an 29.14–15; *supra,* n. 264. Cf. "Nūḥ," *Encyclopedia of Islam,*

Jacob,[314] on Joseph,[315] on Moses[316] and Aaron,[317] on Pharaoh[318] and the Egyptians, on Israel and its passage through the Red Sea,[319] on this people's protracted wandering through the desert,[320] on the land of Canaan that was promised and delivered to Israel, and, as was said, almost all the things that these books relate, he recounts most of them, but with many items subtracted, with many changes, with a pile of lies mixed in besides, in his barbarous and unnatural way of speaking. In this way he mentions certain items from Moses's legislation,[321] while likewise subtracting many things from it. And since for the most part he attests to the truth of the Hebrew volumes, and, as I said above, he does not say that they have been falsified even a little bit, where could this opinion arise among you, which you have not received from your teacher? You could have considered these things much more correctly, much more rationally; you ought to have said this: "And if the Hebrew and Christian scriptures are known to us, nonetheless we conclude that they are true from the fact that in the law our prophet delivered to us he approves of most of what is written there, whereas he rejects nothing either there or anywhere else."

74. From all the things I have written above, I conclude by either a necessary or a plausible argument that the Jewish books were neither lost nor falsified. If Mohammad grafted onto his law (and your law) certain things as they are written among the Jews, as if produced for him in a divine reply, and he did not add that the rest have been lost or falsified, and none of

---

17 February 2015. http://referenceworks.brillonline.com/entries/encyclopae dia-of-islam-2/nu-h-SIM_5966.

314. On Jacob, cf. Qur'an 11.71. See also "Ya'ḳūb," *Encyclopedia of Islam,* 17 February 2015. http://referenceworks.brillonline.com/entries/encyclopaedia -of-islam-2/ya-k-u-b-SIM_7965.

315. Cf. Qur'an 6.84; 11.34; and 12 (*Yūsuf*). See *supra,* n. 268.

316. See *supra,* n. 269.

317. Cf. "Hārūn b. 'Imrān," *Encyclopedia of Islam,* 17 February 2015. http:// referenceworks.brillonline.com/entries/encyclopaedia-of-islam-2/ha-ru-n-b -imra-n-SIM_2745.

318. See *supra,* n. 270.

319. Cf. Qur'an 2.50; 7.138–41; 10.90; 20.77; 26.63.

320. Cf. Qur'an 5.26.

321. Cf. Qur'an 7.142–45.

you can prove what you either suspect or propound concerning these same lost or falsified scriptures, it follows then that they hold the firmest and highest degree of truth (as divine scriptures), lacking any or even the smallest mark of untruth, just as they were produced by their first authors. But one does not read anything about them either in your Qur'an or in any other books of your teaching, nor do you introduce anything anywhere else that could prove that the Jewish books were either lost or falsified.

75. Therefore, it is clear, once the false objections and suspicions have been entirely rejected, that the oft-mentioned scriptures are not partly but are completely true; with no one having the power now to object, it is certain that they are divine. With things being the way they are, I add what I touched on above, that it is necessary either that you accept the Jewish scriptures in their entirety or that you reject the Qur'an. Now, as I have already said, since many things are found in that volume just as they are found in the Jewish books, if they are said to be falsified, then those that have been taken from them or are found just as they are set down there are proved to be entirely false or doubtful. If false or doubtful things have been written down in your law, then actually all that book contains is either false or doubtful. Nothing but what is false and doubtful could be taken from falsified books, just as nothing but what is false or doubtful is set down there. But it happens, as has been said often, that many things have been taken from them or are set down just as they are read in the Qur'an, at least as far as pertains to the meaning. For this reason it follows that that law, then, which I call your law, which you are accustomed to glorify as having been sent from heaven, is not only in part but is wholly—in its totality—false or doubtful. If you refuse to believe or to say that your Qur'an is false or doubtful, you are compelled to confess, with a sure truth that neither deceives nor is deceived urging you on every side, that those books from which Mohammad either took or introduced to your law many things—just as they are read there so far as their meaning—are true not in part but completely true, and that they are not divine in part but are completely divine.

76. Having conceded this, you should receive not only the Jewish volumes as divine, without any mark of falsehood, but moreover, according to this same argument, you should equally and in all respects admit the Christian books. For as I said above, your already mentioned law-giver also mixed many things from them into that same law of yours, and he incorporated them into nearly the entire framework of his volume. If these were taken from counterfeit books, they ought to be rejected, and all those to which they were added ought to be condemned along with them in the manner in which those were above. If you seek to avoid that too, based on a conclusion similar to (or rather the same as) the earlier argument, you will confer the same authority on the Christian books as on the Jewish ones.

77. And although it cannot be denied, although it has become clear from a brief presentation that the Christian books are true and divine, nonetheless let the opinion come forth and proceed to the fore that has been handed down by you—either by all of you, or by some—that even these books have been lost, have been falsified.[322] "At the time of the Roman emperors," they say, "who severely persecuted the Christians for a very long time with exile, proscriptions, and various kinds of death, and who ordered by public edict that their books be everywhere destroyed, both the Gospels and the Acts of the Apostles or the Epistles perished. Afterwards they were recopied and repaired as it pleased the Christians, who had received nothing from the first authors of the books, seeing that a long period of time lay between them and those that followed after them, and they had not even seen the books they created, which had been burned previously, as was said."

78. And is this everything? Is this all, I say, that you have to offer, is this and this alone everything whereby you allege that the evangelical or apostolic writings have perished, whereby

---

322. This assertion that the Christian books had been corrupted clearly concerned not only Peter but also his contemporaries. Godfrey of Viterbo's late twelfth-century *Pantheon* notes that the Saracens declare that Christians have perverted both the Law of the Old Testament and the Gospels, and even allege that Christians have erased Mohammad's name from the Gospel ("Aiuntque nos legem et Evangelia pervertisse et nomen Machomet de Evangelio abrasisse"). See *The Pseudo-Historical Image of the Prophet Mohammad*, 179.

you allege that they have been falsified? If this is all, I will proceed against you in the same way as above; in the same manner
of replying, I will show that what you propose is actually very
weak or rather lacks any force at all. Of course I confess that
Roman emperors, who ruled over all of Europe, over all of Africa, over the largest parts of Asia along with those parts adjacent
either to the Ocean or to the islands of the Tyrrhenian sea,[323]
for three hundred years persecuted almost continuously—at
times severely, at times more mildly—the Christians, who had
already spread everywhere. I also confess that a certain one of
the last persecutors, who was named Diocletian,[324] and who as-
saulted them more ferociously and persistently than the others, had ratified by public edict that throughout all the regions
subject to him, the Christian churches should be destroyed on
the most holy Paschal Feast Day itself, and the Christian books
burnt.[325] Surely I admit this, as I said, acting just as if on behalf
of your position.

79. But what is in that for you? If this edict was also promulgated by that emperor throughout the whole length and
breadth of the Roman empire, if it was fulfilled either in part or
perhaps completely, so far as one considers the destruction of
churches, and if those books that were found also were burned,
did all of the Christian volumes perish in that single event? Was
there no one who lived in such a large Christian population
spread across that extensive empire who, once he heard the
royal edict, would hide some books from among the countless
number of books; was there no one to pull some from the fire;
was there no one to save some of them? And surely, as can be
proved from true histories, in a realm so renowned and extensive there was hardly a city, there was hardly a town, there were
hardly any villages, which did not have a Christian multitude
mixed in among the pagans. Throughout the individual cities

323. The Tyrrhenian Sea is part of the Mediterranean Sea and lies off the
western coast of Italy. The islands mentioned are likely Corsica, Sardinia, and
Sicily.

324. Diocletian (d. 311) was emperor from 284–305; the Diocletian persecution—the last great persecution of Christians in the Roman Empire—bears
his name.

325. I.e., Easter. See Eusebius, *Hist. eccles.* 7.30.22, 8.2.4, pp. 715, 743.

among them there were bishops, presbyters, deacons, and not a small number of clerics who presided over the Christian people and who, with supreme and singular care, safeguarded the sacred books of the Christian Law along with other heavenly sacred things and sacraments entrusted to them. Did every sentence of the Christian religion in them perish, then? Was the love of sacred, divine things so lacking in them that, although they exposed their bodies to the flames, to swords, and to every kind of death in order to preserve God's Law, they would so completely neglect that same Law of God for which they did not hesitate to die?

80. And what will you say about the Persians and the Medes, what about the Ethiopians and the Indians, what about your own Arabia, and what about the other kingdoms which Roman power was unable to subjugate to itself? For since the sound of evangelical preaching had gone out already across the whole earth, with the disciples of Christ crying out everywhere, and almost no corner of the world lay hidden to the Christians who were spread abroad among all the languages of the pagans, did the Christian volumes perish, or were they lost also among them? Did the Gospel perish? Did the apostolic writings perish? Did no people, no languages, no district of Christians preserve the Christian books just as it had received them from their first preachers, lest they be able to perish? But the Gospel was preserved, clearly it was preserved by countless Christian peoples as it was handed down by the evangelists; the apostolic writings were preserved through the most secure lines of transmission and transmitted up to modern times.

81. And, to remain silent concerning the more distant parts of the world and parts less known to us, the Latin church has Gospels handed down to it by Peter, the Greek has them handed down to it by Paul, and both of them handed down to all of Europe the Gospels and the apostolic writings entrusted to them.[326] Since these were highest and chief among the disci-

---

326. For the role of Peter and Paul in transmitting the Gospels and other texts, Irenaeus remarks that Peter and Paul both preached in Rome. Cf. *Against Heresies (Adversus haereses)* 3.1.1, ed. A. Rousseau and Louis Doutreleau, Sources chrétiennes 264 (Paris: Éditions du Cerf, 1979; Turnhout: Brepols, 2010; CD

ples of Christ—one having been taught by him while in the
body, the other invisibly[327]—"beginning with Jerusalem"[328] they
preached the Gospel by the Word of Christ, sometimes together, sometimes separately, at one time themselves, at another
through their followers, as far as the most distant borders of
the West, and handed it down in writing to later generations.
Peter handed down the Gospel of Mark, which he himself had
approved;[329] Paul handed down Luke's Gospel, which he had
written in parts of Greece.[330] Nor was John absent, another of
Christ's disciples, whom Christ chose and taught while he still
tarried among men, handing down to the Christian peoples of
Asia Minor his own Gospel that he wrote. Neither could the
Gospel of Matthew perish, which he had written earlier and
which was handed down by the already mentioned apostles to
the regions and populations on this side of the sea, which, having been quickly transcribed and diffused everywhere, the skill
of many peoples has preserved. In addition to countless other
churches, the Roman church, the head of all the churches of
the world, and through the apostolic pontiffs that followed who
are well known to us from texts, beginning with Peter up until
our own day, has guarded those that were handed down to it
by the already mentioned apostles just as they were written and
very soon after they were written, and this shows that what you
either believe or say—that they have perished—is actually false
and foolish nonsense.

82. Thus too for the apostolic writings: the Acts of the Apostles from the already-mentioned Luke, two epistles from Peter,

---

ROM). Eusebius, *Hist. eccles.* 2.15.2, p. 141, adds that Peter wrote his first epistle
in Rome (which he referred to as Babylon; cf. 1 Pt 5.13) and remarks too that
both Peter and Paul preached in Rome (*Hist. eccles.* 5.8.2, p. 443).

327. Peter the Venerable refers to the fact that although the Apostle Peter
knew Jesus personally, Paul did not; instead Paul saw the risen Christ in a vision while on the road to Damascus (cf. Acts 22.5–10).

328. Lk 24.47.

329. Eusebius identifies Mark as Peter's translator in Rome, who wrote
down the words that Peter spoke. See *Hist. eccles.* 3.39.15, p. 291.

330. Luke is depicted in the New Testament as Paul's companion (cf. 2 Tm
4.11); Luke's Gospel is thought to have been written in Achaia, a region of
Greece on the north coast of the Peloponnesus, but today it is not often alleged
that its author is the same figure identified in Paul's letters as his companion.

three from John in addition to his Apocalypse, and fourteen from Paul, who wrote them in part from Italy and in part from Greece and sent them to churches in different cities, were handed down to the first believers in Christ, and both in Rome as well as in other cities generations of the faithful coming after them preserved them for us today, as was said, with the greatest effort. There remain of the new canon of the Christians the two epistles of the Apostles James and Jude: that is, one of James and the other of Jude. Although these were written in Asia Major,[331] since they penetrated your East and our West at almost the same time, and were immediately joined to the others by the same people I have named, they were preserved with the same zeal as the rest. Thereby they came down to our hands and to those of all the faithful now living, to be safeguarded by us and our posterity "so long as heaven shall be over the earth."[332]

83. Once these things have been dealt with, what remains? Clearly, what remains but this? For it is necessary that those among you who believe or are of the opinion that the Christian books have perished, either show with a sure argument that they have perished or, yielding to the plausible reasons that were set down before, confess that they were safeguarded by the Christians. Now, if it follows that they did not perish, then it follows that they were not falsified. In fact, just as we frequently learn from daily experience, because of the human fickleness that drives us, since the mystery of any secret agreed upon even by a few is unable to remain hidden for long—thus, our French proverb is true: "What two know, everybody knows"[333]— by what strat-

---

331. The Romans split Asia into two provinces: Asia Major and Asia Minor. According to Bartholomew of Lucca (d. ca. 1327), Asia Major began in Thrace where Europe ended and includes the area of Byzantium, where the Emperor Constantine created the capital of the New Rome. See his *Continuatio Thomae de Aquino* De regimine principum, 3.17, in *Opuscula philosophica Thomae Aquinatis*, ed. Raymund M. Spiazzi (Taurini: Marietti, 1954; Turnhout: Brepols, 2013; CD ROM), p. 318.

332. Cf. Dt 11.12.

333. Although I have not found this exact proverb, I have found near equivalents: in old French, "Ce que l'ung ne scet, l'autre scet," in *Proverbes français anterieurs au XVe siècle*, ed. Joseph Morawski (Paris: Librarie Ancienne Edouard Champion, 1925), no. 328, p. 12; and from Spanish: "Lo que saben tres, sabe

agem, by what method could books that are diffused throughout the world, and were preserved, as was said, for so long by
the knowledge of so many people, have been falsified? Did the
whole Christian world assent to such an unholy falsification? Did
Christian wisdom tolerate such a complete corruption of its own
books everywhere? Did none of the many peoples that worshiped
Christ withstand the first corrupters of their books?

84. Now if they were corrupted, they were corrupted at first
by one person or perhaps by a few, or perhaps by many with
mutual consent. Now, how could it have been otherwise, except
that this corruption began with a few? Therefore, this corruption began with a few, or perhaps with more, because in no other way, as I said, could one have been able to keep it secret. But
by the peoples of the entire world? Did they all corrupt at the
same time the books they received, or were they complicit with
the first corrupters? Did everyone really surrender his own eternal salvation, which these books alone preach, either by falsify-
ing them themselves, or by yielding to the falsifiers, either all at
once or gradually? Or could news of such a widespread falsification be hidden, when, as was already set forth, a few can hardly conceal any secret, even after they had been given the very
mysteries (*sacramenta*) of faith? Or did perhaps the whole world
agree to the fraud then, and now the whole world has received
not even a faint rumor of such a general falsification? Clearly, it
surpasses all wonders, all absurdities, that the world corrupted
their books and it did not know that they were corrupted.

85. But perhaps this reached only the Saracens, and was unable to reach only the Christians? Perhaps the corruption or
the loss of the foreign books, which was hidden from Christians for such a long time, was revealed to the former? The Saracens knew matters foreign to them, while the Christians did
not know their own! But what else? What more must one reply
to these empty trifles or to these jokers? What pen earnestly
addresses what one recognizes to be both baldly frivolous and
false? Reason should not attack weakness any longer as if it
were strength, in the same way as, above, it attacked what was

---

toda res"—"What three know, everybody knows." Cf. Henry G. Bohn, *A Polyglot
of Foreign Proverbs* (London: H. G. Bohn, 1857), 229.

presented. Either someone prove with sure arguments what you assert or opine—that the Christian books have been falsified—or, if you do not have anything to offer to the contrary, believe that they are true, believe that they are divine. For they could not have been falsified generally while no Christians protested; nor, if they were falsified, could what was done by the world, so far as concerns the innumerable peoples bearing the Christian name, be concealed from all the Christians in the world.

86. To what I have already said about the Hebrew books, I add that you cannot declare our Gospel to be false, unless you declare as false, equally, your Qur'an. For if the Gospel is false, in this way those things that are contained in the Qur'an just as they are read in the Gospel are either false or doubtful. If they are false or doubtful, then the entire book in which they are scattered throughout is also false or doubtful. In fact, it is clear that nothing can be taken from a falsified book except what is false or doubtful. But if you consider it wicked to say or to believe that your law is false or doubtful, then you will affirm that the Gospel or evangelical scriptures are true and divine, as reason compels you to do, either unwillingly or willingly. Certainly you affirm this, if you say that the evangelical statements scattered throughout your Qur'an are true. For, as has been said often already, either, once these have been rejected, the book to which they have been introduced is rejected, or, once they have been given approval, it receives approval in the same way. With this argument we force you both to believe and to confess that the Hebrew books, as has been set forth, are true and equally divine along with ours, that is, with the Christian books. True, because it is now evident that they are cleared of a mark of deception; divine, because, according to the testimony of your legislator, the Hebrew Law was given to Moses and the Gospel was bestowed upon Christ by God. From this conclusion, it is necessary for you to receive the Hebrew books as the Hebrews do, and to commend the evangelical or apostolic volumes as the Christians do, so far as it bears upon the divine canon.

87. I urge you to be forewarned and forearmed for the reason that when in the course of this task and discourse it is

opportune, I will necessarily attack you on the basis of those that you already hold to be divine; and just as the nature of the disputation recommends should happen, from what you have conceded I will assail also, as I am able, the falsehood in which you are entangled and weighed down beyond all mortals, I think, with the exception of the Jews;[334] and, protected by the shield of truth, with all my might I shall, with God's help, conquer. But let none of you think—because I have said that the evangelical and apostolic writings are ours, whereas I have not written that the volumes of the Jews are ours—that the Hebrew books are not also Christian books, for the Christian accepts the Law of Moses or the prophets no less than the Gospel or the Acts of the Apostles or the Epistles. The Christian "believes with his heart for justice, and confesses with his mouth for salvation"[335] that the canonical scriptures of both races were handed down to both peoples at different times by the same God, the Creator of "[all things] visible and invisible."[336] And although they may strongly disagree with one another, nevertheless the entire Christian world accepts the Jewish scriptures with the understanding that it owes, and it honors them as the greatest strength and foundation of our faith.

88. These things have been said in order to prove, O Saracens, based on that very law of yours in which you believe, that the Hebrew or Christian texts are true and divine and that human fictions cannot withstand their truth; not only does the invincible truth commend them, but even he, your legislator of some sort, confirmed that they are sacred in the manner which I have set forth. The following will reveal, however, that your oft-mentioned law is actually devoid of all truth and that he himself, that he himself was clearly neither a prophet nor a messenger of God, but rather was a seducer and a wicked man.

334. Peter addresses the errors of the Jews especially in his *Against the Inveterate Obduracy of the Jews*. Both in that work and here he stresses that the Jews—and, in particular, the Jews' Talmud—are an important source for Mohammad's errors. See *supra*, n. 243.

335. Rom 10.10.

336. Cf. The Nicene Creed, in *Concilia oecumenica et generalia Ecclesiae catholicae—Concilium Nicaenum I a. 325 (transl. latina)* (Turnhout: Brepols, 2013; CD ROM), 5.

Book Two[337]

89. Now, O Ishmaelites, because firmness should be applied to the statements that had to be presented earlier against a summary of your religion, restrain [your] swords, as I warned before, lay aside [your] stones, open [your] ears, and if anything at all of human wisdom exists in you, having put aside the pertinacious and puerile effort to prevail, listen with attentive minds to the things that follow. This can be useful to you, and if the grace of your God has willed to have mercy on you, it is especially necessary that you examine intently, that you carefully investigate, that while investigating you pay attention to the one to whom you have entrusted yourselves, your salvation (I do not mean only this fleeting and transitory salvation, but that eternal salvation which follows after this), to whom, I say, you have entrusted your bodies and souls, lest there be, according to the renowned prophet Isaiah, "a lie in your hand,"[338] lest you embrace falsehood instead of truth, iniquity instead of justice, diabolical sacrilege instead of divine worship. Referring to idolaters, he spoke in this way: "They have not known, nor understood. Their eyes are covered that they may not see, and that they may not understand with their heart. They do not consider in their mind, nor know, nor have they thought to say: 'I have burnt part of it (that is, of a tree)[339] in the fire, and I have baked bread upon its coals, I have broiled flesh and have eaten, and shall I make an idol from the rest of it? Shall I fall down before a trunk of wood?'—Part of it is ash. His foolish heart adored it, and he has not saved his soul, nor said: 'Perhaps there is a lie in my right hand.' Remember these things, O Jacob, and Israel, for you are my servant."[340]

90. The same thing can have happened to you. You are not idolaters, or so I have heard, and you do not adore wood or stones or the like. But what then? What then, I say, what then? How does it work to your benefit not to receive the creature

337. The *incipit* reads: "Book Two Begins."
338. Is 44.20.
339. This is Peter's explanatory interpolation.
340. Is 44.18–21.

instead of the Creator, if it is not given to you to worship God as he wills and commands that he be worshiped? Consider, therefore, whether inured in an ancient error that you do not disdain to examine now, whether what you have believed until now is false, whether what you have thought false until now is true. It is a sign of the wise to amend errors, even if it causes embarrassment; it is a sign of the stupid not to correct even what is condemned by the world, out of foolish shame. And if it was given to drive out from your hearts a stubborn and destructive feeling of shame at least by contemplation of the widespread nature of error, and so that you do not suppose that only you have erred, I present examples from among foreigners as well as from among our own, who, struck by the Enemy, have not submitted to the multiple portents of error to depart from the path of truth; rather, while a countless number has erred and perished on the wrong path, they alone have not departed from the path of the correct faith already indicated.

91. Consider, carefully investigate ages past, and if you are sensible then observe how often the human race has been implicated in a multitude of ensnaring errors stemming from the very first parent of mortals, incited by that apostate angel who is called Satan, until our own times. God avenged himself upon the wicked that lived at the time of the patriarch Noah, as even your Qur'an confesses,[341] and he destroyed with avenging waters that entire lineage that had withdrawn from divine worship and had filled again the entire earth with an iniquity that must not be tolerated.[342] Then, once the earth had dried out and security was restored as a divine gift, there followed a wickedness, the offspring of earlier ones, not inferior to what had preceded it, and having rejected divine worship—or rather, if I may speak more truly, not having known it—it conferred the honor of the Creator upon the creature, and having progressed from there to idolatry, both by a profane religion as well as by a cursed life, it sprinkled the whole surface of the earth with an increase of iniquities. Only a very few just men were excepted, having been separated by God's grace alone from the universal

341. Qur'an 54.9–13; 71.1–28.
342. Cf. Gn 6.13.

mass of those that perished, and thus with light shining rarely into the dense darkness of the impious that spread everywhere, the prince of darkness possessed the whole world as his entry hall—according to the Gospel that your Mohammad wrote was bestowed upon our Christ—with a lasting and lethal peace, alas, until the time of Moses.[343]

92. Finally, this one people that alone was chosen by God from among all peoples was illuminated by the divine Law through the already mentioned prophet, Moses, and while all the others were abandoned in the darkness of ancient error, it submitted to the precepts given by God and promulgated by him, and it was separated from the general destruction of the impious. Nonetheless, even after it was given the Law the profane and pertinacious enemy did not desist from turning that people away from divine worship, and from trying to join it to the accursed idolatry it had condemned and left behind, to heinous abominations, and to execrable acts, by tempting, enticing, and seducing them again with the clever arts of the pagans (*gentiles*). Finally, the benevolent deity had mercy on perishing humanity, and truth arose on earth as an aid to the wretched; that is, Christ went forth born from a Virgin, and, penetrating the world with his heavenly light, the darkness gradually having been removed, the Gospel of the eternal kingdom, of which he himself was king (as will be shown in its proper place),[344] spread abroad everywhere. You see that his Gospel has spread abroad among all peoples, and that faith in Christ burns in the hearts of all (with the exception of all the Jews and some of you).

93. Nonetheless, there were not lacking to the Christian name many errors that arose in the hearts of Christians, which God's true Church, the follower of Truth, repulsed as soon as it came to know them, which it condemned as soon as it became aware of them. Why do I mention this at the beginning of this book? In order that, as I began to say, you would think and consider that not only the pagans (*paganos*) whom I presented before, not only the Jews, not only Christian heretics, but that even you could

343. Cf. Rom 5.14.

344. In fact, Peter never provides this demonstration elsewhere in this work, which may suggest that he had envisioned a longer treatise.

have been duped, could have been deceived, could have mistaken darkness for light, mistaken what is false for what is true, mistaken a seducer for a prophet, and, as the Jews will do just before the end of the world, mistaken the Antichrist for Christ.[345] And so that the matter is not further delayed, now the spear should be hurled not from a distance, but hand-to-hand combat should be joined, with peace nevertheless, as I said above,[346] and not with anger, with reason and not with madness, with equity and not with iniquity, lest perhaps we be seen not to investigate what is true with a love of truth, but to defend what is false with partisan zeal.

94. I said above and in the last book:[347] I invite you to a salvation that does not pass away but that will endure, not one that comes to an end with a brief life but that will endure in life eternal. It was given to mortals to pursue this, to enjoy this, at the time prescribed by God, but only for those who perceive of God what he is, not what he is not, who worship him not in accord with the phantasms of their heart, but just as he himself wills and commands that he be worshiped.

95. To which you replied: "Far be it that our understanding should think otherwise; far be it that our profession should maintain otherwise. We have not dreamed up anything about God; we have not in fact fabricated anything. We think of him, we confess of him, not according to the figments of our heart, but according to what our prophet, sent by him, has handed down to us. Since he is last in the order of prophets and is just like the 'seal of all the prophets,' and since he is not the author but the bearer of the divine law, not the Lord but the messenger, he received the heavenly commandments God sent to him through Gabriel, containing nothing more nor less, and once he received them he handed them down to us and to our fathers to be observed. We observe them, we guard them, we have dedicated our souls to them, we have dedicated our bodies to them, we have dedicated our life and death to them."

---

345. On the Antichrist, cf. *supra*, nn. 32 and 77, pp. 36, 47. On the Jews and Antichrist, see esp. *Against the Inveterate Obduracy of the Jews* 5, p. 285.

346. *Supra*, book 1.24, and n. 212.

347. *Supra*, book 1.27.

96. Listen, therefore, for the time is at hand, to what you have dedicated your souls, your bodies, your life, and your death. Pay attention to whether you have placed your hope in a safe place, on a sound doctrine, whether you have believed in a true prophet and messenger of God. You call him a prophet; you say that he is the messenger of God. We concede that one must believe a true prophet of God, that one must give assent to a true messenger of God. But it remains to be seen, as I said, whether he was truly a prophet of God, whether he is truly the messenger of God. Consider, one must direct the mind to this: what prophecy is, what it is said to be.

97. The Apostle Peter, first and highest among the apostles of Christ, whose name we believe you know (since it is known to all the world), whose life (in part), whose death, whose tomb[348] I think you know in the chief city of the world, which is called Rome, said: "Prophecy is come not by the will of man at any time," he said, "but holy men of God spoke inspired by the Holy Spirit."[349] In accord with these words of the Apostle, we can correctly define or describe prophecy: prophecy is the pronouncement on things unknown from either the past or the present or the future,[350] not by human invention but by divine inspiration. But the etymology of the noun refers more to the future than to the past or the present; nonetheless, because, by the same divine power by which the future is revealed, both past and present are sometimes known, the revelation of these two time periods is also called prophecy. From a definition of prophecy we can define a prophet: a prophet is one who discloses to mortal men matters unknown either from the past or the present or the future, taught not by human understanding but inspired by the Spirit of God.

98. Moses revealed a prophecy of a past time when he said that in the beginning God created the heaven and the earth, that he created light, that he made the heaven, and placed the firmament in the middle between the waters above and be-

348. Cf. Eusebius, *Hist. eccles.* 2.25.5–6, p. 177.

349. 2 Pt 1.21.

350. Cf. *Rescriptum Christiani*, cap. 27, lns. 1–2, p. 55: "Propheta est ignota predicens, sive de preteritis sive de futuris."

low;[351] that he produced green plants growing from the ground and bearing seed, and an apple tree bearing fruit; that he made the sun, the moon, and the other stars; the fish of the waters and flying creatures as well as four-footed animals on the earth; that he produced creeping things; and finally that he created man to his image and likeness, and that he gave him a helpmeet like himself.[352] These were prophetic words, not pertaining to a future or present time but to the past; they prove themselves to be prophetic for this reason especially, because, as a great man among us said: "A man spoke about that time when there was as yet no man."[353]

99. That same one is shown to be a prophet from a prophecy concerning the present time, as one reads in one of the five books of Moses, which is called Numbers. After those who rebelled against Moses—Core, Dathan, and Abyron—"with their tents and all their substance"[354] were swallowed up into a great opening in the earth by divine vengeance, and when for the same reason the Jews who were murmuring against him wished to slay him, he [Moses] fled to the tabernacle of the Lord. And when he lay prostrate before the Lord on the ground, he said to Aaron his brother, who was then God's high priest: "Take the censer, and putting fire in it from the altar, put incense upon it, and go quickly to the people to pray for them. For already wrath is gone out from the Lord, and the plague rages."[355] His spirit was illuminated, then, with a prophecy of the present when, lying prostrate in the tabernacle of God, he recognized what would happen among the distant and scattered multitude. And immediately thereafter, the same scripture follows with: "When Aaron had done this, and had run to the midst of the multitude that the burning fire was now destroying, he offered the incense; and standing between the dead and the living, he prayed for the people, and the plague ceased. The number of the slain was 14,700 men, besides those that had perished in

351. Gn 1.7.
352. Cf. Gn 1–2.
353. Gregory the Great, *Homiliae in Hiezechihelem prophetam* 1.1, 14, ed. Marcus Adriaen, CC SL 142 (Turnhout: Brepols, 1971; CD ROM).
354. Nm 16.31–32.
355. Nm 16.46.

the sedition of Core."[356] This is also, as I said, a prophecy concerning the present.

100. Who may easily enumerate his prophetic words concerning a future time? He foreknew and he predicted, as God announced to him, that ten well-known plagues would strike Egypt (not all at the same time but one after the other; not on one day but over several different days)—first when water was turned into blood,[357] then when frogs filled everything,[358] then gnats,[359] then flies[360] of different types, then by a very terrible pestilence come upon the animals,[361] then by a dust covering Egypt,[362] then by hail mixed with fire,[363] then by locusts covering the face of the earth,[364] then by a terrible and palpable darkness,[365] then by the death of the firstborn, when in all the land of Egypt there was not a single dwelling in which someone was not dead.[366] There followed the greatest and the last plague providing an end to all the preceding plagues: that is, the drowning of Pharaoh himself in the sea,[367] and the loss of his entire army with none escaping.

101. He foreknew and he predicted the terrible destruction of the already-mentioned rebels; he foreknew and he predicted that a prophet would be raised up by God in Israel, one who would be driven out from a people that will not listen;[368] he foreknew and he predicted so many other things that are ordered in their places throughout his entire Pentateuch, that is, throughout the five books that I named above. Moses, filled with the prophetic spirit as already mentioned, predicted all these things separately before they happened, and made it clear from the effects of the words themselves that he is a true prophet of God. The same holds for some who came before him, like Enoch,[369] Noah, Jacob, and Joseph, and also for many that came after him, like Samuel, David, Isaiah, Elijah, Elisha, Jeremiah, and many others well known to the world.

356. Nm 16.47–49.
357. Ex 7.19.
358. Ex 8.1–5.
359. Ex 8.16.
360. Ex 8.21.
361. Ex 9.3.
362. Ex 9.9.
363. Ex 9.24.
364. Ex 10.4.
365. Ex 10.21.
366. Ex 11.5.
367. Ex 14.27–28.
368. Dt 18.15–19.
369. Gn 5.21–24.

102. But your Mohammad, O Hagarenes, how will you prove that he was a prophet?[370] Was it because he revealed to mortal men past events that had previously been unknown? Was it because he revealed present events that were hidden from others? Was it because he foreknew and predicted some small and trivial future event? How, I ask, is he said to be a prophet? Was it because he often called himself a prophet in his own Qur'an? If he called himself a prophet, let him reveal something that he spoke in a prophetic fashion, something that he did in a prophetic fashion. And you show me yourselves why you believe he is a prophet, why you say he is a prophet, and on what basis he appears to be a prophet of past events, a prophet of present events, or a prophet of future events. Peruse again your oft-named Qur'an, investigate the entire text of that scripture of yours that you think comes from heaven. Reread and reconsider the first surah (that is, prophecy) of that book, which is entitled: "On the Cow, 285 passages,"[371] and, continuing on to the surah, "On the People of Joachim, 200 passages,"[372] carry on a cursory examination through the others that are distributed throughout the whole corpus of this very wicked work, as far as surah 123,[373] which, placed at the end of the book, brings it to a conclusion. Prove from your already-indicated sublime scripture that he offered up even one single prophetic word.

103. And where was it more fitting for him to reveal himself to be a prophet, if he was a prophet, than in a book conveyed from God through Gabriel and transmitted to him, as he wrote, through a heavenly book?[374] Where better should he have revealed himself to be a prophet than in the book to which you cling above all, to which you have entrusted the totality of your faith, to which you have entrusted your salvation, to which, as

370. For Peter's definition of a prophet and prophecy, and its place in his polemic, see esp. Jean-Pierre Torrell, "La notion de prophétie et la méthode apologétique dans le *Contra Saracenos* de Pierre le Vénérable," *Studia Monastica* 17 (1975): 257–82.

371. Qur'an 2. On Robert of Ketton's numbering of the surahs, which omits the first surah, see *supra*, n. 284.

372. Qur'an 3.

373. I.e., Qur'an 114 (123 in Robert of Ketton's numbering).

374. "Book": *per tomos*. Cf. *supra*, n. 49, p. 40.

I wrote above, you have dedicated your bodies and your souls? What reason can there be for God to name him a prophet, and for a prophet called by God, as he said, to announce no prophecy? Which of the earlier prophets was ever called a prophet by God, yet spoke no prophecy himself?

104. Not our Moses, as I said above, nor Isaiah, almost whose entire book resonates prophetically, which foretells things to come in either the near or distant future.[375] Concerning the near future, such as what he said to the king of the Jews, Hezekiah, who was sick and already despairing of life: "Thus says the Lord," he says; "'I will add fifteen years to your days, and I will deliver you and this city out of the hand of the king of Assyria, and I will protect it.'"[376] Which happened, for once he was returned to good health, afterward he lived for another fifteen years,[377] and he was delivered from the hand of the king of the Assyrians, both he himself and his royal city Jerusalem, when God slew in the period of a single hour of the night 185,000 from the army of the blasphemous king;[378] and he was protected by God, such that none of the kings and none of the peoples prevailed against him for the whole of his life. In this way and also by certain other predictions he made that were soon fulfilled, he is proved to have been a prophet of God.

105. He predicted things in the distant future: such as the destruction of Babylon by the Persians and Medes;[379] such as the release from captivity under the Chaldean king that was accomplished by King Cyrus before seventy years passed,[380] whose name, Cyrus, he foreknew and predicted[381] with the keen eye of prophecy almost three hundred years earlier; such as the complete destruction, after many ages, of the aforementioned Babylon, as is seen today, nor was he silent about the fact that it must be returned to desert and that in the future it would be a dwelling place for monstrous animals and poisonous serpents

---

375. Cf. *Rescriptum Christiani* 27, ln. 7, p. 55: "prophetia de futuris duobus modis habetur: dum ea que futura sunt aut in longum tempus previdentur aut in proximum."

376. Is 38.5–6.   377. Cf. Is 38.9; 39.1.
378. Cf. Is 37.36.   379. Cf. Is 21.1–10.
380. Cf. 2 Chr 36.21–23; *supra*, book 1.65 and n. 291.
381. Is 45.1.

instead of humans.[382] Again, he predicted the birth of Christ
for the distant future, when he said: "Behold, a virgin shall con-
ceive and bear a son";[383] you also affirm that to be true;[384] and
he predicted that baptism saves, which he handed down to the
Jews and pagans when he said (while introducing God as the
speaker): "And I will pour upon you clean water, and you will
be cleansed from all your filthiness, and I will cleanse you from
all your idols";[385] and he predicted the miracles of Christ when
he said: "Then the eyes of the blind will be opened, and the
ears of the deaf unstopped, then will the lame man leap just
like a hart, and the tongue of the dumb will be free";[386] and he
predicted the Passion of Christ, when he said: "He is led like
a sheep to the slaughter <...> and he delivered his soul unto
death, and was reputed with the wicked."[387]

106. And what else should I say about such a great prophet?
He foretold so clearly, having been enlightened by the spirit of
God, whatever is understood to have appeared that concerns
Christ, that concerns the Christian sacraments, that concerns
the rejection of the Jews and the calling of the Gentiles,[388] that
concerns the status of the era appearing after this one and belief in the one to come, as, according to the words of a certain
wise man in the past, "he seems to weave the past more than
foretell the future."[389]

107. So after Isaiah, Jeremiah also, to whom God later said,
"I appointed you a prophet to the nations,"[390] declared with
many proofs that he was truly a prophet of God—not only after his death but even while he still lived. After death,[391] from
the seventy years in number which represents the entire period
that the Jews were held captive in Babylonia,[392] as was already

382. Cf. Is 13.19–21.   383. Is 7.14.
384. Cf. Qur'an 3.47.
385. Ezek 36.25, which Peter seems to attribute to Isaiah, in error.
386. Is 35.5–6.   387. Is 53.7, 12.
388. Cf. Is 2.2–4; 11.10; 45.14; 65.1–7; 66.18.
389. Jerome, *Commentarii in Ezechielem* 6.19, ed. F. Glorie, CC SL 75 (Turn-hout: Brepols, 1964; CD ROM), 250.
390. Jer 1.5.
391. Jeremiah was born ca. 645 BCE, and died after 582 BCE, following the last years of the monarchy in Judah.
392. Cf. Jer 29.10.

mentioned. Isaiah foretold their release from captivity, as I wrote above, but he did not indicate the number of years. Because we read and we know that Jeremiah alone indicated that number, and that it was fulfilled after his death, it is clear that he foretold this with a prophetic Spirit, and as a result that he was a true prophet of God. In this way at one time he also foretold the Babylonian destruction already foretold by Isaiah;[393] in this way at another time he also prophesied about Christ and his mother, "The Lord will do a new thing on the earth; a woman will encompass a man,"[394] and many others of this sort.

108. Before death, these things were fulfilled as he had predicted: when he proclaimed and observed that the king of the Chaldeans would come to Syria; that Jerusalem would be besieged by her own princes; that she would be captured after a few years; and that the Jewish people, who were contemptuous of the divine law, would be taken captive.[395] Even this belonged to those prophetic words, this, I say, which occurred among similar ones (for I shrink from recalling and presenting everything, lest perhaps I seem far too prolix to those reading these things): that when King Zedekiah summoned him to a secret conversation and asked him: "Is there any word from the Lord?" he replied, "There is. You will be handed over to the king of Babylon."[396] And when he had added, "I am afraid of the Jews that deserted to the Chaldeans, lest perhaps I be handed over to their hands and they abuse me,"[397] he replied, having been summoned already for the second time on the same matter, "They will not hand you over. I beg you just to listen to the voice of the Lord in what I say to you, and it will go well with you, and your life will be spared. But if you refuse to do so, this is the word that the Lord has shown me: 'Behold, all the women that are left in the house of the king of Judah will be brought out to the princes of the king of Babylon. <...> And all your wives and your children will be brought out to the

393. Jer 50.1–3; 51.41–43.

394. Jer 31.22. For the christological interpretation, see also *Against the Inveterate Obduracy of the Jews* 2, pp. 86–87.

395. Jer 52.1–16.   396. Jer 37.16.

397. Jer 38.19.

Chaldeans, and you will not escape their hands, but you will be taken by the hand of the king of Babylon and he will burn this city with fire.'"[398] The king was unwilling or he feared to yield to the prophet's advice, and he endured what the prophet had predicted to him.

109. So too (to pass over many people and many things) Ezekiel spoke about this same captivity of Zedekiah; although he was in Chaldea for a long time, he foretold what events were about to occur in Judea and those which were already occurring; although he was absent in the body he was present in the spirit. He said: "Can he break the covenant and yet escape? As I live, says the Lord God, in the place where the king resides who made him king, whose oath he has made void, and whose covenant he broke, the covenant that he held with him, he will die even in the midst of Babylon."[399] And in the following sequence of the prophecy, he said: "And all his fugitives with all his bands will fall by the sword, and the rest will be scattered to every wind, and you will know that I the Lord have spoken."[400] All these things happened as the prophet prophesied: King Zedekiah was captured by his enemies, held captive, and later died in Babylon, and all his fugitives with all the bands fell to the sword, and the rest were scattered to every wind.[401]

110. So too the fact that Daniel foretold throughout the entire text of his book events both in the near and the distant future, proves clearly that he was a prophet of God. I have already excerpted a few things from his lengthy volume: to a certain Chaldean king who was called Nebuchadnezzar, and under whose rule he lived himself,[402] who presented a dream to him and demanded from him an interpretation,[403] he said: "My lord, may the dream be for those that hate you, and its interpretation for your enemies. The tree that you saw, which grew great and strong, so that its top reached to heaven and was visible across the whole earth, whose foliage was beautiful and its fruit abundant, and which provided food for all, under which animals of the field lived, and in whose branches the

398. Jer 38.19–23.   399. Ezek 17.15–16.
400. Ezek 17.21.   401. Cf. 2 Kgs 25.1–12.
402. Cf. Dn 1.6–21.   403. Cf. Dn 2.

birds of the air had nests: it is you, O king; you have grown great and strong, and your greatness has increased and reaches to heaven, and your power to the ends of all the earth. The king saw, moreover, that a watcher and a holy one came down from heaven and said:[404] 'Cut down the tree and destroy it, but leave the stock of its roots in the ground, and let it be bound with a band of iron and bronze, in the grass of the field, and let him be bathed with the dew of heaven, and let his food be with the animals of the field, until seven times pass over him.' This is the interpretation of the judgment of the Most High that has come upon my lord king. They will cast you out of human society, and your dwelling will be with the wild animals, and you will eat grass like oxen, and you will be bathed with the dew of heaven. And seven times will pass over you, until you have learned that the Most High has sovereignty over the kingdom of mortals, and he will give it to whomever he will. As it was commanded to leave the stock of its roots, that is, of the tree, your kingdom will remain yours from the time that you learn that power is of Heaven. Therefore, O king, may my counsel be acceptable to you, and redeem your sins with alms, and your iniquities with works of mercy to the poor; perhaps he will forgive your offenses."[405]

111. Since he foretold all these things, illuminated by the prophetic Spirit, he did not leave it unsaid that all were fulfilled within the space of a single year. "All this," he said, "came upon King Nebuchadnezzar. At the end of twelve months the king was walking in the palace of the king of Babylon, and he said: 'Is not this the great Babylon, which I have built to be the seat of the kingdom, by the strength of my power, and in the glory of my excellence?' While the words were still in the king's mouth, a voice came from heaven: 'O King Nebuchadnezzar, to you it is said: The kingdom has departed from you, and they will cast you out of human society, and your dwelling will be with the animals of the field. You will eat grass like the ox, and seven times will pass over you, until you learn that the Most High has sovereignty over the kingdom of mortals and gives it

404. Dn 4.16–20; Vulg.
405. Dn 4.20–24; Vulg.

to whomever he will.' In the same hour the word was fulfilled upon Nebuchadnezzar: he was driven away from among men and ate grass like an ox, and his body was wet with the dew of heaven, until his hairs grew to be like the feathers of eagles, and his nails like birds' claws."[406]

112. "Now at the end of the days, I, Nebuchadnezzar, lifted up my eyes to heaven, and my sense was restored to me, and I blessed the Most High, and I praised and glorified him that lives forever, because his power is an everlasting power, and his kingdom is from generation to generation, and all the inhabitants of the earth are counted as nothing before him. He does what he will, both to the powers of heaven and to the inhabitants of the earth, and there is none to resist his hand and to say to him: 'Why have you done it?' At that time my sense returned to me, and I came to the honor and glory of my kingdom. And my shape returned to me, and my nobles, and my magistrates sought me out. And I was restored to my kingdom, and greater majesty was added to me. Therefore I, Nebuchadnezzar, now praise and magnify and glorify the King of heaven, because all his works are true and his ways just judgments and he is able to bring low those that walk in pride."[407] When he was consulted, concerning the writing on the wall,[408] by King Balthasar, who was already called the king's successor,[409] he replied in this way, that it was to happen suddenly that night, the same night as when he spoke.[410] And thus as a prophet he foretold many great and wondrous events both in the near and distant future, as I said, and declared himself truly to be a messenger of God, truly to be a prophet of God, by the outcomes of the things that were foretold.

113. Thus too at the time of Rehoboam, the son of Solomon who ruled over two tribes of the Jewish people,[411] there came a

406. Dn 4.25–30; Vulg.
407. Dn 4.31–34; Vulg.
408. Dn 5.25. The writing on the wall was *Mane, Thecel, Phares,* which was said to mean that God had numbered the days of his kingdom, which would be divided among the Medes and the Persians.
409. Cf. Dn 5.1–2.
410. Cf. Dn 5.30, which describes Balthasar's death on that same night.
411. Rehoboam reigned ca. 932–917 BCE over the southern kingdom of

certain man of God, truly a prophet, whose name is not mentioned, to a certain other, idolatrous king that ruled over ten tribes of this same people;[412] when he found him sacrificing on an altar to idols, he said: "O altar, altar, thus says the Lord: 'A son will be born to the house of David, Josiah by name, and he will sacrifice upon you the priests of the high places who now offer incense upon you, and he will burn the human bones upon you.' And he gave a sign on the same day, saying: 'This will be the sign that the Lord has spoken: Behold, the altar will be torn down, and the ashes that are upon it will be poured out.' And when the king heard the speech that the man of God cried out against the altar at Bethel, he stretched out his hand from the altar, saying, 'Seize him!' But his hand that the king stretched out against him withered so that he could not draw it back to himself. The altar also was torn down, and the ashes poured out from the altar, according to the sign that the man of God had expressed before by the word of the Lord. And the king said to the man of God, 'Entreat now the face of the Lord your God and pray for me so that my hand may be restored to me.' So the man of God entreated the face of the Lord God, and the king's hand was restored to him, and became as it was before."[413]

114. See how this great prophet foretold both the distant future and the present moment. He spoke about the distant future when he named the king that would be born at least two hundred years in the future: "A son will be born to the house of David, Josiah by name."[414] About the present moment, when he said: "This will be the sign that the Lord has spoken: Behold, the altar will be torn down, and the ashes that are upon it will be poured out." And as soon as he stopped speaking, the altar was torn down, and its ashes were poured out.

Judah, comprising the two tribes Judah and Benjamin, after Solomon's death. Cf. 1 Kgs 11.43; 12.23; 14.21.

412. I.e., Jeroboam, first king of the northern kingdom of Israel (consisting of the other 10 tribes), who reigned from ca. 931–910 BCE.

413. 1 Kgs 13.2–6.

414. King Josiah ruled over Judah ca. 640–609 BCE; thus, he ruled almost 300 years after Jeroboam.

115. So too Elijah,[415] so too Elisha,[416] so too others beyond number, foretold many things and great things past numbering which it is too troublesome to repeat; the events that were fulfilled without restriction taught that the prophecy was true in all respects, as it was foretold. And in order to mention some prophecies, moreover, from among those men I have named, what Elijah had foretold when he threatened an idolatrous people was fulfilled: "As the Lord lives <...> if there will be (that is, there will not be) either dew or rain [...] except by the word of my mouth."[417] After all dew and rain had been suspended for three years and six months, at length, in response to his prayers, both heaven provided rain and the earth brought forth its fruit. And this too was fulfilled that he foretold in prophetic fashion for a certain king of the Jews:[418] "Because you sent to inquire of Beelzebub the god of Ekron," he said, "as if there were no God in Israel from whom you could ask for a declaration, therefore you will not get down from the bed on which you lie, but you will surely die."[419] And another was fulfilled that not he, but the sons of the prophets said about him (not just once but twice) to Elisha his disciple: "Do you know that today the Lord will take your master away from you?" And twice, since he had been asked twice, he said, "Yes, I know. Keep silent."[420] And the fiery chariot and fiery horses that separated master and disciple showed that that was fulfilled, and Elijah himself was carried up in a whirlwind to heaven.[421]

116. And what about Elisha? He begged Elijah that his spirit would arise twofold in him, but even though that would be very difficult to accomplish, as the same prophet attests, he accomplished what he requested.[422] But when will his prophetic spirit and intellect, just like a careful investigator and the truest

---

415. A ninth-century BCE prophet active in the northern kingdom of Israel.

416. Another ninth-century BCE prophet in the northern kingdom of Israel, viewed as Elijah's successor.

417. 1 Kgs 17.1. Words in parentheses are Peter the Venerable's.

418. King Ahaziah reigned in Israel ca. 853–852 BCE. Because after an injury he sought an oracle from Beelzebub (Baal-Zebub), the god of Ekron, Elijah prophesied that he would die (cf. 2 Kgs 1.2–17).

419. 2 Kgs 1.6.   420. 2 Kgs 2.3, 5.

421. Cf. 2 Kgs 2.11.   422. Cf. 2 Kgs 2.9–10.

discloser of things present as well as future, be revealed? He had promised to cleanse the king of Syria's leprous leader from leprosy, and he had commanded that he immerse himself in the waves of the Jordan so that he could be cured.[423] Although at first he was indignant at the commands, he complied with the advice of the servants, and from the obedience he showed to the prophetic command he was rewarded with the health he desired.[424] His servant, Gehazi, was afflicted with a deadly and familiar greed only too common among wretched mortals; and what God had freely given to the prophet, he insisted upon selling for a great deal of silver and for the value of clothes; but at once, along with the illicitly desired wealth, he was himself suddenly made a leper; he actually took upon himself the leprosy of the prince who had already been cured.[425] This did not escape the notice of the prophet even though he was absent, nor, once the servant returned to him, did he indicate that it had escaped his notice. For he said to him: "Where have you been, Gehazi?" He answered, "Your servant has not gone anywhere at all." And he said: "Was not my heart present when the man turned back from his chariot to meet you? So now have you accepted money and clothing, to buy olive orchards and vineyards, sheep and oxen, and male and female servants? Therefore, Naaman's leprosy will cling to you and to your seed forever." And then Scripture added: "So he left his presence leprous, as white as snow."[426] See that not a lying but a true prophet, not a false but a true messenger of God both foreknew and foretold that one would be cured of leprosy, and so it was done, and he foreknew and foretold that the avaricious servant would be covered with the leprosy from which the man was cured, and so it was done.

117. O Hagarenes, did your prophet, did yours, did he clearly, like so many and like such great prophets, foreknow or foretell even any lowly or trivial thing at all? Let his book be put on

---

423. The Syrian general Naaman was a leper who sought a cure from the prophet Elisha. After having fulfilled Elisha's instruction to bathe seven times in the Jordan River, Naaman was healed (cf. 2 Kgs 5.10–14).

424. 2 Kgs 5.13–14.   425. Cf. 2 Kgs 5.20–24.

426. 2 Kgs 5.25–27.

display, let his Qur'an, which is so sublime and heavenly as to be called scripture—according to you—let it be read over, let it be unveiled word by word with not a single surah left out; let that prophet of so many peoples come forth publicly, and let him show that he foretold anything, prophetically, even something lowly or trivial, as was said, from the book which he left to you.

118. But let us return once more to Elisha: "And the king of Syria," says the Hebrew and Christian Scripture, "warred against Israel, and took counsel with his servants, saying: 'In such and such a place let us lay ambushes.' And the man of God Elisha sent to the king of Israel, saying: 'Take care not to pass through that place, for the Syrians are there in ambush.' And the king of Israel sent to the place which the man of God had told him, and seized it in advance, and guarded himself there not once nor twice, and the heart of the king of Syria was troubled on account of this. And calling together his servants, he said: 'Why do you not tell me who it is that betrays me to the king of Israel?' And one of his servants said: 'No one, my lord O king, but Elisha the prophet who is in Israel tells the king of Israel all the words that you have spoken in your privy chamber.'"[427] Do you hear? The prophet, who was filled with a prophetic spirit, foreknew and told the king of Israel in advance of the ambushes of the Syrians, and the enemy's battle array was unable to escape that invisible eye in any place by any stratagem. The subtle and perspicacious insight of the prophet penetrated to remote lands, to deep valleys, to hidden woodlands; the prophetic hearing was present at secret counsels and could not be repulsed by fortress walls or by barred gates, and it was not absent from the royal bedchambers; and with messengers always passing between them, the prophet revealed to his king everything that his far distant adversaries plotted so shrewdly and with such hostility.

119. Why then did a prophet so renowned, according to you, not offer advice with even some small spark of prophecy to himself, not to mention to anyone else, during his frequent expeditions against enemies? Why, since he often fled from battles as the vanquished, did he not foresee that he would be overcome by enemies? Why, on a certain battlefield of his on which

427. 2 Kgs 6.8–12.

he himself was present, did he not foresee and guard against a tooth from among his lower teeth being knocked out,[428] a lip from being cut, the wounds that the enemies would inflict upon his forehead and his face? But why am I waiting either for you, O Ishmaelites, or for him to produce from the already mentioned Qur'an (that is, your law), anything that your prophet foretold in a prophetic manner, not to mention anything from among things foretold that actually occurred as he foretold them? Indeed, what could arise among the things he foretold when it is clear that he foretold nothing at all?

120. But perhaps one of you will object and place before us another text just as important that contains his genealogy and some of his deeds and battles.[429] There one reads that he foretold that twelve men from his own race or family, which is called Ḳuraysh,[430] would rule after he had died, succeeding one another, one after the other; it is written that he named the first three of them: Euobacaras, Aonar, and Odmen.[431] But it is not so; diabolical deception will be unable to benefit his faction in this way, nor will Satan prevail to cast darkness over splendor, to cast blackness over the angel of light.

121. And who, O Hagarenes (whom I name as often as the matter taken up compels me to do), in order to prove that the one with whom we are concerned was not a prophet of God, who, I say, can be found better suited to prove that for us than the very one you say is a prophet of God? Clearly, if he himself denied that he is a prophet, will you say that he is a prophet, in opposition to him? How so? Listen, and if any rational intellect

428. Cf. Petrus Alfonsi, *Dialogue* 5, p. 155; cf. *Rescriptum Christiani*, cap. 23, lns. 2–5, p. 50.

429. As Glei points out (p. 292, n. 496), this is not a reference to the *Liber generationis Mahumet*, translated by Herman of Dalmatia, but rather to the *Fabulae Saracenorum*, translated by Robert of Ketton.

430. "Ḳuraysh": the name of the Meccan clan or tribe to which Mohammad belonged. See W. Montgomery Watt, "Ḳuraysh," in the *Encyclopedia of Islam*. University of Tennessee at Chattanooga. 25 February 2015. http://reference works.brillonline.com/entries/encyclopaedia-of-islam-2/k-urays-h-SIM_4533.

431. I.e., Abū-Bakr (r. 632–634 CE), ʿUmar (r. 634–644 CE), and ʿUthmān (r. 644–656 CE), the first three caliphs—according to the Sunni reckoning—after the death of Mohammad.

remains in you, pay attention.[432] And lest I hold you too much in suspense by drawing this out too long, listen to what he says in your Qur'an, a scripture you think it very wicked for anyone to contradict: "Whatever you find written about me," he says, "compare with the Qur'an, and if it is not in agreement with it, then know that I am not responsible for that text, and it is not mine."[433] Therefore, compare the aforementioned text with the Qur'an, and see whether it agrees with it or whether it disagrees with it.

122. It says, as was already mentioned, that he foretold that twelve men from his stock or race, which was called Ḳuraysh, would rule one after another over his dominion after him; he named the first three of them, as was set forth. Indeed, someone other than he introduced this in that text. Whereas, on the other hand, he himself, not someone else, [said]: "Whatever you find written about me, compare with the Qur'an, and if it is not in agreement with it, then know that I am not responsible for that text, and it is not mine." It does not agree with the Qur'an,[434] however, seeing that the entire text of that book does not have any statement that he made in a prophetic fashion, and it records that he did not foretell anything pertaining to the future. Therefore nothing (as both ecclesiastical and Roman—rather, divine as well as human—legal processes attest, and as reason herself teaches), nothing ought to be believed more than what one has confessed oneself. Therefore, such writings, wherever they appear, must be put aside, and they should be made subject to a book that, according to you, has such great dignity because, with Mohammad as your witness, if there is any scripture (to use his words) that does not agree with his Qur'an, he is not responsible for it, and it is not his.

123. Do not these suffice, O men, in order to prove that he is not a prophet? But let others follow these, and let them declare

432. Whereas here Peter merely questions whether his Muslim opponents retain a rational understanding, elsewhere he despaired that Jews had lost all rationality. Cf. *Against the Inveterate Obduracy of the Jews* 5, p. 211.

433. In fact, this passage is not in the Qur'an; Peter's error can be traced to the *Rescriptum Christiani*, cap. 31, lns. 53–54, p. 60, from which he takes this verbatim.

434. I.e., the prophecy Peter has cited above.

that he is a faithless, rather a most depraved, man, who is far removed from all prophetic grace, as he himself confesses. For, while introducing God speaking to him as if in a poetic fiction, the wicked and mendacious man says this in the Qur'an: "You will never come to them with God's manifest miracles, seeing that they reject them as hateful and pernicious, and they have contradicted the truth coming to them."[435] And again: "If we did not know that they will not believe you, \<just as they did not believe others\>, we would give you signs and wonders."[436] What shall I say? Who can be sufficiently surprised, who can utter, who can find words appropriate to mock the man's great stupidity, or rather insanity?

124. And, in order to turn to him whom the words concern: Is this not the entire reason, O Mohammad, why you were sent by God to come to men without miracles, because they would reject them as hateful and pernicious, and would contradict the truth coming to them? Is this not the reason, I say, that you were not given signs and wonders—because God foreknew that they would not believe you, just as they did not believe others? If, as you say, God told this to you, then God's foreknowledge is indubitably false, it is plainly false. For how, in accord with what you propose, is God's foreknowledge not false, if he foreknew that even if you were sent with signs and wonders, humans would not believe you, when without miracles, signs, and wonders many people believed your very foolish fables, gave assent to your most nefarious teaching, and submitted to your infernal doctrine without hesitation? And for whom does your remark, clearly for whom does it not appear weak, fragile, and senseless?

125. Choose, then, surely choose which of the two you prefer. Either say that God has erred in his foreknowledge, say that he lied when he said that men would not believe you even with signs and wonders, since the Arabs, the Persians, the Syrians, the Egyptians, and the greater part of the Africans believed even without miracles; or if you are afraid to say that God has

435. Cf. Qur'an 6.4–5.

436. Peter does not cite Robert of Ketton's translation of the Qur'an here, but rather Ps. Al-Kindi's *Rescriptum Christiani*, cap. 28, lns. 21–22, p. 57; cap. 30, lns. 2–3, p. 57. Cf. Qur'an 17.59.

erred, that God lied, remove the falsehoods, remove the blasphemies from your book, or rather, what will be saner advice,
condemn your entire Qur'an, which is sprinkled throughout
with errors, lies, and blasphemies.

126. But what is the meaning of what I presented earlier, when
you introduce God saying to you: "If we did not know that they
will not believe you," and then you add, "just as they did not believe others"? Who are the others that men did not believe? Was
it perhaps Moses? Or was it perhaps Christ himself? No others
present themselves, clearly no others present themselves about
whom I could conclude that you thought this, about whom I
could conclude that you said this. Indeed these are the highest
and the sole lawgivers in the world—Moses for the Jews, and
Christ for all nations. Moses came with signs and wonders, and
Christ came with even more signs and wonders. Once they saw
the signs and wonders, the Jewish people believed Moses; and
the world believed Christ and his apostles once it saw the great
and countless miracles. Of whom, then, did you say "just as they
did not believe others"? For men were inspired by God to believe
those who performed miracles, whereas men who were deceived
by you believed you without signs when you spoke empty and
false things. Your statement, then, is false in which you imagine
that God told you that men had not believed them, and that they
would not believe you.

127. But I return to what I proposed to prove with your own
testimony, that you are not a prophet. For when you assert
that God did not give you signs, surely you deny that you are a
prophet. What is more remarkable than prophecy, what sign is
greater than prophecy? What is more correctly called a sign, a
wonder, a miracle, than either to report the past so far as it is
unknown to men, or to disclose the present, or to foretell the
future? Since, then, prophecy is among the clearest signs given
by God, when you declare that God did not give you signs, certainly you deny that you are a prophet. Either admit that God
gave you signs, then, and remain a prophet, or if he did not
give you signs, cease to be a prophet. To be sure, a compelling
argument presses you on every side, so if, as was just said, you
have denied that signs were given to you, you disavow equally

that you are a prophet. If you said they were given to you, then necessarily you accuse God of a lie, and it is necessary for you to correct what you wrote falsely.

128. And because your monstrous words, words never heard before, force me almost to be struck with amazement, who, O wretch, from the community of all the prophets has said that he is a prophet in the way that you do, who has wanted to be thought to be a prophet in the way that you do? As true and humble servants of God, they shied away from the glory of that great name, and although truly they were prophets of God, they refused to call themselves prophets so far as they could while preserving the truth. For that reason, to those who said to the one among them who was called Amos, "Do not prophesy in Bethel, and do not preach at the house of an idol," he replied, "I am no prophet, nor a prophet's son, but I am a herdsman, and a dresser of sycamore trees."[437] And John, whom your prophet refused to call "the Baptist," but instead called him the son of Zachariah and extolled both him and his parents in his Qur'an with much praise, replied, "I am not," to the invidious priests and Levites of the Jews asking him, "Are you a prophet?"[438] They were truly prophets of God, nonetheless, but they said they were not prophets in another sense that does not concern you so long as you remain infidels, to preserve the expression of their truth. Nevertheless, in their books they left behind prophetic signs of which there can be no doubt, and what they foretold either they showed was fulfilled in their own time, or they declared that it would be fulfilled, as became clear to their descendants later.

129. But yours (and I cannot be surprised by this too often), yours calls himself a prophet, and he introduces God to his texts calling him a prophet. And although he claims, asserts, and repeats almost *ad nauseam* that he is God's prophet, he says nothing about the future, he says nothing prophetic, he does not disclose anything that has been foretold or fulfilled by him, but neither does he foretell what will be fulfilled. I remain silent over the pleasures he promises in paradise or the fanta-

---

437. A conflation of Am 7.13, 16.
438. Jn 1.21.

sies in hell,[439] by which he cannot appear as a prophet before
they are confirmed as fulfilled by those who were in paradise
or hell. It was not difficult for him, nor would it be difficult for
me to call myself a prophet, if I wished; nor would it be difficult
to write that and to introduce God to a text to call me a prophet; nor would it be difficult to proclaim to men that I am God's
prophet. I could make up whatever I want about things that will
come to pass or not come to pass after the end of the world or
after the destruction of things, and I could not be proved to be
a liar in this lifetime when foretelling things which may or may
not come to pass after this lifetime.

130. Let him be silent concerning the fragile, senseless, and
weak diabolical fiction, as I said above, because one cannot be
believed to be a prophet by predicting things that will come
to pass after the end of this world, unless he proves himself to
be a prophet in and from things that exist before the end of
the world. If he wants to be thought a prophet, let him take
the proofs of his prophecy not from among the dead but from
among the living, not from what he promises will be fulfilled
after death, but from what he shows have been fulfilled before
death. A Christian believes in his prophets in this way and by
just such manifest proof: not just because they called themselves prophets, but because they proved that they are prophets, without a trace of doubt, by manifest signs, clear miracles,
and from the outcomes of the things they foretold. Therefore,
O Mohammad, either show that you are a prophet by such indi-
cations, or, if you cannot do this, cease—you who are damned
and worthy to be damned—to call yourself a prophet. And although what I have presented could suffice to demonstrate that
you are far removed from prophetic grace, nonetheless I will
embark as if on another beginning to show the readers that you
are not a prophet.

131. Of the prophets, some either were or were said to be

___

439. According to the *Rescriptum Christiani* (cap. 28, lns. 18ff., p. 56), Mohammad's apparent ignorance of the real nature of paradise should be enough
to show that, unlike a true prophet, he was also ignorant of the past and the
future. On the pleasures of paradise and the torments of hell, see *supra, Summary* 9.

good, and others bad. Among the good prophets, some foretold universal events, and others foretold particular ones, and still others foretold what were at the same time universal and particular. Of the bad prophets, some were deceivers, and others truthful. In addition to these, there are those that are not called prophets but, in common terminology, are said to be divines, such as augurs, soothsayers, diviners, magicians, and fortune-tellers. Therefore, let the pen pursue the differences among the individual prophets, according to the order in which they were proposed. The good prophets are those whose life is praiseworthy, whose prophecy or prediction is true. Among their number are those I wrote down above: Moses, Isaiah, Jeremiah, Ezekiel, Daniel, and many others. Among them also is Christ himself, who, although he is God and the Lord of all the prophets, is called a prophet nevertheless because he made many prophecies. The Gospel which you yourselves confess was given to him attests to this, O Saracens, just as one reads there what the multitudes said about him: "A great prophet is risen up among us,"[440] and just as he said about himself: "It cannot be that a prophet perish outside of Jerusalem."[441] As one as truthful in life as in his prophecy, as was fitting for one bearing testimony in the same Gospel to the Jews disputing with him, he said: "Which of you convicts me of sin?"[442] Indeed, none of them was able to convict him of sin who was without sin. So much for his life; but what about prophecy? "If I speak the truth to you, why do you not believe me?"[443] For Truth could reveal nothing but what was true. Therefore, he is himself a good prophet with the other good prophets, and he is even superior to them.

132. But who are the bad prophets? The ones that led a reprobate life, whose prophecy or prediction was false. Such were those at the time of Elijah, those about whom one reads in the book of the kings of Israel and Judah, the 450 prophets of Baal, and also the 400 prophets of the groves.[444] The ones whom the same Elijah, after having offered a sacrifice to God and after it was consumed by heavenly fire, had caused to be dragged by

440. Lk 7.16.
442. Jn 8.46.
444. Cf. 1 Kgs 18.19.

441. Lk 13.33.
443. Ibid.

the people, bound at his command, to the Wadi Kishon; and, glowing with the fervor of divine zeal, he slew them as the worst idolaters.[445]

133. Among the good prophets who foretold universal events (that is, foretold things that pertain to all people), as I mentioned, are those that I named in part above, along with almost all the others that are called good prophets, whose life is praiseworthy, as I mentioned above, and whose prediction is truthful. What they foretold about Christ actually pertains to all, [Christ] who, as in fact a certain great, just man said in the Gospel, "is the one set for the fall and for the resurrection of many."[446] His life, his prophecy, his miracles, his death, his resurrection, his descent from heaven and his return to it, brought life for those that believe and death for those that do not believe. Finally, at the end of the age, at his universal and Last Judgment, he will distribute everlasting thrones to the entire mass of mortals gathered by divine power before his tremendous majesty, either delivering each and every one to perpetual fire or restoring him to everlasting life with him, as determined by his individual merits. In this way too, all the rest that one reads in the prophetic words or books that pertain to everyone and not just to certain individuals—whether taken in a good or bad sense—concerns those I call universal prophets.

134. I call those particular prophets who have not foretold what pertains to all, but who predicted by a prophetic Spirit what pertains to certain peoples, or what pertains to certain individuals who are explicitly named. Among them is Jonah,[447] who was sent by God only to the pagan people of Nineveh;[448] although his mission presaged the calling of all the nations, the fact that he was plunged beneath the waves,[449] eaten by a fish,[450] and that he remained unharmed in its belly, that he remained safe while escaping from the whale and from the sea, prophesied with action and not with words that the salvific death of

---

445. 1 Kgs 18.40.
446. Lk 2.34. The "just man" is Simeon, who recognized the child Jesus in the Temple as the Messiah.
447. Cf. Qur'an 37.138–48; 21.87.   448. Cf. Jon 1.2.
449. Cf. Jon 1.15.   450. Cf. Jon 1.17.

Christ and his resurrection from death must be set above all miracles. Among them, too, is Samuel,[451] who did not predict universal events but those that pertained specifically to certain individuals: such as to the priest Eli those events that would come to pass for the descendants of his house,[452] such as to Saul, the first king of the Hebrews, first concerning the asses of his father Kish that were lost and then found,[453] and afterwards of the transfer of his kingdom to a relative and a rival,[454] and about certain other matters, in cases pertaining either to the Jewish people alone or to certain other persons. Among them too is a prophet of the same era, who is called a man of God[455] by his sacred scripture and is not explicitly named by a proper name, and, after he had foretold many things that would happen to the already-mentioned Eli, he added even this: "And this," he said, "will be a sign to you, that will befall your two sons, Hophni and Phinehas: in one day both will die."[456] Which also happened.

135. Among them, too, is one whom the same text calls a prophet, while remaining silent concerning his name, and whom it introduces as speaking to a certain king of Israel[457] about a king of Syria who pursued victory: "Go, and strengthen yourself and know and see what you should do. For the next year the king of Syria will come up against you."[458] And again another prophet without a name said to the same king: "Thus says the Lord: Because the Syrians have said, 'The Lord is God of the hills, but is not God of the valleys,' I will deliver all this great multitude into your hand, and you will know that I am the Lord."[459] This was fulfilled at once on the seventh day, and just as had been predicted. For once the battle against the Syrians was begun, the Hebrews "struck 100,000 of their foot soldiers in one day. And those who remained fled to the city, and a wall fell upon the 25,000 men that were left."[460] These things that the already-mentioned proph-

---

451. Samuel "judged Israel all the days of his life." Cf. 1 Sm 7.15.
452. Cf. 1 Sm 3.1–18.   453. Cf. 1 Sm 9.1–20.
454. I.e., David. Cf. 1 Sm 15.28.   455. Cf. 1 Sm 2.27.
456. 1 Sm 2.34.
457. Namely, Ahab (r. 875–854 BCE).
458. 1 Kgs 20.22.   459. 1 Kgs 20.28.
460. Cf. 1 Kgs 20.29–30.

ets foretold were not universal events, but were things shown in advance that concerned either particular races, or certain individuals and their own fortunate outcomes. Among them is also the great Elijah; among them is Elisha, who does not appear to be inferior to him with respect to miracles. One of them, as I said above, threatened King Ahaziah with death and, as it had been predicted, he died; the other foretold frequent triumphs for another king, who is called Joash,[461] over the king of Syria,[462] which also happened, and certain other, similar things that they predicted also were fulfilled, as had been said.

136. Therefore, these are the ones I have presented—and there are many others of their number about whom I have remained silent—that I call particular prophets, because by the prophetic Spirit they foretold what concerns not everyone but certain individuals. But one must distinguish between the latter and the former, and one must observe cautiously and carefully that universal prophets (that is, those that foretell what pertains to everyone) could not have existed from the time of Christ to now nor can they exist from then until the end of the world.[463] For whatever concerns the common condition or fault of mortal man or of the world itself, whatever concerns true or false religion, whatever concerns the duties and universal ends of the good or the evil, has all been foretold already by those mentioned who are called universal prophets; and they have handed it down in texts for instruction and as a historical account for those coming after them. What has already been fulfilled in large part is preserved because it must be fulfilled entirely by the end of the time.

137. Therefore, once the prophets had ceased and with John —whom we call the Baptist and you call the son of Zachariah (not that we deny that he is his son)—once they had entirely disappeared, I say, from among the Jewish people, who had been the only caretaker of the divine Law until Christ, that entire type of prophecy that pertained to the universal condition ceased because it was no longer necessary once it had been fully present-

---

461. Elisha prophesied to Joash, who was king of Israel from 799–784 BCE.
462. 2 Kgs 13.14–19.
463. I.e., the age of universal prophecy has come to an end.

ed to everyone it concerned. Therefore your Mohammad was not, as you say, the "seal of the prophets," that is, the last among the prophets, but rather John the Baptist,[464] about whom Christ said in the Gospel which, according to you, was given to him: "the Law and the prophets until John."[465] Clearly these were the prophets who would foretell what pertains to all, not those who would prophesy things concerning specific persons.

138. After John the Baptist they often prophesied various events for individual persons or times with a prophetic spirit, and the Church of Christ has often possessed and experienced it in different times and different parts of the world, such as in the Apostle Paul, who foretold many things about the future that were fulfilled or are yet to be fulfilled. Fulfilled, as in you and in the Jews, when he said: "For there will be a time when they will not endure sound doctrine," and, in the same verse, "and will indeed turn away their hearing from the truth, but will be turned to fables."[466] Now, it is obvious to the world—all except to you and to them—that both you and they (as will be proved in its own place) have turned your hearing away from the truth and have turned it to fables: you have turned away from Christian truth to the fables of Mohammad; the Jews have turned away to the fables of the Talmud. He foretold things yet to be fulfilled when he wrote that "the man of sin, the son of perdition who opposes and is exalted above all that is called God, or that is worshiped,"[467] would be revealed, and that the one we call Antichrist would sit in the temple of God.

139. And so too there were others among the apostles, others among their disciples, who both were called prophets and who showed that they are prophets from the outcomes of what were foretold. Among such as these there was also one who was called Agabus, who, binding his own feet with Paul's belt when Paul was going to Jerusalem, said: "The man whose belt this is,

---

464. According to the *Rescriptum Christiani* (cap. 45, lns. 20–21, p. 63), Jesus claimed that John the Baptist would be the last of the all the prophets: "cum dicatur michi a Domino meo Ihesu Christo quod in Iohanne Babtista finis sit omnium prophetarum."

465. Lk 16.16; Mt 11.13.   466. 2 Tm 4.3–4.

467. 2 Thes 2.3–4.

the Jews shall bind in this manner in Jerusalem."[468] After a brief period of time had passed, when he [Paul] came to that city, he was seized by the Jews, bound by a tribune,[469] scourged by the Romans, which revealed that he was a prophet who speaks the truth. And who will reveal the number of prophets of this sort who, coming after Christ, gleamed brightly among the Christians both by their life and by their prophecy?

140. If one should speak to the faithful and those believing in Christ, he would reveal an enormous field. For when could such a large number of prophets be treated—by me or by anyone at all—that foretell not universal events, as I already presented, but individual ones, as I said, from Christ up until our own era? If I should want to disclose one after the other the names or the number of those who were renowned in terms of a prophetic grace of this sort, drawn together according to events that were true, you would refuse, I think, to give credence to the words. For how in fact could you believe God's prophets when you still do not believe God himself? But I know this to be your understanding, I know this to be your creed: that you believe the true God and believe in the true God. But the following argument will make clear whether this is true, vanquishing you through the spirit of God.

141. Meanwhile, let a discourse based on reason pursue the matter proposed. For that discourse and that argument was one that concerned the mode of universal prophecy according to the distinction already presented; the one that follows after that one was concerned with the mode of individual or personal prophecy according to the division proposed, for that mode of prophecy is clearly, I say, one by which individual events are foretold, as I said, and not one by which universal ones are prophesied. Certainly that mode of universal prophecy arose from almost the very creation of the first man, so to speak, but it was brought to an end, as I said, with John. Whereas the particular or personal mode was given to many prophets both before and after John, and will perhaps still be given to many more. After having described this double division of prophetic

468. Acts 21.11.
469. Cf. Acts 21.33.

grace, let the discourse return to those who were universal and particular prophets at one and the same time, and let it indicate who they are from the texts.

142. From among their number once more I bring forth Isaiah, who, just as he was shown to have foretold universal events, in the same way it has to be proved as well that he foretold individual events pertaining to certain nations, or personal events pertaining to certain persons. He prophesied to specific nations, such as what he prophesied against Babylonia,[470] against Moab,[471] against Damascus,[472] against Egypt,[473] against the Edomites,[474] against Arabia,[475] against Tyre,[476] as a reading of his book indicates. He prophesied to certain individuals, such as what he prophesied concerning the king of the Assyrians, Sennacherib,[477] or the king of the Judeans, Hezekiah,[478] and concerning certain others, just as one reads there in scattered places.

143. Jeremiah, written about above, follows after him; in the same way, just as he foretold many things that pertain to everyone, so too he did not remain silent concerning many individual or personal ones. Filled with a prophetic spirit, he prophesied individual ones that concerned certain nations, such as those he prophesied against the Philistines,[479] such as those against Moab,[480] such as those against the sons of Ammon,[481] such as those against the kingdoms of Hazor,[482] such as those against Elam,[483] such as those against Babylonia.[484] He prophesied personal ones, such as when he foretold that King Zedekiah would be seized and held captive by the Chaldeans,[485] and just as when he threatened a certain false prophet, Hananiah: "The Lord has not sent you," he said, "and you made this people trust in a lie. Therefore, thus says the Lord: 'Behold, I am going to send you off the face of the earth. Within this year you will be dead. You

---

470. Cf. Is 13.19.
471. Cf. Is 25.10; Is 15.1; 16.2–7.
472. Cf. Is 17.1.
473. Cf. Is 19.1–24.
474. Cf. Is 11.14.
475. Cf. Is 21.13.
476. Cf. Is 23.13.
477. Cf. *Rescriptum Christiani*, 27, lns. 9–10, p. 55.
478. Cf. Is 37.21.
479. Cf. Jer 47.1–7.
480. Cf. Jer 48.1–47.
481. Cf. Jer 9.25–26; 25.20–21.
482. Cf. Jer 49.28, 30, 33.
483. Cf. Jer 25.25.
484. Cf. Jer 50.1–51.64.
485. Cf. Jer 37.18.

have spoken rebellion against the Lord.'"[486] And so too when he said to two others: "Thus says the Lord of hosts, the God of Israel, to Ahab the son of Kolaiah, and to Zedekiah the son of Maaseiah, who prophesy to you in my name falsely: 'Behold I will deliver them up into the hands of Nebuchadrezzer the king of Babylon, and he shall kill them before your eyes.'"[487]

144. Daniel, too, is a prophet of universal and personal prophecies at the same time, who (as I set forth much earlier), filled with each charisma, often foretold both what pertains to everyone and what pertains only to individuals. To everyone, as when he foretold what the dream of the king of Chaldea presaged, which the same king had been made to forget.[488] For he had seen a statue whose head was gold, whose breast and arms were silver, whose stomach and thighs were bronze, whose legs were iron, whose feet were part iron and part clay;[489] these presaged that the greatest kingdoms of the earth would follow after him, one after another, and would have different courses and outcomes. These would extend for such a great length of time, succeeding one another, until, struck by a rock cut out from a mountain without hands,[490] they, too, will come to an end as the world comes to collapse. Again, there is what he prophesied to everyone, as the last part of his prophecy indicates, which, if any one of you reads it, he will find it there. There truly are prophecies to certain individuals, such as those he foretold to king Nebuchadnezzar and those he foretold to king Balthasar.[491] Daniel is like the two mentioned above, then: not only a prophet of the universal or only of what concerns a person, but he is at one and the same time a prophet of the universal and of the personal.

145. But perhaps one of you will be surprised because I propose the Hebrew prophets to you just as if you were Jews; but let him hear what follows so that he will cease to be surprised:

486. Jer 28.15–16.

487. Jer 29.21.

488. The king had not forgotten his dream, but Daniel was indeed the one who was able to interpret its meaning for the king. See Dn 2.

489. Dn 2.32–33.   490. Cf. Dn 2.45.

491. Cf. Dn 5.1–2.

the aforementioned prophets are indeed Hebrews, but even though they are Hebrew prophets they are also yours. But you may say, "How ours? For what does an Arab have to do with a Hebrew? What does an Ishmaelite have to do with a Jew?" Clearly, quite a lot: first, that Ishmael and Isaac were brothers, although the one was born from the maidservant Hagar, and the other from the freewoman, Sara.[492] Second, in addition to the fact that the line of consanguinity and language is almost shared both in terms of the forms of the letters and in speech, you have also set yourselves apart by the singular and ancient sign of circumcision just as it was derived from the father of both peoples, Abraham, either from the native practices of all nations or from laws handed down by them. Third, that you ought to accept that the Hebrew and Christian prophets with whom we are concerned are inspired by the divine spirit and replete with prophetic grace, as was shown by clear and invincible reasons in the previous book. If you have given careful attention to what went before, it is superfluous to reconsider them completely and to treat them in writing anew.

146. But if, perchance, either you have not listened attentively, like ones who are contemptuous of what concern us at present, or if you have consigned those things read or heard to a lethargic forgetfulness with the general indolence that besets almost all but those who are scholarly, I briefly repeat what was said in various places above, and, if you have sufficient concern for your salvation, you will be able to recall them. From all this you have to believe that the Jewish and Christian prophets, about whom a long discussion has taken place, are also yours, and that you should give credence to them as to your own, if, that is, your obstinacy (which has been struggling against the obvious truth of what I wrote above) is removed and, once every cloudy mist has been put to flight, irrefutable reason will make it clear. And how will it make clear what I say? Rather, it already has made it clear, and were I not speaking to unbelievers and to those who are entirely estranged from God, I would shrink from reiterating things that have been said so often. But

492. Cf. Gal 4.22.

let the pen bear all patiently, and let it humor heretics or heathen people with the salvific constancy of faith and truth.

147. What do you want from me, Ishmaelite, how should I
prove that my prophets are yours, how should I fight against you
with their words, which have been admitted as if by you? Clearly
I have, I have many times. Which? Listen! Why do you accept
anything taken from my books, which are much older than
yours, when I am a Christian and you are, as I said, a heretic or
a heathen? What belongs to me and what belongs to you? I take
nothing from your books; why do you steal something from my
books? Are you jealous of mine? Do you want to become, perchance, a Christian? And O, would that were so, clearly would
that it were so, would that you would turn to the true God after having abandoned a foolish, lethal error that is lacking all
reason, that is devoid of all truth, that is fleeting because of its
worthless phantasms and unheard of foolishness; would that
you would come to know "Christ as the power and wisdom of
God,"[493] and once freed from the snares of the nefarious and
exceedingly dishonorable man, you could sing with David, king
and prophet, to whom, that wicked one wrote, God gave the
Psalms: "The snare is broken, and we are delivered."[494]

148. If you overlook this, leave mine to me and guard your
own for yourself. I will add nothing from your Qur'an to my
books, so you should not mix anything from my Gospel with
your texts. Leave my Moses alone, put aside my prophets, do
not fashion a monstrous mixture and one that should not be
tolerated by any rational soul, such that either you add the
words of a heavenly prophecy to infernal writings, or you will
befoul them with a mixture of nefarious fables and one that
on all sides is surrounded by a heap of lies. And for what reason, rather by what insanity, have you mixed something from
the false Hebrew or Christian books (as you believe and assert
them to be) into your Qur'an, which you esteem as sent from
heaven? For what purpose have you added Jewish or Christian
lies, as you consider them to be, to your true scripture? For if
our books lie, excerpts taken from them are also false. But if

493. 1 Cor 1.24.
494. Ps 123 (124).7.

the excerpts are false, then also the texts to which they have been added are false. But it is true that they have been added to your Qur'an. Therefore, it is certain that your own Qur'an is false on account of the falsehood mixed into it, false not only in part but entirely false. To be sure, even if perhaps there are some truths in it, they are corrupted by an admixture of falsehoods and they are not now worthy of belief.

149. Do not the judgments of all peoples agree on this? Everywhere across the globe that law thrives![495] If I have been found to be a false witness in one word, I will not be heard in the true ones, nor will I deserve trust in the true ones. On the basis of this just rationale, I reject your Qur'an; on the basis of this judgment of fairness I condemn not just some of its parts, but I condemn your entire Qur'an completely. Choose, then, one of the two alternatives I provided for you above: either cast aside the Qur'an owing to the falsehoods that have been taken from books that you say are false, and that have been added to your book, or, if you are unwilling to do this, then confess that the Hebrew and Christian books from which they have been taken are true.

150. And because no other pathway appears by which you could otherwise avoid this impasse, I believe you would rather choose to admit that our books are truthful, lest all that you have previously safeguarded by paternal law perish at one and the same time with the very author of this law. If you choose that course, you will trust in the already oft-named books, that is, the Hebrew and Christian ones, as you do in your own scriptures. For these reasons I placed the Hebrew prophets before you, and I will place Christ and Christ's disciples before a Hebrew just as if before a Christian. Therefore, since I intend to prove something, I offer examples (as reason instructs) from what has been admitted, just as from those with which you already agree.

151. And seeing that the already mentioned books, O Hagarenes, are made common for us and for you, let this discourse return to the beginning, and let it indicate why it has brought

495. I.e., if a part is false, then the whole is false.

into the open so many examples on behalf of prophets. It was proved thoroughly from the above that Mohammad, your law-giver, was not a prophet or messenger of God, but still it must be proved according to the divisions set forth because it will provide more evidence for the readers. For, as I wrote above, some of the prophets were or were said to be good, and some bad. Among the good, some foretold universal events, others particular ones; some of the same prophets foretold universal events and particular or personal ones at one and the same time. I have introduced some by name, and I have described which grace from the threefold division of prophetic grace has come down to each, one by one. For this reason, as every one of you names Mohammad a prophet, asserts that he is a prophet, you should show that he was a prophet and you should prove— from an authority or by reason—either that he belongs among the universal prophets by foretelling something universal, or among the particular ones by foretelling something particular, or among the personal ones by foretelling something personal.

152. But why should I take up the useless effort? Why should I struggle in vain? I have invited and I do invite, I have challenged and I do challenge you to explain with what power, with what reason, with what truthful or lying fiction you say that this man, you believe that this man, O you Arab, is a prophet. Has he fore-told anything pertaining to the universal salvation of the world, whereby he could be called a prophet of what is universal, in accord with the division already set forth? Has he foretold any-thing whereby he could be called a prophet, foretelling some-thing particular pertaining to certain individuals and not to everyone? Has he foretold anything whereby he could be proven a prophet, prophesying some true things before they occur, not to certain people as a group but to certain individuals person-ally? But why, soldiering on very stubbornly in your error and in opposition to your own salvation, why do you run from what pertains to salvation and why do you pursue what is harmful? Tell me, tell me now, if you have anything to say! In accord with some part of the aforementioned divisions, show that your Mo-hammad is either a universal prophet, or a particular prophet, or both at the same time, or that he prophesied what pertains to

a person, that is, not to all or to many, but to some individuals.

153. But how will you do that? Why do you hold me in suspense? Tell me if you have something to justify it. Indeed, these are God's words, but both after him and along with him they are also mine. If you can produce from your Qur'an, mentioned so many times as to become tedious, a great or even a trivial or modest thing that was said or written by a prophetic spirit, then produce it, make it known! Do you find anything, as was already said above, in that entire book of yours—which is sacred to you, but according to us ought to be cursed—anything said prophetically by him, your prophet, about things past, or things present, or things future? For, as already set forth, in this threefold division consists the sum total of prophetic grace. For whatever events are foretold prophetically are either, as was said, about the past, or the present, or the future, whether they are those that are said about universal events, particular or personal ones, or whether they are foretold for the present moment, or the near or distant future. Therefore, in which division of prophetic grace, so subtly and carefully investigated, will you, O Arab, be able to find your prophet, against whom I take aim?

154. But I refuse to present again what I have already presented. For I have proved that he is not a universal prophet, nor a particular or personal prophet; I have shown that he has not revealed anything about the past, made known anything for the present, or prophesied anything for the future. If this is the way things stand, this one is not your prophet, or anyone's prophet, as you claimed. But, as one gathers from the things already presented, one reads that he did not say or write anything prophetic. He is not, then, a prophet.[496]

496. The *explicit* reads: "Here ends the second book of Lord Abbot Peter of Clairvaux, *Against the Teaching of the Saracens.*" In the margin one finds the remark: "There are two books missing that I have not been able to find." With regard to the "missing" books, see the Introduction, p. 16.

APPENDICES

LETTER OF PETER OF POITIERS

POITIERS

(*Epistola Petri Pictaviensis*)

1. To a unique and singular father and to his lord, the lord abbot Peter of Cluny, the least of his sons, Peter, [sends] joy always in Christ.

2. Since, according to your practice, you always handle everything in a philosophical manner, you have quite expertly sent to me, who both suffers and deserves many sufferings, a passion tale that should be read.[497] It is thanks to your kindness that on this occasion at least I hold your letter and the grace of a paternal greeting from which, meanwhile, I bear the burden of your absence (which always weighs most heavily on me) far more lightly. Nonetheless, after I came to understand that you have it in mind to cross over to England, with the Lord guiding you, I became very anxious for you and for your companions, and began to offer up prayers and vows of supplication to God Almighty both on behalf of your entire journey and for your propitious return to us, as he grants it. But I also will take pains to entreat those to do the same who are more devoted to you and those whom I know to be more dedicated to holy prayer, and I will entreat them more and more, as Christ grants. May the Holy Spirit direct your journey and your counsel, and let our joy at your return to us be complete.

497. The Latin text is especially troublesome here. One is right to reject Kritzeck's translation of *passionem legendam* as "a passion for reading" (see Kritzeck, *Peter the Venerable and Islam*, 59), which Lemay insisted "really is a howler"; see Lemay, "Apologetics and (bad) Latin," 44. Lemay suggests instead that Peter the Venerable "had offered him (*misistis*) the advice to 'read Christ's passion'"; Lemay, "Apologetics and (bad) Latin," 44, and cf. Glei, 300, n. 502. Yvonne Friedman noted, however, the existence of an unpublished text of Pe-

3. As you ordered, I am sending you the chapter headings that John lost, and I believe that they are much more clearly arranged than they were before. So, to be sure, they have been given titles just as you began to do, or at least in the order you will give them, as it seems right to you, against those that truly are the enemies of the Cross of Christ. Whereas, with the great assurance that I knew your intention, if I have presumed to add or change anything, and if this has pleased you, let it remain. If not, it is for you to correct where we erred. May the chapter found there that concerns abusing wives in a very depraved fashion[498] not scandalize you in any way, because truly it is in the Qur'an, and, as I was assured in Spain by Peter of Toledo,[499] whose associate I was in the work of translation, and as I heard from Robert [of Ketton],[500] now the archdeacon of Pamplona, all Saracens do these things at their pleasure, as if according to a precept from Mohammad. I want you to confound them, then, just as you have confounded the Jews[501] and the heretics[502] from our region. Indeed, in our time you are the only one who has

---

ter the Venerable's letter to Peter of Poitiers in Madrid, Biblioteca Nacional MS Latin 4464. The letter contains a reference (at fol. 62a) to "the passion which a certain pilgrim suffered while on pilgrimage." See *Petri Venerabilis Adversus Iudeorum inueteratam duritiem*, ed. Yvonne Friedman, CC CM 58 (Turnhout: Brepols, 1985), p. lxi and n. 33. More correctly, the text refers to "a foreign passion of a certain martyr the like of which is hardly read anywhere and which in a unique way proclaims the love on which the whole law and the prophets depend (cf. Matt. 22.40)" ("peregrina cuiusdam martyris passio cui similis pene nulla legitur et qua singulariter caritas in qua uniuersa lex pendet et prophete predicator"). I would like to thank both Professor Ryan Szpiech for providing me with a scan of the manuscript, and Professor Frank A. C. Mantello for his transcription. It seems likely, then, that Peter of Poitiers alludes to the passion tale mentioned in Peter the Venerable's letter.

498. See below, Peter's Chapter Headings, 2.vi. This material is not treated in *Against the Sect of the Saracens*.

499. As noted in the Introduction, Peter the Venerable assigned Peter of Poitiers to assist Peter of Toledo in translating from Arabic the *Apology of* [Ps.] *Al-Kindi*, which appeared under their Latin title *Epistola Saraceni cum Rescripto Christiani*.

500. For the translation work of the Englishman Robert of Ketton, see the Introduction, p. 21.

501. Cf. Peter the Venerable, *Against the Inveterate Obduracy of the Jews*.

502. Almost certainly a reference to Peter's polemic *Against the Petrobrusians*.

cut down with the sword of the divine word[503] the three greatest
enemies of holy Christianity—I mean the Jews, the heretics, and
the Saracens—and you have shown that Mother Church is not
so deprived or despoiled of good sons but that she has still, by a
gracious Christ, such ones as can supply "to each one demanding it a reason for the hope" and faith "that are in us,"[504] and
can humble all the devil's arrogance and pride "that raises itself
up against the height of God."[505]

4. Health and prosperity and every good to you, in the first
place, and then to your companions that are both yours and
ours, namely, the lord Hugh the Englishman, and John (who
lost the chapter titles), and to our Bartholomew,[506] to the lord
constable Godfrey,[507] to Gerard the German (if nonetheless he
is with you) and to all the rest. I beg you, ignore my tardiness
and my weakness, because the Lord knows, although I have

503. Cf. Eph 6.17.   504. 1 Pt 3.15.
505. Cf. 2 Cor 10.5.

506. Possibly a reference to the physician Bartholomew of Salerno (fl.
1150–1180), who treated Peter and offered him medical advice. For an effort
to identify him, see esp. *The Letters of Peter the Venerable,* 2: 302–304. The two
maintained a correspondence, as evidenced by *Letters* 158a and 158b (likely
written in 1151); see *Peter the Venerable: Selected Letters,* ed. Janet Martin (Toronto: Pontifical Institute of Mediaeval Studies, 1974). These may be found in
translation in *Medieval Medicine: A Reader,* ed. Faith Wallis (Toronto: University
of Toronto Press, 2010), 406–409, and reprinted in *Reading the Middle Ages.
Sources from Europe, Byzantium, and the Islamic World,* ed. Barbara H. Rosenwein,
2d ed. (Toronto: University of Toronto Press, 2014), 2: 342–45.

507. *Godefredus Constabulus* (i.e., one in charge of the stables) is also mentioned as a witness to restitution made to Peter the Venerable and the monastery of Cluny, to bring an end to a controversy. See *Bullarum sacri ordinis
Cluniacensis,* ed. P. Symon (Lyon: Antonius Jullieron, 1680), 60; available at
http://www.uni-muenster.de/Fruehmittelalter/Projekte/Cluny/Bullarium/
bullarium.php?p=060. Cf. *The Letters of Peter the Venerable,* 2: 263–64. Yvonne
Friedman notes, however, that Godfrey/Godefridus was constable during
1146–1147, whereas Leontfridus is named constable in a letter from 1149,
which suggests 1147 as a *terminus ante quem* for this letter. (See *Adversus Iudeorum inueteratam duritiem,* lxi–lxiii.) This complicates the dating of *Against the
Saracens;* she concludes on the basis of the dating of this letter: "Either Peter
wrote the book in England before he received the outline [i.e., the chapter
headings] and in that case the date would seem to be 1148–1149, or if the
journey took place as late as 1154, the book was written towards the end of
Peter the Venerable's life and never completed" (ibid., lxiii).

willed much, hindered by the burden of the entire body and especially by the accustomed weakness of [my] feet, I was not able to send this to you earlier. In fact, I have also written all of these things in a larger book, fearing that even this letter may be lost on the journey, just as the chapters were lost. That was very wearisome.[508]

508. The *explicit* reads: "The epistle ends."

PETER OF POITIERS'
CHAPTER HEADINGS

(*Capitula*)[509]

1. *The chapter headings of the first book* of Peter, lord abbot of Cluny, against the wicked teaching of the Saracens:

I. Prologue to the Saracens,[510] admonishing them and summoning them to listen patiently, and to understand rationally what follows.

II. How foolishly and ridiculously they say that the Jews have lost their Law, and that now they have only a false and deceptive one.[511]

III. This opinion of theirs is proved to be foolish and vain, with a rational argument.[512]

IV. Because they assert in the same way that Christians have lost the Gospel and the apostolic writings, it is shown how easily that can be refuted.[513]

V. That the falsification of the Gospels could not have escaped the notice of Christians, especially when, scattered throughout the entire world and distributed among a great variety of languages, they all actually have the same Gospel, and because no Christians of any era depart from the truth that the Gospel is one and the same.

---

509. For Peter of Poitiers, see *supra*, n. 30, p. 10.

510. For the prologue, see *supra*, pp. 51–75.

511. It was increasingly common to charge, in medieval religious polemics, that Jews had falsified the Scriptures, or that Christians had. See my "Falsification of Scripture and Medieval Christian-Jewish Polemics," *Medieval Encounters* 2/3 (1996): 345–80. Peter treats this theme in Book One, 55–64.

512. See Book One, 65–75.

513. See Book One, 76–82.

VI. That if the Gospel were falsified, this could not have escaped the notice of people both studious and wise, of so many tongues and races, nor would such men have permitted themselves to be deceived by such a bald deception, nor, having abandoned truth, would they have embraced what is false in place of the things that are true, nor things uncertain in place of those that are sure.[514]

VII. That if they receive part of the Gospel, then it is proved that of necessity they also have to receive the whole of it.[515]

2. *Chapter headings of the second book:*

I. That one ought not to say or believe that Mohammad is a prophet,[516] for these reasons.

II. That he was a thief; and that is proved from what follows.

III. That he was a murderer and, moreover, a murderer of many relatives.

IV. That he was a traitor, often murdering those who were unaware or sleeping.

V. That he was a wicked adulterer, saying in his Qur'an that the practice of adultery was something granted to him by God.[517]

VI. That, beyond that, he taught sodomy and the most depraved practices, commanding it in his Qur'an as if the person of God were speaking in this way: "O men, penetrate the women subject to you in whatever part pleases you."[518]

514. See Book One, 83–85.

515. See Book One, 86–88.

516. See Book Two, which treats this theme extensively.

517. On the women permitted the prophet, see Qur'an 33.50–52. Although Peter does not address this theme in this work, he does treat it above in the *Summary* 10 (and see n. 67, p. 44).

518. Qur'an 2.223. As Glei noted (301–2, n. 617), Robert of Ketton added an interlinear gloss to his translation of the Qur'an that suggested a proclivity among Muslims for sodomy, and Peter of Poitiers saw this passage as pointing to unnatural sexual practices generally. A similar accusation appears in the Latin text of the *Liber denudationis* 10.3, translated in the later thirteenth century from an Arabic exemplar composed near the end of the 11th or early 12th C. For the Latin and English of this text, see Thomas E. Burman, *Religious Polemic and the Intellectual History of the Mozarabs*, pp. 342–43.

VII. That very often there is something in his Qur'an that contradicts itself, at one moment denying and at another affirming the same thing that earlier it had denied.

VIII. That no miracles have endorsed his legislation, although Moses, the legislator of the Old Law, and Christ, the author of the New Testament, confirmed by many and by extraordinary miracles that the Laws that they gave were divine and holy.[519]

3. *Chapters of the third book:*

I. It is proved that Mohammad could not have performed miracles, on the basis of his wicked life mentioned above.

II. That he himself confessed in his Qur'an that God did not give him signs.[520]

III. How frivolous, or rather how empty is the reason that he presented there, as to why he may perform no miracles, introducing God speaking to him in this way: "We would give you signs and wonders, if we did not know that they would not believe you."[521]

IV. That therefore he even contradicts it when he calls himself a prophet, and affirms that nonetheless signs were not given him, since prophecy is itself a very great sign.

V. That necessarily he was deceived in one of these two, because if he were a prophet then he received prophetic signs, and if he did not receive signs then he was not a prophet.[522]

VI. That there was never a light, as the myth of his birth and upbringing maintains, enclosed within Adam's ribs and thereafter within the ribs of Noah, and thus throughout all the generations up to Mohammad himself; that is the most laughable claim of all.[523]

519. See Book Two, 126. Qur'an 2.253 also notes that Jesus performed miracles.

520. See Book Two, 123.

521. Cf. *Rescriptum Christiani* cap. 28, pp. 56–57; cf. Qur'an 17.59.

522. See Book Two, 127.

523. For the claim that God had placed a light within Adam's ribs, which passed down the generations to Mohammad himself, see Robert of Ketton,

VII. That they say that he foretold those who would succeed him in the kingdom (first Abubarcharus, second Aomen, third Odmen, fourth Hali);[524] and certain other things may be shown to be false from the narrative of the very historian that reports this.

VIII. It will be proved, again, that he could not have been a prophet, on the basis of the Gospel of Christ, which they believe in part.[525]

4. *Chapters of the fourth book:*

I. That the words spoken by the Lord in the Gospel: "the Law and the prophets until John,"[526] should not be said concerning all prophets, but only of those before Christ who foretold the universal salvation of the world that was achieved by Christ.[527]

II. That even after John or Christ there were other prophets, or perhaps there will be others, who did not foretell or perhaps will not foretell human salvation in a specific way through that extraordinary operation, but foretold (or perhaps will foretell) by means of a prophetic spirit only what is relevant to their own races, lands, or persons; many examples of which we embrace.[528]

III. That Mohammad, who belonged to neither the one group nor the other, did not foretell the salvation that was achieved by Christ, although he lived long after Christ, nor did he say anything at all that pertained even a little to prophecy.[529]

IV. That this is revealed from his Qur'an, in which he wrote nothing that is actually prophetic; since reason does not actually support the claim that he said anything in a prophetic manner anywhere, and that he remained silent

Mistake-Laden and Ridiculous Chronicle of the Saracens (*Chronica mendosa et ridicula Sarracenorum*), in *The Pseudo-Historical Image of the Prophet Mohammad*, 93.

524. That is, the first four caliphs, according to Sunni reckoning: Abū-Bakr, ʿUmar, ʿUthmān, and ʿAlī. Cf. Book Two, 120.

525. See Book Two, 136–37.   526. Lk 16.16.

527. See Book Two, 137.   528. See Book Two, 138–39.

529. See Book Two, 151.

about this in his scripture that alone (according to him) is sublime, where, although he called himself a prophet, nonetheless he makes no prophecies.[530]

V. That the entirety of Mohammad's scripture is nothing other than the frightful dregs and the foul residue of heresies that were condemned and buried five hundred years before he was born by the universal, sacred Church of the entire world—especially [the heresies] of the Manicheans, and of apocryphal books, and especially of that execrable book of the Jews, the Talmud. The Saracens have accepted these heresies, because they do not read or know how to read truthful histories and ecclesiastical acts, and they have never heard that those times or that those heresies existed, and for this reason these animals and wretches received that Satan[531] as if he were speaking what is wondrous and new.

VI. An exhortation and admonition for them to come to true and holy Christianity through the ritual ablution of sacred baptism, at least at the End Time, when the end of the age is already near, rejecting the fables and fantasies of the devil, and believing in Christ's Cross and death, in which alone there exists the true and entire salvation of men.[532]

530. See Book Two, 153.
531. I.e., Mohammad. See *Summary* 6–7.
532. The *explicit* reads: "The chapters of the fourth book end."

INDICES

GENERAL INDEX

Aaron (Moses's brother), 113, 128

Abdia(s), the Jew, 78, 104

Abraham, 100, 112, 155

Adam and Eve, 78, 112

Africa, 45, 57, 66, 110

Agrippa Castor, 54

Ahaziah, King, 150

Alexander III, Pope, 6

Alfonso VI, Emperor, 14, 19

Alfonso VII, Emperor, 19, 72

Al-Furqān (Qur'an), 78

Anastasius the Librarian, 37

Angles, 96, 97

Antichrist, 36, 47, 126, 151

Antoninus Pius, Emperor, 69

Apelis (Apelles), heretic, 52

Apollinaris of Hierapolis, 54, 69

Apollinaris of Laodicea, 70

Apollonius, 54

apostle(s), 7, 32, 36, 51, 52, 67,
    73, 83, 92, 93, 105, 118, 119,
    127, 144, 151; James, 119; John,
    67, 118, 119; Jude, 119; Paul,
    117, 118, 119, 151, 152; Peter,
    118, 127

Arabia, 39, 110, 117, 153

Arabs, 38, 45, 66, 75, 143

Archelaus, Bishop of Mesopotamia, 58

Arians, 55, 56, 59, 60, 61, 70

Arius, heresiarch, 46, 47, 60

Ark (of the Covenant), 106

Armannus, abbot of Manglieure, 7

Armenians, 66

Arnobius of Sicca, 70

Asia, 45, 66, 69, 116, 118, 119

Assyrian(s), 108, 131, 153

Athanasius of Alexandria, 59, 70

Augustine of Canterbury, Saint, 97,
    98

Augustine of Hippo, Saint, 32, 48, 59,
    62, 71

Augustine of Hippo, Saint, works: *The
    City of God*, 48, 71; *The Harmony of
    the Evangelists*, 48

Baal, prophets of, 147

Babylonia, 107, 110, 132, 153

Babylonian captivity, 133

Balthasar, King, 136, 154

baptism, 46, 64, 132, 171

Bardesanes of Edessa, 64

Bartholomew (physician?), 165

Basil of Caesarea, 61

Basilides, heretic, 52

Bernard of Clairvaux, 7, 9, 15, 27

Bethlehem, 5

Bibliander, Thomas, 23

Bouthillier, Denis, 14

Britain, 96

Burnett, Charles, 19

Carthusian Order, 6

Cataphrygians, 53

Chalcedon, Council of, 63

Chaldea, 108, 134, 154

Chaldean(s), 108, 131, 133, 134, 153

Christ, 117, 118, 119, 120, 121, 125,
    126, 127, 133, 144, 147, 149, 150,
    152, 156, 157, 163, 165, 169, 170;
    birth of, 132; Church of, 151; cross
    of, 164, 171; passion of, 132

Christians, 12, 19, 20, 48, 67, 76, 88,

INDEX OF HOLY SCRIPTURE

Deutero-canonical Books

INDEX OF QURANIC REFERENCES